# MOSCOW
# STATION

# MOSCOW STATION

## HOW THE KGB PENETRATED
## THE AMERICAN EMBASSY

# Ronald Kessler

Charles Scribner's Sons

NEW YORK

Charles Scribner's Sons
Macmillan Publishing Company
866 Third Avenue, New York, NY 10022
Collier Macmillan Canada, Inc.

Library of Congress Cataloging-in-Publication Data
Kessler, Ronald.
Moscow station.
Includes index.
1. Espionage—Soviet Union.   2. Soviet Union. Komitet
gosudarstvennoĭ bezopasnosti.   3. United States. Embassy
(Soviet Union)   I. Title.
UB271.R9K46  1989     327.1'2'0947     88-30575
ISBN 978-1-5011-9417-7

Macmillan books are available at special discounts for bulk purchases
for sales promotions, premiums, fund-raising, or educational use.
For details, contact:

Special Sales Director
Macmillan Publishing Company
866 Third Avenue
New York, NY 10022

10 9 8 7 6 5 4 3 2 1

Designed by Jack Meserole

PRINTED IN THE UNITED STATES OF AMERICA

For my mother,
Minuetta Kessler

# Contents

# Acknowledgments

I could not have undertaken this project without strong support from my family and friends. My editor, Edward T. Chase, was enthusiastic and a pleasure to work with. My agent, Julian Bach, provided wise counsel and encouragement. My wife, Pamela Kessler, accompanied me in my encounter with the KGB, gave me the benefit of her good judgment at every turn, and put up with the sounds of my typing at 4:30 A.M. Through their own hard work and tenacity in college, my children, Greg and Rachel Kessler, provided an example for me to follow.

Several friends in the intelligence community, my friend Daniel M. Clements, and my wife read the manuscript and gave me invaluable and insightful suggestions. My friend Nick Gage worked his usual magic on the subtitle. I am grateful to each of them for the important contributions they made.

While some must remain anonymous, those who gave of their time in interviews or otherwise helped include:

Kenneth L. Adelman, Goethe W. (Bud) Aldridge, James M. Baker, David R. Beall, Jacob D. Beam, Raymond E. Benson, Shirley Benson, Ladislav Bittman, Dr. Charles E. Brodine, Lane M. Bonner, Corporal Arnold Bracy, Frieda L. Bracy, Theodore Bracy, Master Gunnery Sergeant John G. Bradley, Thomas E. Brannon, Virginia Broich, Thompson P. Buchanan, Frederick B. Bunke, Donald F. Burton, Charles Carter, Lawrence D. Cohen, Richard E. Combs, Gary M. Comerford, Sergeant Donald S. Cooke, Alexandra Costa, Sharon Credit, Robert T. Crowley,

Miranda Daniloff, Nicholas Daniloff, and Kenneth E. deGraffenreid.

Also Colonel C. Sean Del Grosso, Richard N. Dertadian, Sergeant Albert D. Diekmann, Joseph E. diGenova, Victor Dikeos, John J. Dion, Timothy Dixon, Dusko Doder, Staff Sergeant Vincent O. Downes, John Drotos, Golnar S. Duchateau, Phillipe Duchateau, Yvonne Dupont, Ilya Dzhirkvelov, Pete Earley, John T. Elliff, Robert M. Embry, John A. Fahey, William S. Farmer, David A. Faulkner, Lieutenant General Lincoln D. Faurer, Chris Frost, Paul Gaffney, Gunnery Sergeant Paul A. Gasparotti, William Geimer, Charles Geiss, Gennadi I. Gerasimov, Robert K. German, Richard J. Gilbert, Culver Gleysteen, and Sergeant Joseph Goddard.

Also Galina N. (Galya) Golotina, Rear Admiral John E. (Ted) Gordon, Arthur A. Hartman, Donna Hartman, Lake W. Headley, Major David H. Henderson, Rudolf Herrmann, Lance Corporal John S. Hlatky, Walter D. Huddleston, Patrick J. Hurt, Donald F. B. Jameson, Louise R. Jameson, Curtis W. Kamman, General Paul X. Kelley, William Kelley, George F. Kennan, Teresa Kenney, Richard W. Keifer, Lieutenant Commander James R. Kirkpatrick, Samuel C. Klein, Richard H. Klingenmaier, Kenneth G. Knauf, Foy D. Kohler, Boris S. Korczak, Major Allen Kris, Ronald Kuby, and William M. Kunstler.

Also E. Charlene Kurth, Rear Admiral Ronald J. Kurth, Robert E. Lamb, James W. Lannon, Anthony Lauck, Taina A. Laurivuori, Stanislav Levchenko, Spencer G. Lonetree, Thomas R. Maertens, John L. Martin, Sergeant John A. Martinson, Thomas E. Marum, Sergeant Richard W. Mataitis, Ambassador Jack F. Matlock, Jr., Frank Matthews, Lanny E. McCullah, Frederick A. Mecke, James E. Nolan, Jr., Phillip A. Parker, Corporal Duane B. Parks, James P. Pender, Corporal Gary T. Pitman, Rodney Pope, Lieutenant Colonel Michael L. Powell, Carl Provencher, Roger A. Provencher, and Colonel Michael E. Rich.

Also Gailon C. Roen, Sergeant Todd M. Roen, Raymond W. Rugen, John K. Russell, Cecilia Serrano, Lieutenant Colonel John Shotwell, L. Britt Snider, Nancy D. Snyder, John F. Sopko, Christopher A. Squire, the late Walter J. Stoessel, Jr., Lee Stufflebeam, Staff Sergeant Robert S. Stufflebeam, Michael V.

Christopher A. Squire, the late Walter J. Stoessel, Jr., Lee Stufflebeam, Staff Sergeant Robert S. Stufflebeam, Michael V. Stuhff, Robert Surprise, Malcolm Toon, Sally F. Tsotie, Jaraslav Verner, Paul C. Vincent, Kent E. Walker, Major Richard (Rick) Walton, Dana Weant, Sergeant John J. Weirick, Helen Westwood, Angelic White, Corporal Robert J. Williams, Master Gunnery Sergeant Joey E. Wingate, and F. Mark Wyatt.

I am grateful to the following individuals for permission to reprint selected material from their books: Leo D. Carl, author of *International Dictionary of Intelligence,* to be published by National Intelligence Book Center in Washington, D.C.; Ilya Dzhirkvelov, author of *Secret Servant,* published in the U.S. by Harper & Row and in the United Kingdom by William Collins Sons & Co.; and Samuel C. Klein, the lawyer for Irvin C. Scarbeck, who gave me access to his late client's unpublished manuscript.

# PART I

# CHAPTER 1

# The Jewels

THE JEWELS to the CIA's Moscow station were shielded by a metal shack behind a vault door on the ninth floor of the American embassy. Known as the Communications Programs Unit, or CPU, the shack was a metal chamber within a room as large as the situation room of the White House. Made of galvanized steel, the CPU looked like a walk-in refrigerator. Each square foot of the walls, ceilings, and floors had cost twenty-five dollars to build.

The cartoons that festooned the CPU's inner walls did little to relieve its essential homeliness. Yet to the dozen CIA, National Security Agency, and State Department code clerks who worked inside it, the CPU was a thing of beauty. For it protected some of the most sensitive information in the arsenal of the United States government.

The CPU resembled the Russian metrushka dolls that tourists bought in Moscow: decreasing in size, there was a doll within a doll within a doll. In the same way, within the CPU, near the southwest corner of the embassy, was a smaller version of the larger CPU. This was the CIA's code room, the inner sanctum of the mustard-colored, Beaux Arts embassy building on Tchaikovsky Street. Here, gleaming gray cipher machines encoded and decoded messages that were transmitted by commercial satellite at 9,600 characters a second between Moscow and Langley. These machines were the jewels, the most precious commodity at Moscow station.

Through these machines flowed the top-secret details of CIA operations targeted against the Soviet Union. Other crypto machines in other sections of the CPU transmitted the results of NSA eavesdropping on Kremlin communications and instructions from Secretary of State George P. Shultz to Ambassador Arthur A. Hartman on dealing with the Soviets, including details of American positions on arms reduction talks.

If the Soviets could ever read the messages, they would know how to counter American negotiating strategies and how to evade NSA eavesdropping techniques. Most damaging of all, they would be able to identify the CIA's informants or assets in the Soviet Union. For such informants, this would almost certainly mean death by firing squad.

The CIA was supremely confident that the codes couldn't be broken. Yet there was reason for concern. In recent years, the KGB's efforts to penetrate the embassy had grown from a drizzle to a downpour. In part, that was due to the growing sophistication of the FBI's counterintelligence program in the U.S. While the KGB still recruited its share of important spies, the FBI was making it more and more difficult. The logical solution was to target Americans overseas.

The KGB had even established a new branch, the Sixteenth Department of the First Chief Directorate, that targeted the communications of the U.S. and its allies. This department ultimately directed the spying activities of former Navy warrant officer John A. Walker, Jr., who compromised Navy communications. So compartmented was the operation that only Walker's KGB case officer was supposed to know his identity.

By 1984 the KGB had achieved extraordinary success in breaching the embassy's tightly wrapped cordon. It had managed to implant tiny, highly sophisticated bugging devices in thirteen IBM Selectric typewriters used in secure areas of the embassy in Moscow and the American consulate in Leningrad. The bugs recorded the movements of the typing elements—the balls that rotated in the typewriters to imprint letters on paper—and transmitted the information in fragmentary, coded bursts to a KGB listening post in a Soviet apartment next to the embassy. As a result, all of the highly classified data prepared on the typewriters in Moscow—including names of CIA officers stationed at the embassy—found its way to the KGB's forbidding headquarters, a ten-minute taxi ride from the embassy.

Several of the typewriters had been shipped to the embassy as long ago as 1976, and the batteries that powered the bugs were dead. But more recent versions of the electronic devices tapped the typewriters' power supply. They were transmitting perfectly when the NSA, acting on information given to the French by a defector, finally discovered them in 1984, first at the American embassy in Moscow and later at the consulate in Leningrad.

In a classic display of turf consciousness, the CIA noted smugly that it had been suspicious of the typewriters all along and had not used them. However, the secretary to the deputy chief of mission, who also typed for Ambassador Hartman, was using one. A State Department security officer was using another. Because records were so chaotic, there was no way to tell who had used them before that.

But bugging typewriters and breaching the sanctity of the jewels' inner chamber were entirely different matters. All the ingenuity and technical resources of U.S. intelligence agencies had been marshaled to make sure the embassy's communications were secure. NSA designed the cipher machines, which substituted random digits for each letter of the alphabet. The digits that were substituted constantly changed according to a complex algorithm, or mathematical formula, prepared by NSA and built into the cipher machines. NSA prepared keys for the machines in a separate, guarded communication security facility the length of three football fields near its headquarters at Fort Meade, Maryland. Embedded in magnetic strips were lists of numbers that changed the way the cipher machines substituted digits for letters. Without the keys, there was in theory no way to decipher the encoded messages.

Every twenty-four hours, NSA changed the keys. In addition, the CIA often substituted new keys for particular messages or for particular words within those messages. Furthermore, the CIA double-encoded all its messages, passing them through two cipher machines.

Because of advances in cryptography, the keys no longer had

to be sent by courier to Moscow. Instead, they could be multi-plexed—sent in fragmentary bursts of a millisecond each—over many different circuits, just as the messages themselves were sent.

If there was an Achilles' heel to the system, it was the teletypes and printers that carried the "clear text" or uncoded messages before they were coded or after they were decoded. In the parlance of code clerks, the "red side" of the communications circuits carried the plain text. The "black side" carried the coded version. If the KGB could somehow penetrate the CPU and place bugs on the "red side," it could conceivably tap into CIA communications.

That was why the CPU was so important. It blocked any electronic signals from entering or leaving the code room. Without a way to get a signal out of the CPU, any bugs placed on the printers and teletypes would be useless. No effort had been spared to make sure that didn't happen. The CPU, in effect, was like a giant balloon. If even a microscopic hole developed in its skin, radio waves could penetrate it, allowing the KGB to pick up signals from bugs placed within.

Built by Rayproof Shielding Systems Corp., the CPU was a precision instrument made of steel that had been meticulously purified to remove any contaminants. The thousands of screws used to erect the metal sheets were engineered to create their own threads as they were turned into the steel, thus forming a seal against radio-wave penetration. The door was made of surgeon's steel that was flanged to give it a knifelike edge. Beryllium coated the steel to ensure a smooth fit when the door closed.

The utility lines that supplied the CPU with air, power, and communications were most vulnerable to attack. To make sure they were sealed against signals, the air vents contained honey-combed filters made of thousands of one-inch pipes about an eighth of an inch thick. Because of the way radio waves travel, the pipes blocked all but the shortest waves from entering or leaving the CPU. Those signals were so weak they could only travel a few feet. To ensure that the communication lines did not emit stray signals, the CPU converted the data into light beams that traveled over thin strands of optic fiber. Without physically tapping into the lines, there was no way to pick up any stray signals. Since the

CPU was raised off the floor, all sides of it could be inspected at any time for bugs on the communications lines.

The power line presented the greatest problem. If the KGB could place bugs on the printers, it could transmit the signals out through the electrical supply and listen in from anywhere in Moscow. To prevent that, the city power was only used to run a generator which provided clean electricity to the CPU. All the lines passed through special electronic filters and circuits that blocked any foreign emissions.

There was a final check to make sure the CPU was winning this electronic war: test equipment costing more than a half million dollars periodically verified that no unwanted emissions left or entered the CPU. With its computer programs and plot printouts, the equipment was the bottom line on whether or not the CPU was doing its job.

The system seemed foolproof, yet the United States had underestimated the KGB before. Outside on Tchaikovsky Street, the Soviet Union was a Third World country. Guests at the best hotels in Moscow could not get milk for their coffee or orange juice for breakfast. The people stood in lines, grim and resigned, to get chocolate, shoes, or thousands of other items that stores in the U.S. stock every day. Even brick buildings were considered a luxury. During the depths of the Great Depression, Americans were not as deprived as Soviets are today. But when it came to technology for security, the Soviets equaled and in some areas surpassed the U.S. Eavesdropping was one of those areas. When NSA scientists and engineers examined the more recent bugs found in the IBM Selectrics, they were astounded. The circuitry was far superior to anything the CIA had devised.

For all the equipment and the redundant safeguards, it was always possible that if the KGB got into the CPU, it could find some way to transmit signals out.

That was why the Marines were there, to guard the jewels with their honor and their lives. They were the front line of defense, the ones, as a Soviet commentator put it, who "so ably guard the American embassy." From the halls of Montezuma to the shores of Tripoli, they had served their country with distinction. Of all the services, they had the reputation for being the fiercest, the most patriotic, the toughest. In boot camp, they learned to call everyone "Sir!," to refer to a wall as a bulkhead and a bed as a rack, and to be loyal to their brothers. Each day they did hundreds of bends and thrusts, push-ups and side-straddle hops, along with leg lifts, side lunges, squat benders, and sit-ups. They learned to shoot to kill, and most of all they learned to obey orders. Their motto is *Semper fidelis*—always faithful.

The Marine Corps proclaimed that it selected only the finest Leathernecks to become security guards. For six weeks, in a school outfitted like an embassy on a tranquil hill at the Quantico Marine base outside Washington, each Marine trained with a .38-caliber revolver, a Remington 870-P 12-gauge shotgun, a Uzi 9-millimeter submachine gun, and MPG tear-gas grenades. They learned to use handcuffs, Mace, and the side-handle baton; to react properly to suspected explosive devices; and to release noxious gases in the event demonstrators stormed an embassy.

They were the pride of America, young men you would want on your side, and they held their heads high.

As visitors entered the embassy in Moscow, a Marine guard was the first thing they saw. He stood, erect, behind bulletproof glass at post number one. His hair cut "high and tight," his dress blues perfectly creased, he symbolized America's honor in a foreign and often hostile land. A second Marine, one visitors would not see, stood post number three, guarding the entrance on the ninth floor to the CPU and the secure areas of the embassy. A third Marine, the roving sergeant-of-the-guard, checked up periodically on the other Marines. Finally, the State Department's regional security officer, known as the RSO, lived in the embassy with the Marines and other embassy personnel. At any moment, he could appear to make sure the Marines were doing their duty.

On paper, the setup looked perfect. For the KGB to enter the CPU, it would have to send its officers past the Marine at post number one, then past the Marine at post number three. The KGB would have to know the combination of the vault that enclosed the CPU, and penetrate the cipher lock on the inner door of the CPU. The only other way was to recruit a CPU code clerk, someone with cryptographic clearance that went beyond top-secret.

Certainly, the KGB had made use of corrupt Americans in the past. Besides Walker, Ronald W. Pelton had given the Soviets details of NSA operations. William P. Kampiles had sold them the manual to the supersecret KH-11 spy satellite. But given the quality of the Americans sent to Moscow, it was unthinkable that such a thing would happen there.

Since the Soviet Union was considered the most important diplomatic post in the world, the State Department sent only its most distinguished foreign service officers to Moscow. Ambassadors to the Soviet Union had always been chosen with an eye to history. Many had become legendary figures—W. Averell Harriman, George F. Kennan, Charles E. Bohlen, Llewelyn E. Thompson.

Since the Soviet Union was its main target, the CIA sent only its most capable and clever officers. The NSA, likewise, sent only its best linguists and engineers. And the Marine Corps sent only its most qualified, most mature guard school graduates.

So far as anyone knew, CIA communications had never been compromised since the agency's founding in 1947. Just in case all the locks and humans failed, there were additional safeguards to make sure that never happened. Throughout the ten-story embassy, motion and noise detectors, heat detectors, entry alarms, door counters, and video cameras tracked every movement at night when the CPU was not manned. Besides the communicators, only the Marines had the combinations for entering the CPU. In the event of a fire, they were to smash the cipher machines before the KGB could get to them. A special plastic envelope inside a safe near post number three held the combinations. If the envelope were ever opened, the plastic could not be reconstructed, so no one would take a chance opening it. Every morning, a CPU officer checked to make sure the envelope was intact. Moreover, each component of the cipher machines had been sprayed with a distinctive, clear plastic coating. If any part were replaced, the differences would be detected immediately under ultraviolet light.

Nothing had been left to chance, it seemed, and yet there was something wrong—something terribly wrong—at Moscow station.

Ever since the U.S. and the Soviet Union established diplomatic relations in 1933, the Soviets had been trying to compromise embassy employees and gain access to the code room. If the KGB could find any weakness, any vulnerability, any hidden desire, it would exploit it by slowly ensnaring American embassy employees in a subtle but deadly trap. By the time an American realized what had happened, he was subject to blackmail and terrified of being found out.

The first step in this process was sizing up or assessing each employee assigned to the embassy. The Soviets wanted to get a feel for what each individual was like. Then they could decide which approach might work best. What better way to do that than by assigning KGB officers and informants to work in the embassy right alongside the Americans?

At first blush, it seems inconceivable the Americans would allow such a thing. Certainly neither the CIA nor the State Department would ever allow a Soviet national to work at their headquarters in Washington, not even to sweep the floors. Nor had the Soviets ever allowed an American to work inside their embassy in Washington.

But over the years, the Soviets had woven a cocoon around the Americans so the Americans actually wanted Soviets to work inside the embassy. When they came to Moscow, the Americans experienced profound culture shock. Besides the lack of consumer goods, everything from looking up a telephone number to hiring a plumber took an inordinate amount of time. Just buying tickets to the Bolshoi Ballet was like applying to college. To buy a book or a dress, they had to wait in three lines—one to look at the item, one to pay for it, and one to pick it up. There was no such thing as fast food. Going to a restaurant required reservations. If the Americans wanted to go for a ride in the country, they had to get Soviet government approval, entailing delays and possible disapproval of the request. Moreover, the atmosphere of Moscow was depressing. While the people could be warm and animated, the city was sterile and gritty. In winter, the sun rarely shone—the sky stayed a perpetual murky gray. People prayed for snow; it would brighten things up. The city's finest hotels reminded the Americans of New York tenements circa 1930.

These were conditions that every Soviet put up with, but the

KGB manipulated them to control the Americans. If the Soviets disapproved of an American initiative, or the FBI had just arrested a Soviet spy in New York, the Soviets would tighten up on the goodies available to the embassy, perhaps denying a visa to a repairman who could fix the embassy's elevators or claiming planes that were half empty were booked. If the Americans were behaving themselves, they might get their Bolshoi tickets a little faster and their trips within the Soviet Union approved a little quicker.

The Americans had gradually grown to accept these manipulations and to let the Soviets have their way. For the most part, the same diplomats populated the embassy year after year. Soviet specialists who spoke Russian fluently, they would do a tour in Moscow, return to Washington to work on the Soviet desk, then do another tour in Moscow. They had long ago accepted the Soviets' contention that it was easier and cheaper to employ Soviet nationals at the embassy to cut through Moscow's bureaucratic jungle. And which Soviets would the Americans employ? Those chosen by the Soviets, of course. Only Soviets supplied by UPDK, a state agency controlled by the KGB, could work in foreign embassies in Moscow.

The Americans fell for the scheme. It was comfortable—part of the protective cocoon—and an interface between the two societies. The explanation was always "there are larger issues at stake," when no issue short of nuclear war was more important than preventing espionage. So the Americans used the Soviets to drive them to the ballet, cut their hair, fix their radios, and even answer their phones at the embassy switchboard. A frightened would-be defector had to talk first with a Soviet before he could plead for help from an American.

The FBI was just as interested in penetrating the Soviet embassy in Washington as the Soviets were interested in penetrating the embassy in Moscow. For the purpose, the bureau would have given anything to have one American working in the Soviet embassy. Yet the KGB had 206 Soviet informants working in the U.S. embassy. They outnumbered the Americans.

If the Americans were gullible, they were also lazy. Certainly they worked long hours and had to endure tremendous hardships in Moscow, not only because of the living conditions but because of the stress they were under. They realized they were constantly being observed, constantly being followed. At any time, the Soviets could set them up and eject them from the country in retaliation for something that may have happened back in the U.S. But the Americans also wanted their creature comforts. That was one of the benefits of being in the diplomatic corps. The thought of going without a Soviet driver for his Mercedes made Ambassador Hartman shudder. He was convinced an American driver could not negotiate Moscow's streets without getting lost. Moreover, an accident involving an American driver could be messy. The Soviets might create a provocation by charging the driver with reckless driving. Never mind that the Soviets managed quite well in Washington with Soviet drivers.

The foreign service officers did not want to replace their Soviet staff with American blue-collar workers. They looked down upon them—they would be less educated than their supervisors and from Indiana instead of New York, and might compete for the limited resources of the embassy. Far better to have Soviets who could be controlled, who would not become part of the embassy community, and who would not cut into their perquisites. In any case, things had always been done that way. Why change them now?

To preserve their dukedoms, Hartman and some of his predecessors had come up with a curious formulation to explain why it was better—even safer—to employ Soviets rather than Americans. According to this rationale, at least they *knew* the Soviets reported to the KGB and so would be more careful around them. Because they were Americans, the diplomats might blurt out secrets to the blue-collar workers who would replace the Soviets. The blue-collar workers would be more susceptible to Soviet recruitment efforts because they lacked commitment.

It was snobbery of the worst kind and had no basis in counterintelligence fact. Generally, the Walkers, Peltons, and other traitors have been professionals, not blue-collar workers. Nor were the Soviets interested in recruiting electricians or gardeners. They targeted diplomats, CIA officers, and code clerks.

Following the diplomats' reasoning, it would be better for banks to hire bank robbers because the management assumes they will try to steal money. Likewise, the CIA should hire KGB officers as secretaries because the agency would know they were trying to steal secrets.

If the reasoning was illogical, it also belied a basic misunderstanding about intelligence work. Hartman would point out that the Soviets did not work in the secure areas of the embassy and thus had no access to classified documents—the "money" of the embassy. But the Soviet workers were not there to grab documents. They were there to provide information so the KGB could compromise the Americans in the embassy. The KGB wanted to know which Americans were alcoholics or loners, flirts or homosexuals, immature personalities or malcontents. While the Soviets could learn a lot about the Americans by bugging their apartments and following them, nothing could substitute for the kind of daily office contact the Americans allowed the Soviets to have.

The KGB also wanted the Soviet workers in the embassy so they could compromise the Americans directly. Like motorcycle riders going without helmets, the Americans recklessly allowed the Soviets to place KGB "swallows" in their midst—enchanting young women used to entrap the Americans in compromising relationships.

For years, the FBI and CIA warned the State Department of the dangers and tried to pressure it to replace the Soviets with Americans. Since they ran the embassy, the diplomats were in a superior position. They repeatedly sabotaged the intelligence community's efforts by claiming that it was all part of a plot to break relations with the Soviets.

Hartman was a leading proponent of that view. An avuncular man with thinning white hair, a large nose, blue eyes, and a round face, he projected an aura of newborn innocence that was disarming. In some ways, he mirrored the views of the State Department, which saw security as a threat to its own hegemony. But in other ways, Hartman's approach was almost a caricature of those views. A protégé of former secretary of state Henry A. Kissinger, Hartman was the senior career ambassador and one of the brightest officers within the distinguished corps of the foreign service. A graduate of Yale University and Harvard Law School, he had been assistant secretary of state for European affairs in the Nixon and Ford administrations and had held a series of prominent posts in London, Saigon, Brussels, and Paris before President Reagan named him envoy to the Soviet Union in 1981.

So adept at plumbing the subtleties of the Soviet mind, the New York native insisted on portraying security questions in black and white terms. Thus he linked security with diplomatic relations, as in a cable he sent to Shultz in November 1984.

"I have watched with amazement the expanding activities of a small group of people inside and out of the government who, by wrapping themselves in the mantle of defenders against hostile intelligence operations, are making mischief that can set back indefinitely any movement towards dealing seriously with the Soviet Union," Hartman wrote of a new effort to replace the Soviets with Americans. Hartman said the "misguided" effort ignored "the questions of efficiency, vulnerability to entrapment, and logistic support for our employees."

In truth, there was no relationship between security and smooth relations with the Soviets. The State Department tended to take the long view of the U.S.-Soviet relations. Playing the traditional role of the mother in a family situation, it was more interested in preserving peace than in forcing issues and presenting a macho image. Whatever the merits of that approach, it had nothing to do with simple self-protection. A desire to shelter one's home from intrusion does not suggest hostility toward one's neighbors. State Department and CIA officers assigned to develop Soviet sources could meet with them twenty-four hours a day, so long as they did not bring them into the CPU and the embassy's secure areas. It was the difference between inviting guests into one's living room and leaving the front door wide open all night.

Hartman chose not to see the distinction. He would tell his staff that he *wanted* the Soviets to hear 80 percent of what was going on in the embassy. By that he meant that it was his job to articulate American views to the Soviets. If they had a better

understanding of American values and aspirations, tensions between the two countries would diminish. But that was not what he
said. It was like a bank manager exhorting his staff to give out
money: the fact that he really only wanted tellers to process
legitimate withdrawals and attract more business got lost in the
translation.

Hartman was too experienced and too intelligent to be unconcerned about the KGB threat. But the impression he conveyed
was quite different—an impression reinforced by the State Department's institutional aversion to security.

And so it was not surprising that by 1985 the Marine security
guards were issuing some 200 security violations a year within the
embassy; that safes in the embassy containing top-secret documents were routinely left wide open; that embassy security
officials told the Marine guards to ignore certain types of security
violations; that many Marines considered security practices at the
embassy to be worse than at American embassies in Somalia or
Zimbabwe; and that the Soviets working in the embassy were
trusted to escort the Marines into mechanical areas of the embassy
that were off-limits to most employees.

Nor was it surprising, given the priorities set by the State
Department and Hartman, that alarms went off three or four
times a night for no reason and that no steps were taken to replace
the alarm system; that many Marines slept through the alarms;
that the alarms in the CPU could be silenced by a Marine on post
number three and no record would show when they went off; that
the video cameras either did not work or were so fuzzy the
Marines could not distinguish between men and women; that for
budgetary reasons the CPU was not manned twenty-four hours a
day as it had been in the past; that a single Marine guard at post
number three controlled access to the entire embassy at night;
that the gate blocking Soviet cars from entering the embassy
courtyard frequently stuck in the "up" position; that the Marines'
requests for replacement of inoperable locks and security gates
were ignored; and that some of the typewriters that wound up
containing bugs had originally been allowed to sit overnight in a
Soviet customs warehouse.

It was not surprising, either, that the Americans stored

materials for construction of the new embassy in a "secure" warehouse that employed four Soviet workers; that the Americans let the Soviets form the precast concrete and girders for the new embassy in their own plants; that the materials were not rigorously checked for bugs before they were installed on site; and that ultimately the new embassy was found to be riddled with hundreds of different kinds of bugging devices. So contemptuous of American security practices were the Soviets that they arranged different colored bricks in a wall of the new embassy to read from a distance "C.C.C.P."—the Cyrillic letters for "U.S.S.R."

Constricted by unrealistic rules against having women in their rooms, and further constrained by Soviet rules against unmarried couples in hotel rooms, the Marines meanwhile wound up frequenting prostitutes at local bars controlled by the KGB. Despite prohibitions on contact with Soviet bloc nationals, one Marine had two Polish women in his bed at the Marine House in the embassy at one time. Another Marine, with the knowledge of other Marines, went with the daughter of a Soviet intelligence officer for six months, leaving her pregnant. An assistant commander of the Marine detachment guarding the embassy and another Marine had sex simultaneously with a pretty hitchhiker who was most likely a Soviet. And several Marines succumbed to the wiles of a handful of embassy wives—known as "the Home-wreckers"—intent on taking on as many Marines as they could, thus subjecting both themselves and the Marines to possible Soviet blackmail attempts.

If the embassy was a microcosm of Peyton Place, it was also rife with double standards. Influential members of the embassy community actively fought security rules. Hartman only encouraged disrespect for the rules by allowing Yugoslavian women to dance with the Marines in the embassy disco, even though Marine rules prohibited the Marines from having contact with Yugoslavian nationals. He also permitted attractive Soviet employees to attend the annual Marine Corps ball and "Thank God It's Friday" parties at the Marine House.

In a classic display of poor leadership, Hartman, under pressure from a defense attaché's wife, overrode his own orders to the Marines to bar from the embassy a Soviet hairdresser who had been caught in recruitment activities, allowing her to enter again.

In fairness to Hartman, some of the security breaches were beyond his control. For example, an interagency committee headed by the CIA developed the disastrous security program for construction of the new embassy, which was around the corner from the old one. But Hartman set the tone, and he was responsible to the President for security at the embassy.

Many of the Marines began to wonder why they should obey orders that restricted their lives when some of the more powerful members of the embassy community did as they pleased— engaging in prohibited black-market activities, seeing Soviet prostitutes, refusing to show identification when asked to do so at the embassy entrance. Adding to the Marines' sense of impotence, Hartman even prohibited them from carrying loaded weapons, contrary to their training as Marine guards.

If the Marines saw Soviet women on the sly, or engaged in black-market activities themselves, or saved from incineration interesting documents marked "secret" to read in their racks, or threw shredded classified documents down on the heads of Soviet militiamen as a lark, or altered the logs to show they had not violated curfews, they could rationalize that the ambassador did not care about security. Everyone else was allowed to break the rules. Why shouldn't they?

But these were surface manifestations of deeper problems— problems that led back to Washington and fierce power struggles among the agencies represented at the embassy. While the State Department ran the embassy, only a third of its 191 American employees worked for State. The rest worked for the CIA, the NSA, the Defense Intelligence Agency, the various branches of the military services, the U.S. Information Agency, and the Agriculture and Commerce departments. While State was responsible for security at the embassy, the CIA, by executive order, had overall responsibility outside the U.S. for counterintelligence. That included repelling the KGB from embassies overseas.

If a penetration occurred, it was done on the CIA's watch as much as the State Department's. Moreover, it was the CIA's secrets, more than any other agency's, that most required guarding.

In the end, it was NSA that found the chilling evidence—the sinister devices in the CPU that showed that the KGB had penetrated the code room and had been able to read all of the embassy's communications. Corroborated by secret information from defectors and a rash of executions of CIA assets, it was evidence so shocking, so devastating, so damaging that the CIA and the NSA tried to cover it up, primarily to hide their own embarrassment.

While President Reagan had been briefed on the find, very few others within the CIA, NSA, FBI, and National Security Council knew the truth. Since the intelligence community almost trusted the Soviets more than it trusted the State Department, it kept State in the dark. As a result, the State Department triumphantly leaked stories to the press that no evidence of a penetration had been found, ensuring that the atmosphere of neglect that had led to the security lapses would continue.

But to those within the government who knew, it was one of the biggest scandals in U.S. history—a penetration that decapitated the CIA and its operations in the Soviet Union, that exceeded the damage done by Walker, that surpassed the Iran-Contra scandal as an example of government stupidity and culpability. It was, in the words of one government official who helped prepare briefing papers on it for Reagan, a "bungle beyond imagination."

The question remained: Who did it?

# CHAPTER 2

# The Great Seal

EFFORTS to co-opt the Americans began almost immediately after the U.S. and the Soviet Union established diplomatic relations on November 16, 1933. The American diplomats set up offices in the National Hotel across from the Kremlin. Built in 1903, the hotel had once been home to Vladimir I. Lenin. Besides William C. Bullitt, the ambassador, only three diplomats staffed the temporary embassy. They had no codes, no safes, no couriers, and no security officers.[1]

The following year, the delegation expanded to forty members. They made their offices in a neoclassical home known as Spaso House, just a few blocks from the present embassy and a quarter mile from the Moscow River. Built in 1914 by a wealthy prince, the home has an eighty-two-foot-long ballroom. It is now the residence of the U.S. ambassador.

In his memoirs, George F. Kennan, then a secretary of the embassy and later an ambassador to Moscow, recalled that Sergei, a Soviet national, lived in Spaso House and tended the furnace.[2] The Americans accepted this intrusion just as they accepted Moscow's dreary skies and temperatures of forty degrees below zero.

Spaso House had only one telephone line with two extensions, one upstairs and one downstairs. "These tinkled halfheartedly and indiscriminately, day and night; and when one answered them there was often no reaction at the other end, only labored breathing and a baffling verbal silence," Kennan wrote.

According to Kennan, a Soviet aide had explained to him, in a rather embarrassed confidence, that Georgi V. Chicherin was in the habit of using the phone to summon Sergei to clean his apartment next door. Chicherin, a former Soviet government official who had gone into disfavor, was reluctant to speak directly over the phone, so his method of signaling took the form of calling Spaso House and maintaining a charged silence.

No doubt this was the way the Soviet security police, then called the OGPU, summoned Sergei for consultations on how to further co-opt the Americans. But Kennan felt it had even more to do with the fact that Sergei must be a Soviet government functionary who was the only one authorized to see Chicherin. Kennan recognized, nonetheless, that Sergei probably had "other connections and responsibilities" beyond tending the furnace.

Charles E. Bohlen, who joined the delegation in 1934, put it more bluntly:

"It was generally assumed from the beginning that Spaso House was insecure and that Sergei was an agent of the Soviet security police," he said.[3] "We suspected that Sergei's apartment contained espionage devices, but his door was always locked and we had no key to it. Years later, when I was ambassador and Sergei was still caretaker, I insisted on having a key. After a delay of several weeks, one was produced, but the apartment had been cleaned out."

Thus, for two decades, the Americans suspected that Sergei was probably bugging their premises. In fact, a bugging device was found in a wall of the ambassador's office almost as soon as he moved in. But like sheep being led to slaughter, the Americans simply accepted their fate, leaving Sergei to his devices and treating the security question as if it were an amusing if distasteful part of their existence.

The Marine security guard program did not start worldwide until 1949, but Bullitt early on requested six Marine guards for Moscow. The Marines lived at the Savoy Hotel along with the rest of the staff.

One day Bohlen was sitting in the lobby of the hotel when a heavily made-up Soviet woman pranced to the desk and asked for Sergeant O'Dean's room number. As Bohlen recalled it, the desk clerk looked up at her suspiciously and asked, "Why do you want to visit Sergeant O'Dean?"

She replied airily, "I am his Russian teacher."[4]

By 1935 the embassy had moved into more permanent quarters in an office building on Mokhavaya Street next to the National Hotel. According to Bohlen, Bullitt urged the staff to mingle with the Muskovites as a way of establishing closer ties. The Soviets took that literally and flooded the embassy with ravishing ballerinas. Several of them made themselves at home at the embassy, eating lunch and dinner there and talking and drinking with the diplomats into the early morning hours.

"In those day, the ballerinas were given free run of the diplomatic corps, and many temporary liaisons were formed," Bohlen said.[5] "One of the girls had an unrequited passion for Bullitt, and she spent hours talking of her undying love for the ambassador, describing him as her sun, her moon, and her stars." Bullitt even took her on a boat ride up the Moscow River.[6]

Within two years, the pattern of lax security had been firmly established. While relations between the two countries then were not as tense as they are today, the Soviets made it plain that they intended to overthrow the capitalist structure and replace it with Communism. The Soviet secret police was an instrument of terror. Even if the Soviet Union were an ally, there was no reason to permit the kind of snooping the Soviets engaged in. Yet the Americans, like diplomats from other countries, had accepted Soviets within the embassy as a fact of life. Like a plant that grows according to the nutrients it is given, the embassy had developed an institutional blindness to security that continued into the present.[7] If there were any doubt about it back then, it was dispelled by a 1940 FBI memorandum that got passed along to President Roosevelt.

Having heard that secret information from the embassy was leaking out, J. Edgar Hoover, then the FBI director, sent a special agent to investigate. Posing as a courier on temporary duty, the agent reported back that the Soviets working at the embassy— thirty-three—almost outnumbered the Americans—thirty-five. They typed, delivered messages, translated, and answered the phones.[8]

"Not being able to find normal female companionship," the

agent reported back, "the men attached to the embassy turn to a group of Soviet prostitutes for companionship. These prostitutes form a regular embassy ring with headquarters in the National Hotel. It is reported all of these girls report constantly to the GPU [a predecessor of the KGB].

"The GPU maintains a watch in front of the embassy building at all hours," he continued. "When a girl of the regular group is seen in the company of an American embassy attaché, no attempt is made to follow her. However, if a strange woman appears in such company, she is followed until she leaves the company of her escort and is then taken into custody and questioned."

According to the agent, the Soviet prostitutes went out with the embassy employees in groups of two or three and pretended they did not speak English.

"Consequently, the men, being unable to talk with the girls, discuss matters among themselves in the presence of these prostitutes," the memo said, citing several examples of secret matters discussed in their presence. "It is reported the girls actually do understand English," the agent added.

The agent found that one of the male code clerks and a male secretary to the then ambassador, Laurence A. Steinhardt, had engaged in "sexual perversion" in the embassy's code room. A few years later the KGB used William J. Vassall's homosexual orientation to entrap him into spying for the Soviets, first when he was a clerk in the British embassy in Moscow and later when he returned to London working for the Admiralty. In addition, the FBI agent in 1940 found a high-ranking embassy employee had been associating with a Soviet woman who had been the paramour of Tyler G. Kent, a former embassy code clerk later convicted by the British for making unauthorized use of classified documents while working as a code clerk at the American embassy in London.[9] The agent reported that another code clerk was living with a Soviet woman.

The FBI agent visited the embassy's code room at night and found all the safes and code books out, with messages lying on the tables. At one point, the code clerk left the undercover agent alone in the code room for forty-five minutes. During that time, the door to the code room was left wide open. At any time, the

Soviet employees who worked a few feet away could have come in and scooped up the secret messages.

The agent also reported that a messenger burned secret messages in the basement. No guards were present to make sure the papers were destroyed.

"It is the custom of the Soviets to loiter in the basement of the building, and usually when the paper from the offices is burned at the close of the day, they gather around and watch the fire," the FBI agent said. "Paper bundles such as the bundles of confidential messages do not burn readily, and even after being in the fire for several minutes, many messages still may be removed and read. Only the Soviets usually know whether the paper thrown into the fire is completely burned."

Steinhardt corrected the abuses after they were pointed out to him, and the code clerks were transferred. But it did not take long for the lackadaisical attitude to return.

When Kennan became ambassador in 1952, he noticed that the interior of Spaso House had just been painted. Checking, he found that Soviets had done the work without any American supervision. No doubt they had left bugs along with their paint.

"We had long since taught ourselves to assume that in Moscow most walls—at least in rooms that diplomats were apt to frequent—had ears," Kennan wrote in his memoirs.

In September 1952, near the end of Kennan's brief tour, two technicians arrived from Washington to check further for bugs. Having found nothing, they asked the ambassador if he would go through the motions of dictating to his secretary in the den. Perhaps the sound of his voice would activate the bugs. As he later reported:

I droned on with the dictation [as] the technicians circulated through other parts of the building. Suddenly, one of them appeared in the doorway of the study and implored me, by signs and whispers, to "keep on, keep on." He then disappeared again but soon returned, accompanied by his colleague, and began to move about the room in which we were working. Centering his attention finally on a corner of the room where there was a radio set on a table, just below a round wooden Great Seal of the United States that hung on the wall, he removed the seal, took up a mason's hammer, and began to hack to pieces the brick wall where the seal had been. When this failed to satisfy him, he turned these destructive attentions on the seal itself.[10]

In the seal the technicians found a cavity resonator that modulated microwaves beamed at it from the building across the street. By converting the reflected beams back into sound waves, the Soviets could reproduce every sound in Kennan's office.

The day after finding the bug, Kennan noticed that his Soviet servants were unusually quiet, even hostile. The tranquil mood of Spaso House had been shattered. The thought of offending them weighed on him. Perhaps, he thought, he should not have assisted the technicians after all.

"Had I been right, I wondered, to lend my person to this deception?" Kennan wrote. "Was it proper for an ambassador to involve himself in this sort of comedy? Or would I have been remiss, in the eyes of my own government, if I had refused to do so? I am not sure, even today, of the answers to these questions."[11]

It was not that Kennan was soft on Soviets—they eventually expelled him because of remarks they did not like. Yet instead of being outraged at the invasion, he was inexplicably filled with trepidation about having played a role in uncovering the bugging device. Through his aide, I asked Kennan to explain his ambivalence.

"He felt that as the ambassador he should not be involved in espionage or counterespionage," the aide reported back.[12] "He wouldn't have done it except for the fact it was in his office and he had to speak in order to activate it."

Kennan's ambivalence then is as difficult to understand as Hartman's approach to security was thirty-five years later. There are those in the State Department who attribute this antipathy toward security to a backlash against the late Senator Joseph McCarthy, who used witch-hunts for imaginary Communists in the State Department to bolster his own power. But the aversion to security predates McCarthy. In any case, the fact that vigilance about security matters is perceived as anti-Communist zealotry only underscores the State Department's deep-seated aversion to security, an aversion that borders on masochism. Neither the right nor the left has any corner on the instinct for self-preservation.

Instead of being rooted in anti-McCarthyism, the State Department's attitude probably is a variation on Henry L. Stimson's view, advanced shortly after he became secretary of state in 1929, that "gentlemen do not read each other's mail."[13] The occasion was his veto of continued funding for the Black Chamber, a cryptographic unit that had broken the codes of Germany, Japan, and the Soviet Union, among others. The fact that these countries were all engaged in trying to break American codes did not seem to matter.

A disinclination to protect one's privacy certainly goes beyond Stimson's desire to avoid intercepting other countries' communications. But the underlying attitude, incomprehensible as it may seem, is the same: that any involvement in protective measures sullies the diplomat, tarnishing his elitist brow.

Just before the Americans found the bug in the Great Seal in the fall of 1952, Joseph Stalin decided he did not want the British or the American embassies near the Kremlin any longer. By stalling, the British managed to stay where they were, since the Soviet leader died the next year. The Americans dutifully moved to their present location on Tchaikovsky Street, slightly more than a mile west of the Kremlin.

Just built, the new quarters was an apartment house that the Americans had to renovate for use as an embassy. Faced with stucco, it was a monstrous-looking building, almost as hideous and oppressive-looking as the J. Edgar Hoover Building in Washington. The inside was a rabbit warren of miniature rooms, stairways wide enough for only one person, and elevators that held no more than three or four people.

Then as now, Soviet construction methods were primitive. The walls were insulated with sawdust and ashes, while the floor was laid on beams made of rough-hewn logs.[14]

To convert the building to an embassy, the Americans knocked out walls and connected rooms to create suites. As in 1979, when they began construction of the latest American embassy in Moscow, the Americans placed security last on their list of priorities.

Bohlen, who was by then ambassador, recalled that " . . .

security men from the embassy were on guard all day to prevent the installation of microphones on the two top floors . . . where I had my office. Unfortunately, because of carelessness and to save money, there was no watch at night."[15]

The guards, of course, were needed at night rather than during the day, when Americans supervised the construction workers. Like turtles turned on their backs, the Americans exposed themselves to whatever devices the Soviets wished to plant in the embassy.

While he was ambassador, Bohlen forbade embassy personnel from getting involved with Soviet women. Nevertheless, at least twelve embassy employees fell prey to Soviet recruitment tactics, usually involving women. Typically, he said, "The secret police took incriminating pictures, then tried to recruit the Americans for espionage."

With the Americans in their new home, the Soviets began a different kind of penetration—microwave bombardment. At first, the microwaves came from a Soviet apartment house to the west of the embassy. Later, they came from the roof of an apartment house to the east and also from an office building to the south.[16]

U.S. intelligence agencies decided the microwaves probably picked up emanations from cavity resonators similar to the one found in the Great Seal. They later realized they could be used as well to track the movement of CIA personnel within the embassy and to trigger false alarms to harass, weardown, and confuse the Marines at night.

Malcolm Toon, the director of the State Department's Soviet desk in the 1960s, suggested to Dean Rusk, then secretary of state, that they tell the embassy employees about the microwaves. Toon felt they should decide for themselves if they wished to continue to live there. Rusk told Toon to check with the ambassador, Llewelyn Thompson. Thompson said telling the employees would mean that the embassy would have to complain to the Soviets about the bombardment. He did not want to ruffle their feathers over something as minor as the health of American workers.

"He was reluctant to do it," Toon said. "He felt it might be an abrasive element in our relations with Moscow. So I lost the battle."[7]

When Walter J. Stoessel, Jr., became ambassador, the Americans finally complained about the microwaves. The State Department commissioned a special study by Johns Hopkins University. The study concluded that the level of radiation over the years had been well below the levels considered safe by the Environmental Protection Agency.

Although the Soviets turned off the radiation temporarily, they soon resumed the bombardment. Toon, who became ambassador after the controversy erupted in February 1976, kept a cartoon from the Fort Worth *Star-Telegram* in his den showing the American ambassador having dinner. The chef comes in and says, "I've got good news and bad news. The good news is that they've turned off the radiation. The bad news is I had the roast in the window."[18]

For the children of the diplomats who lived in the embassy, the new building was a haven, with places to explore and new friends to meet. They looked up to the Marines who lived in the embassy as big brothers who taught them to box and wrestle. Every several weeks, new employees moved in, and they brought with them packing crates that could be used as forts.

The children flooded an area of the back courtyard and used it as an ice-skating rink. For the children, as for their parents, a favorite sport was broom ball, a quaint game that combined hockey and curling. Instead of skates, the children used shoes with rubber suction cups. Instead of a puck, they used a hard ball slightly larger than a tennis ball. Instead of a hockey stick, they used a broom with its bristles wrapped tightly together, then dipped in water and frozen in the cold air.

One day in 1964 the children found a new toy—a tunnel that led from the basement to the bowels of Moscow. So they could see in the dark, the children placed candles on the gas pipes that lined their new play area.[19]

The Americans sealed off the tunnel, but new ones kept appearing, both at the embassy on Tchaikovsky Street and later at the new embassy around the corner. Some of the tunnels were utility conduits. Others appeared to have been designed for the purpose of breaching the embassy's security.

The Soviets had outfitted the embassy with other unwelcome intrusions. On May 16, 1964, the Americans found forty microphones cleverly hidden in bamboo tubes built into the walls. The tubes ran horizontally from the inner walls to the mortar behind the outer facing of the embassy. Because they were made of wood, the tubes could not be spotted by metal detectors. Only a tiny pinhole appeared where the bugs met the inner walls. Because the holes appeared behind radiators, they did not fill up with paint. Nor were the Americans likely to remove the radiators to check for bugs.

Nearly invisible wires led from the microphones in the tubes through the mortar to collection points that ran to nearby Soviet apartments. Microwaves controlled the microphones so they could be turned off in the event of an electronic sweep.

For ten years the bugs had been transmitting conversations from the secure areas of the embassy, including the CIA's and the ambassador's offices. The Americans finally discovered them when the heat was turned off for the spring and they removed the radiators.[20]

The technicians found another fifty microphones hidden in the apartments within the embassy. Foy D. Kohler, then the ambassador, dispatched Stoessel to complain to the Soviet Foreign Ministry.

"He came back with bugs that they had found of ours. So that was that," Kohler said.[21]

Even if they could find all the bugs in the embassy, the Americans knew that trying to remove bugs from their apartments outside the embassy would be like emptying the ocean with a cup. While the Americans were working, the Soviets could always break into their apartments. Soviet nannies and maids who worked there could let them in. If they had sensitive information to discuss, the Americans would try to communicate in writing or take a walk in the park. But even the outdoors was not safe. The Soviets would try to pick up their conversations with parabolic microphones, or they tried to read their lips.

The Americans learned that the best way to direct their Soviet help was by talking to the walls. One evening in 1971, Roger A.

Provencher, then the embassy's administrative counselor, went out with his wife, Josiette. When they returned, she opened the refrigerator and noticed that two pounds of butter had disappeared.

"The maid must have taken it," she said.

The next morning, the Provenchers heard the Soviet maid let herself in, open the refrigerator, then slam it.

"There's your butter!" she announced.[22]

When Toon became ambassador, his wife found that if she talked to the walls, the maids at Spaso House took her complaints about the way they made the beds far more seriously.[23]

Almost as soon as they moved in, the Americans began planning for a larger embassy that they would design. The Soviets, meanwhile, wanted a new embassy to replace the former private home they owned on Sixteenth Street in Washington.

As early as January 1963 the Soviets began negotiating for land for their embassy. They chose a site in Chevy Chase, D.C., but a court blocked the acquisition because of zoning regulations. The U.S. General Services Administration proposed instead a site called Mount Alto. The second-highest point in Washington, Mount Alto would give the Soviets a tremendous advantage in intercepting microwave communications in Washington.

At first, the Soviets were more interested in Tregaron, the estate of the late Joseph E. Davies, who followed Bullitt as ambassador to Moscow. The site was in a lower part of the city but gave the Soviets more privacy. Congressman John J. Rooney, who controlled the State Department's budget with an iron fist, lived two blocks from Tregaron in Washington's Cleveland Park.

"I'd rather have a nigger living next to me than a Russian," he told the realtor representing Davies's heirs.[24]

As a result, the Soviets accepted the Mount Alto site, while the Americans agreed to a low-lying plot for their own new embassy, around the corner from the existing one.

On May 16, 1969, the two countries signed the Embassy Sites Agreement giving each the right to build their respective embassies on land leased for eighty-five years. The agreement linked the two projects so that both would start at the same time. According to a 1975 State Department memorandum, strict reciprocity was needed, since the Soviets had been dragging their heels on making the necessary arrangements for the project in Moscow.[25]

Nevertheless, in March 1977 the State Department signed a protocol allowing the Soviets to start on their embassy before the Americans started on theirs. In return, the Soviets gave the Americans additional space for apartments and some price reductions. The Soviets then delayed agreeing to a construction contract for the Moscow project. By the time it was signed in 1979, the Soviets had already built a portion of their new embassy in Washington.

The Americans wound up paying roughly twice what they had anticipated. The 1976 State Department cost estimate had been $75 to $100 million. By 1987, Congress had appropriated $192 million for the new embassy, including $37 million for additional security measures.[26] The cost for the new Soviet embassy came in almost exactly as projected.

Security precautions followed the same pattern. While the Soviets insisted on watching the Americans pour concrete for the embassy in Washington, the Americans blithely let the Soviets manufacture precast concrete for the American embassy in Soviet plants. While the Soviets surrounded their construction site with high fences and armed guards, the Americans had unarmed Marines watch four video screens, whose cameras usually didn't work. While the Soviets paid $50,000 extra so the American contractors would delay installing girders while the Soviets X-rayed them, the Americans let the Soviets install girders without taking X-rays of them first, on the assumption that any bugs could be removed later.

The differences in approach would soon create an eavesdropping monster in Moscow.

# CHAPTER 3

## The Station

THE CIA STATION in Moscow consisted of a dozen intelligence officers who operated out of the seventh floor of the embassy. The chief of the station was Murat Natirboff, a crusty, sixty-year-old former Marine whose family came from White Russia.[1]

In running spy operations in Moscow, the CIA officers faced an almost impossible task. The Soviets controlled their citizens like battery-operated toy cars. They could not travel from one city to another, rent an apartment, write an article, use a photocopying machine, choose an occupation, be admitted to a university, or change jobs without government approval. Unless they received permission, they could be shot for leaving the country. Just to make sure no one got away, the Soviets locked passengers in their berths on overnight trains between Moscow and Leningrad.[2]

The CIA officers operated undercover, ostensibly carrying out the functions of State Department officers. For the most part, the KGB knew who they were anyway. If they had served at other posts, the KGB had a record on them and had probably spotted them as spooks in the past. If they were new, the Soviets assumed they must be intelligence officers, figuring the Americans would send only experienced diplomats to an important post like Moscow.

In the end, it did not make much of a difference. The Soviets, being highly suspicious, assumed all foreigners were spies. And that certainly included Americans assigned to the embassy.

The KGB was everywhere—listening in on calls, bugging apartments, beaming microwaves at them, picking up vibrations from voices off windows, and following anyone who left the embassy. The KGB used the latest video recorders to film activities in a room through concealed lenses just a sixteenth of an inch in diameter. They carried briefcases fitted with cameras whose lenses were concealed by flaps that automatically opened and closed. While following people, they used secure communications systems on Moscow's subways to keep in touch with one another.[3]

According to Stanislav Levchenko, a KGB major stationed in Tokyo until he defected in 1979, the KGB deploys hundreds of officers around the American embassy, ready to follow anyone who leaves. In fact, the Soviet apartment building attached to the south wing of the embassy is so filled with KGB officers it is practically a KGB barracks.

"They're selling ice cream, they're riding bikes, they're inside the apartments across the street," Levchenko said.[4]

"They own the real estate," a former CIA official said. "They don't have any manpower problems. Since they control the situation, they can take control of anything—traffic, telephones, the fire department. They have very extravagant facilities across the street [from the embassy] for surveillance. A lot of it is stationary surveillance. There is no one in the rearview mirror. But your passage is recorded.[5]

"You're never really sure you're not dealing with the cops, even if the guy winks or smiles," he said. "So you have no resources. You don't have the manpower. If you do get a guy who is legitimate, and he wants to put something in your palm, it's entirely possible that by the time you see him again, he's been brought under control. He's under new management."

Besides conducting surreptitious surveillance, the Soviets stationed militiamen at the front door of the embassy. They worked for the ministry of internal affairs, or MVD. In the guise of protecting the embassy from terrorists, they checked the identification of everyone who entered, including Americans. If Soviets tried to enter the embassy without the permission of their government, the militia men arrested them or beat them.

For good measure, the Soviets sprinkled "spy dust" in the embassy to help them track CIA officers. No doubt applied by the Soviets working in the embassy, the dust was a chemical known as NPPD. The wife of an embassy officer first noticed the yellowish powder on her husband's coat in 1985.[6] Apparently, the Soviets had been sloppy and had left too much of the substance around.

Checking further, embassy security people found the dust sprinkled on doorknobs that might be used by CIA officers. In addition, the Soviets had dabbed it on the steering wheels and door handles of cars used by CIA officers. CIA officers left their car windows open in case anyone wanted to leave messages for them, so it was easy for the KGB to leave the dust in their cars.

The explanation pieced together by the intelligence agencies was that the Soviets used the dust to spot Soviets who might be in contact with the CIA. If a suspect had shaken hands with a CIA officer or touched the same doorknob, the NPPD would rub off on his hands and transfer to his belongings. The Soviets applied a chemical to the desk, filing cabinets, or steering wheel of the suspect. On contact, the chemical made the "spy dust" turn pink, heralding the fact that the hapless suspect had had unauthorized contacts with CIA officers. The Soviets might then set up video cameras to try to catch the suspect in the act of stealing secret documents.

On August 21, 1985, the U.S. lodged a complaint with the Soviets about their use of "spy dust" in the embassy. Concerned that it might be carcinogenic, a team of scientists led by the National Institute for Environmental Health Sciences visited Moscow and took samples back to the U.S. After testing the chemical on animals, they concluded that the spy dust, like the microwaves, posed no threat to health.[7]

Beyond the external threats, CIA officers assigned to Moscow experienced a certain amount of stress because of internal friction. Many State Department officers considered the CIA an obnoxious presence. A former consul general to Leningrad said that ideally an embassy would have no intelligence officers. One reason for the resentment was the CIA officers' special position within the embassy.

"He [the CIA officer] sees the ambassador directly. That's something, because you're waiting in line to do that. This guy is younger than you are. Also they don't talk about what they're doing. They don't join the club and swap war stories. There's also resentment about housing. The CIA guy might go into a place where his predecessor was. It might be more desirable housing," a former CIA official said.[8]

For their part, many State Department officers felt that the CIA looked upon an embassy as a cover for their own activities and did not appreciate the importance of diplomacy.

"Some in the intelligence community feel the only thing the embassy is important for is a platform for covert intelligence," a State Department official formerly assigned to the Moscow embassy said. "The rest of it is sort of Ivy League, mushy stuff mainly useful at cocktail parties. We feel that what the embassy does across the board is important. While intelligence gathering is an important part of what the embassy does, it's by far not the only thing and arguably not the most important thing."[9]

On the other hand, a former CIA official said of State officers: "Their position is to not take a position on anything: 'We won't argue and will let it pass. We won't respond to provocations.' It's as if they all had lobotomies."

In communicating with Soviets developed as agents, the CIA used a panoply of signaling devices ranging from chalk marks left on walls and newspapers arranged in certain positions to radio transmitters that sent coded messages in bursts to satellites.

In sending reports back to Langley, the CIA officers were supposed to use cryptonyms to hide the names of their agents. In addition, they transmitted a constant stream of nonsense because an increase in traffic might signal to the Soviets that something was in the offing. If they developed a new and important source, the CIA officers were supposed to get on a plane and fly to Washington to report it. But sometimes that rule was honored in the breach.[10] In any case, the traffic that went back and forth through the CPU contained enough details about CIA operations that the Soviets could deduce, if they could read the messages, identities of CIA assets. For example, the cables included the dates of expected document pickups, amounts of money to be paid, and the types of information obtained.

The CIA was established in 1947 but it did not send an officer to Moscow until 1953, in part because of State Department objections.[11] State felt the presence of intelligence officers within the embassy would impair its diplomatic mission. The Soviets, meanwhile, had been sending spies to the U.S. for years. There was, for example, Rudolph Abel, an "illegal" who slipped into the U.S. using a false passport in 1949. When the FBI arrested him at Manhattan's Latham Hotel in 1957, the agents discovered enough spy paraphernalia in his room to stock an intelligence museum— microfilm concealed in nickels, secret writing materials, and hollow pencils and shaving brushes containing film. So important was he to the Soviets that they traded him in 1962 for Francis Gary Powers, the pilot of the U-2 reconnaissance plane shot down over Russia.

Abel never publicly admitted his guilt, but according to documents obtained under the Freedom of Information Act, two of his lawyers told the FBI after he was convicted that he had admitted to them he was a Soviet intelligence officer engaged in spying activities.[12]

Peer de Silva, the chief of operations of the CIA's Soviet bloc division, recounted in his memoirs sending the first CIA officer approved by the State Department to Moscow in 1953. Like any intelligence officer, it was the CIA man's job to run agents, usually locals with access to information. The CIA already had a valuable agent in Moscow, and the CIA officer was to locate dead drops—nooks and crannies in trees and telephone poles where the agent could leave documents for him. But the agent reported back to the agency that the dead drops selected by the officer were inaccessible and useless.

"What are you trying to do? Kill me?" he asked.[13]

The CIA dispatched another officer to Moscow. He reported back that within a week of arriving in Moscow, the first officer had begun sleeping with his KGB maid. The officer had confessed to Bohlen, then the ambassador, who quickly sent him home. Without referring to the officer as a CIA man, Bohlen, in his memoirs, mentioned that one of the twelve Americans compromised while he was ambassador was a "security officer."

"His work was not only worthless, but much had been fabricated," de Silva wrote of the CIA officer.

Over the years, many CIA officers sent to Moscow have been daring and cunning. But like the first officer sent to Moscow, a disproportionate number have been alcoholics, people suffering from psychological problems, or con artists. Some of the first CIA officers were linguists who knew nothing about spying.

"In those days, we learned about spying from novels," a CIA officer from the 1950s said. "The training division figured they knew about it in novels."

The former officer said some CIA officers pretended to have sources that did not exist.

"One case officer fabricated a complete network of agents by hiding them behind cryptonyms and pseudonyms," he said.[14]

For years, the CIA sent its newest recruits to Moscow on the theory that the KGB would have a harder time identifying them as CIA officers. Thus the CIA assigned Edward Lee Howard, who had never had a foreign post, to Moscow.

When he applied to the CIA in 1980, Howard admitted that he used illicit drugs, but he promised to stop. Almost as if the CIA were looking for trouble, it hired him anyway. Just before he was to leave for Moscow, another polygraph test revealed he was still using drugs and was an alcoholic as well.[15]

The CIA compounded its initial error by firing him instead of finding him another job first. Thus he became a walking time bomb, full of secrets he had learned about Moscow station. He admitted to another CIA officer that he had thought about selling all he knew to the Soviets to get revenge. Yet the CIA took a year to alert the FBI. Meanwhile, Howard met with the KGB in Vienna and fled the U.S. in September 1985. Eventually, he defected to the Soviet Union. There, he helps the KGB identify CIA officers assigned to the embassy.

In part because spying in Moscow is so difficult, about 95 percent of the CIA's information on the Soviet Union comes from technical sources—spy satellites that distinguish numbers on license plates, interceptions of Soviet communications, and sensors ranging from radar to seismic devices that track Soviet missiles, airplanes, and other weapons systems from ships, ground stations, and satellites. While the CIA analyzes the results, other agencies do much of the collection work. NSA, for example, intercepts communications. The National Reconnaissance Office, operated jointly by the Air Force and CIA, is in charge of lofting of spy satellites.

The CIA wants to know the capabilities of existing Soviet weapons, military strategies, and plans for development of new weapons. Over the years, the CIA has been able to spot every new weapons system deployed by the Soviets.[16] Each system follows a natural progression, from inception to manufacture. Often, the process takes twenty years. When one system is finished, the CIA looks for another to take its place in military test facilities.

In preparing the National Intelligence Estimates that go to the President through the National Security Council, the CIA and the intelligence community analyze both technical and human sources of information, the latter known as HUMINT. Not all human intelligence entails covert spying. Some of it comes from diplomats, who pick up a wealth of information from Soviet officials on the organization of Soviet agencies, the background of government officials, religious and political developments, and the latest internal intrigues.

Besides CIA officers, military attachés assigned to the Defense Intelligence Agency obtain information in Moscow on Soviet military strength and pass it along. Finally, the CIA sifts through information from the open press and from reports of doctors, economists, and scientists who visit the Soviet Union.

In this process, intelligence from CIA operatives in Moscow is considered icing on the cake. It cannot be relied on in any given year. Nor is it always accurate. The Soviets, for example, often feed the CIA misinformation through double agents. On the other hand, some information cannot be obtained any other way. A spy satellite cannot plumb the thinking of a scientist. Nor can interceptions of communications normally pick up discussions about a new weapons project.

The object of Moscow station is to develop and run Soviet agents who can provide that kind of information, preferably in the form of documents outlining military plans, the workings of military installations, and the details of Soviet research.

As a result of the close scrutiny given CIA officers in Moscow, a former CIA officer said flatly, "You can't cultivate people in Moscow."[17]

Because of the difficulties, the officers assigned to the station usually wound up handling agents who had been cultivated by others. In some cases, the CIA developed the agents when they were outside the Soviet Union. For example, Anatoli N. Filatov, a colonel in the GRU, or Soviet military intelligence, approached the CIA in the mid-1970s when Filatov was stationed in Algiers. After he was transferred to Moscow, the CIA assigned a case officer to work with Filatov there. It did not take long for the KGB to catch on. Just over a year later, the KGB arrested Filatov and expelled the case officer. The Soviets sentenced Filatov to fifteen years in prison.[18]

Over the years, no CIA asset has been as prolific as Oleg Penkovsky, another GRU officer who agreed to spy for the West in 1962. For sixteen months he provided the British MI-6 and the CIA with running accounts of Soviet military strategies, Soviet plans during the Cuban missile crisis, and details of KGB and GRU operations targeted against the U.S.[19] In addition, he gave the CIA a series of articles from a top-secret military magazine which had asked Soviet military leaders to express their views on policy. The articles provided insight into the Soviet military mind.

Penkovsky initially approached a CIA officer in Moscow but the CIA rejected him, thinking he was a Soviet plant.[20] After another unsuccessful attempt with a Canadian, he eventually approached Greville Wynne, a former British intelligence officer who was visiting Moscow on business. Wynne introduced the GRU officer to the British MI-6. The CIA then agreed jointly to finance and run the spying operation with the British.

Another method used by the CIA for developing agents is to send traveling contract employees for brief visits in the Soviet Union. Boris Korczak is an example of such an operator.

Brash and swaggering, Korczak is a Lithuanian émigré who offered his services to the CIA in Copenhagen in 1970. According to Korczak's account, he became a CIA contract employee whose cover was that of an electronics importer and exporter.[21] Motivated by a fierce hatred of the Communist regime, he visited a Soviet exhibition in Copenhagen in 1973, where he began developing contacts with KGB officers.

While the Soviets were aware of Korczak's anti-Soviet background, he convinced them that he wanted to make amends and return to the Eastern bloc.

"I never admitted I made a mistake," he said. "But I said I'm ready to do what I need to in order to go back home. You can't tell them suddenly you are convinced you were wrong."

In 1975 the KGB recruited Korczak to gather information in the Far East. At first, the KGB gave him little tasks—he was to report on the appearance of an electronics firm's office, for example. Gradually, the KGB asked him to do more important operations, like obtaining secret electronics manuals. He was now a double agent, ostensibly working for the KGB. In fact, he was reporting to the CIA.

In visits to Moscow, Korczak became acquainted with a KGB officer who drank heavily and was dissatisfied with his slow rise within the organization.

One night over vodka, the KGB man said he hated himself for working for the KGB.

"I am going to shoot myself," he said.

"That's so stupid," Korczak said. "There are other ways. How about getting even?"

Korczak offered to introduce him to a CIA officer, who began obtaining information from him on Soviet naval secrets. In 1979, according to Korczak, his career as a double agent came to an end when a drunk CIA officer in Copenhagen blurted out his identity at a reception. To this day he carries a gun and claims to have been the target of a KGB assassination plot.

In theory, one of the functions of Moscow station was to counter any Soviet attempts to penetrate the station and the embassy. In practice, the CIA was far more interested in the glamorous activity of running spies than it was in the tedious work of guarding the embassy from hostile intelligence threats.

Incredibly, the CIA was not all that interested in developing expertise on the workings of the KGB, a prime requirement in any effort to counter the work of the opposition. When the National Security Council wanted the latest information on the KGB, it turned to the FBI, not the CIA.

"The CIA does not try to learn about the KGB. Their interest is in running operations," said a high-ranking U.S. intelligence official.[22]

"Within the CIA, studying the KGB is for fifty-year-olds who have been pushed aside in the hierarchy," a former CIA official said.[23]

The result was that defending the embassy fell to the RSO— the State Department regional security officer. The RSO reported to the administrative counselor, who reported to the deputy chief of mission, who reported to the ambassador. By any standard, he was a minor figure in the power structure of the embassy, a mere handmaiden to the important work of the diplomats.

The Soviets, on the other hand, accorded top priority to penetrating the embassy and had developed such intrusions into an art form.

# CHAPTER 4

# The Opposition

THE KGB has certain natural advantages over the CIA. The CIA has to recruit new employees mainly through job fairs and ads in newspapers. The KGB does not have to recruit. It simply decides which of the best university graduates it wants. Unlike the CIA, the KGB is not hindered by interagency rivalries. Beside the Communist Party, the KGB is the most powerful organ in Soviet society. Its officers are layered within all the other agencies of the government and within the governments of Soviet satellites. Its role is not only to spy on foreigners but to spy on Soviets as well. The KGB is not constrained by constitutional protections that guarantee due process as in the U.S. Nor does it have to worry about exposure in the press.

To carry out all its functions, the KGB has 1.2 million employees plus hundreds of thousands of informants. The fact that its operations are centralized makes it far more efficient than American law-enforcement and intelligence agencies with an equivalent number of employees.[1]

Within the KGB, the Second Chief Directorate, or counterintelligence division, has general responsibility for targeting foreigners and embassies. The Seventh Directorate carries out the surveillance.

According to Ilya Dzhirkvelov—a KGB defector who worked in both the First Chief Directorate, which conducts intelligence operations overseas, and the Second Chief Directorate—compromising embassies and foreigners who worked for them is one of the KGB's top priorities.

41

"Before a foreigner who applies to enter the Soviet Union receives his visa, he is carefully screened by the KGB on the basis of its vast records and of a report received from the KGB *rezidentura* in his country of origin," Dzhirkvelov wrote in his book *Secret Servant*.[2] "If the foreigner turns out to be 'clean,' he may not be kept under constant surveillance, though he will be surrounded by informers. But if there is any doubt about him, he will be kept under observation until he leaves and, depending upon the KGB's plans, appropriate prophylactic measures or special actions may be put into effect, such as attempts to compromise, blackmail, or even expel him from the country."

According to Dzhirkvelov's own experience in tracking foreigners for the KGB's Second Chief Directorate, the KGB wanted not only to render diplomats, journalists, businessmen, and military attachés harmless, but also to recruit them as sources of information or even as agents of influence. He said others might be selected for expulsion. If the Soviets could compromise them, he said, they could arrest them and accuse them of engaging in some kind of spying or espionage activity.

Dzhirkvelov said the monitoring service for listening to telephone conversations is a vast organization that employs translators familiar with every language, including Swahili. Any phone conversation can be assumed to be monitored, and conversations in restaurants were not immune from listening. The more fashionable restaurants have bugging devices in areas where foreigners are seated.

Typically, Dzhirkvelov said, the KGB knows about a diplomat's interests before he arrives. For example, when the KGB assigned Dzhirkvelov to compromise a young Near East diplomat, the KGB was able to tell him before the man arrived that the man was not connected with any intelligence service, that he liked literature and history, and that his main interest was European women. Once he arrived, the KGB men noticed that he liked visiting restaurants with Middle Eastern cuisine and would become friends with the waitresses. They also took note of the fact that the young man was still living at the Metropole Hotel because UPDK, a branch of the Foreign Ministry, had not yet found him better accommodations.

According to Dzhirkvelov, UPDK in fact is a department of

the KGB, which used it to manipulate the diplomats' environment. Besides providing living quarters, the agency supplies embassies with Soviet employees. If a car needs repairing, the embassy must call UPDK. If a diplomat wants tickets to the Bolshoi, the embassy calls UPDK. If a diplomat wants to travel outside a twenty-five-mile limit around Moscow, UPDK must approve. When the Soviets feel like turning up the heat on a diplomat, they instruct UPDK to make it difficult for a diplomat to find an apartment.

Roger A. Provencher, the administrative counselor in the American embassy in the early 1970s, recalled that UPDK continually outfoxed the Americans. "UPDK had the same people in the 1970s as in the 1960s," he said. "The Americans tried to conceal their personal lives as much as possible from the Soviet workers, knowing full well that the Soviet staff was trying to find information that could be used to compromise the Americans." But Provencher said that through eavesdropping and other intrusions, UPDK repeatedly obtained the information the KGB wanted.[3]

By observing the diplomat, Dzhirkvelov knew that he favored the Uzbekistan restaurant and liked blondes. So he arranged for a sexy, blonde KGB plant to get a job as a waitress there—a woman whose taste in entertainment ran to orgies and who had been working for the KGB for several years. The first time he visited the restaurant, she caught his eye, and he pressed her to spend the evening with him. She had been instructed not to agree so easily—to play the part of a respectable young woman.

Later, she moved in with the diplomat. The KGB recorded their sexual activites on cameras. Meanwhile, the KGB had told UPDK not to give the diplomat an apartment. Upset that he was still living in a hotel, he complained to his new girlfriend, who arranged a casual meeting with Dzhirkvelov in a restaurant. Of course, the man was not told that Dzhirkvelov was a KGB officer.

The two chatted about Moscow and the theater. The diplomat commented that he was struck by the freedom he enjoyed after having been told foreigners were followed or compromised in Moscow. But the diplomat complained that for three months he had been forced to live in the hotel.

Dzhirkvelov looked surprised and asked whether he would

object if he looked into the matter. He said he had some friends in the Foreign Ministry who might help. The diplomat's face lit up at the suggestion. He gave Dzhirkvelov his card and said he should phone him if he could help him. Claiming he worked for the Institute of Oriental Studies, Dzhirkvelov gave the man a phone number that rang at his desk at the KGB. In the phone book, the number was listed as a number for the Institute.

Within a few days, Dzhirkvelov told the diplomat a flat had been arranged, but the matter must be kept secret. The diplomat happily agreed.

The diplomat, and his girlfriend, continued to meet with Dzhirkvelov. Usually, Dzhirkvelov brought along another KGB officer whom he introduced as his wife. During their talks, the diplomat discussed his government's aims in domestic affairs and its participation in national liberation movements. Once the diplomat had moved into his new apartment, he opened up even more and discussed the diplomats he knew from the American, French, and British embassies.

"This was not simply because I had done him a favor or was on the surface very open with him, criticizing some aspects of life in the U.S.S.R. It was rather because what we called the 'familiarity factor' was beginning to come into play: eventually even the most cautious person drops his guard and forgets that the person he is talking to represents a foreign state," Dzhirkvelov said.[4]

Eventually, Dzhirkvelov turned the screws on the diplomat. The KGB wanted to know the identity of a Soviet citizen who had scrambled over the wall of the diplomat's embassy. Dzhirkvelov apologized for placing the diplomat in an awkward position, but he said he had been asked for the information from the Foreign Ministry official who had helped the diplomat get his apartment. After some internal debate, the diplomat revealed the defector's identity to Dzhirkvelov. The KGB man then suggested that keeping the man would be harmful to relations between the two countries and was not worth it. Whereupon the diplomat persuaded his ambassador to hand the man over to the Soviet authorities.

Later, Dzhirkvelov turned the screws several more rotations. He instructed the girlfriend to incite the diplomat to beat her up. Gloomily, Dzhirkvelov told him that the woman had complained to the courts and had a medical statement documenting that she had bruises and a fractured rib. He told him this could lead to his expulsion.

Eventually, the diplomat began working directly for the KGB while feigning loyalty to his own country.

The greatest possible coup for the KGB was the penetration of an embassy. It was virtually impossible in the 1950s to break into the American, British, or French embassies, so the Soviets instead targeted embassies that had friendly relations with those countries. One was Turkey, a member of NATO. The KGB wanted to obtain documents, notes, codes, and code books that would give insight into relations between Turkey and its allies.

"After carefully studying the possibilities of penetrating the Turkish embassy, we came to the conclusion that there was a 100 percent guarantee of success," said Dzhirkvelov.[5] He said his superiors, after clearing it with the Central Committee, gave permission to carry out the operation.

For the penetration, the KGB chose a Sunday during the summer because most of the employees of the embassy would be on vacation or not working. At the KGB's request, Soviet citizens and foreigners living in Moscow invited the few employees who remained in the embassy to social functions that day.

A special group of agents placed the streets around the embassy under surveillance, and other KGB men replaced the traffic police in the area. The embassy guard had been collaborating with the KGB and was paid to let the KGB in. If he were found out, he was told, he would be guaranteed a comfortable living in the Soviet Union.

The operation lasted several hours, according to Dzhirkvelov. Experts at cracking safes even opened the ambassador's safe, and photographers took pictures of documents, which were then resealed as if they had never been opened. The KGB officers photographed more than a thousand sheets of documents and notes. They also installed new microphones to replace the ones put in earlier by the KGB. Many had become obsolete or had simply worn out.

The KGB officers had no confidence in the walkie-talkies of that day and did not use them. Instead, a technician had set up a communications system within the embassy so that the officers could talk with the director of the operation, who remained outside. Suddenly, the KGB men got a message that one of the diplomats who had been invited out had become apprehensive and was returning to the embassy. They began putting everything back in order, Dzhirkvelov said. If the Turks discovered them before they escaped, the KGB men had decided they would pretend they were ordinary thieves. They realized the story would be barely credible.

As it turned out, the director of the operation arranged for the Turkish official to have a minor traffic accident. The driver of the other car demanded that the traffic police be summoned to establish who was to blame for the accident. An inspector arrived, witnesses were questioned, and a report was written. By that time, the KGB officers had left the embassy.

"In the same way we penetrated the Egyptian, Iranian, Syrian, and other embassies, for which we were rewarded with inscribed watches and the title of Honored Chekists," Dzhirkvelov said.

By allowing Soviets to work in the American embassy, the Americans made the KGB's job that much easier. According to Levchenko, the former KGB major who defected from Tokyo in 1979, the policy was "naive."

"That was really smart having Soviet operators and employees," Levchenko commented sardonically.[6]

Dzhirkvelov told me each Soviet worker at the embassy was a KGB informant or agent who reported at least once a week to his KGB case officer.[7] Besides compromising Americans and picking up information inside the embassy, they were useful for keeping track of them, he said.

"It is practically impossible to keep every foreigner under surveillance," he said. "If the drivers [chauffeurs] work with you, then you know where they went and at what time."

What Dzhirkvelov called the "familiarity factor" worked especially well with the Marines, who were generally shunned by the rest of the embassy staff. Rather than discouraging fraternization, the State Department permitted them to invite Soviet workers at the embassy to social functions like the annual Marine Corps ball. It was almost as if the State Department dared the Marines to go to bed with Soviet women.

In 1971, when Jacob D. Beam was ambassador, the Marines extended their usual invitations to the Soviet workers to attend the Marine Corps ball. One of the Soviet guests was a twenty-four-year-old knockout who was so pretty the embassy hesitated to employ her when UPDK assigned her to work there. The woman showed up half an hour late, so her entrance was spectacular.[8]

"Her hair was well done, she had a beautiful face, a body like you've never seen before, and a bright red dress that was like paint on her body. There was nothing underneath. You could see the nipples and pubic hair," recalled Provencher, then the embassy's administrative counselor.

An hour later she disappeared. Comparing notes, the diplomats realized one Marine was missing. At 6:30 A.M., the man stumbled in. He told his detachment commander he couldn't help himself.

"She took me to her place," he said. "Then she took me to a friend's house. There were two or three other men, and two or three other women, and they did a lot of drinking, and there was some intercourse," he said.

The detachment commander brought the Marine to the regional security officer and then to Provencher.

"Well, do you have anything to say for yourself?" Provencher asked.

"Yes, sir," he said. "Best piece of ass I ever had, sir."

The marine was sent home that day. But other compromises did not end so neatly.

"Suddenly, the almost oppressive stillness was literally shattered by the demandingly incessant ring of the unusually loud telephone bell at the reception desk switchboard," Irvin C. Scarbeck, the second secretary of the American embassy in Warsaw, said in describing the way his downfall began in December 1960.[9]

"During the day, the bell could ring a hundred times and I could never hear it; at night, in the high-ceilinged, ancient old converted town house, it sounded like a burglar alarm. But then, I thought, it has to be. The Marine guard can be all over the building, shaking down the rooms for unlocked safes, classified documents inadvertently left lying around, and other security violations. The bell had to be loud."

The Marine guard answered the phone and asked Scarbeck if he would take it. On the line was a woman speaking Polish.

"If I had had even the slightest smidgen of hunch in my makeup; if I had possessed even the most infinitesimal particle of clairvoyance; if I could have had the faintest glimmerings of what must inevitably and inexorably result if I so much as said the first word into that telephone, I would have probably fled the embassy shrieking in terror and thenceforth regarded the place as the abode of the damned," Scarbeck said. Instead, Scarbeck, who was the general services officer, picked up the receiver and heard a voice that intrigued him.

"It had a sort of metallic quality which gave it a unique bell-like sound when she pronounced certain words," he recalled. "The bell-like quality carried over into the peals of laughter which came from her following each of my floundering attempts to elaborate on my obviously unclear explanations."

The woman introduced herself as Urszula Discher, a Polish woman who said she worked for an American diplomatic family. She said she was calling because she wanted another job; her present job entailed working late into the evening. They talked for half an hour, and Scarbeck asked her if she would like to meet for coffee. After all, his wife had just left with their children to visit her family in West Germany, and Scarbeck was looking for excitement. He picked her up in his car.

"As I pulled away from the curb, I looked over at her to find her staring at me with the biggest, darkest eyes I think I had ever seen," he said.

They talked, and the next day the twenty-two-year-old Discher called Scarbeck to say she needed help urgently. Her landlord was about to kick her out because she was three months behind in the rent. In all likelihood, the Polish security police concocted the story. They must have been amazed when Scarbeck fell for it.

"Now on the one hand I was suspicious as hell," Scarbeck said. "Just got to know the gal the night before, and here she was the very next day giving out with a hard-luck story and asking for financial assistance. On the other hand, she certainly did have great, frightened doelike eyes; she was really quite attractive; and the story of her life as she had told it to me did seem to ring true."

When he asked how much money she needed, she said ten dollars. Scarbeck agreed to meet her in a park across from the embassy. As he handed the money to her, she kissed the back of his hand.

Scarbeck had received thorough briefings from the State Department about attempts to blackmail diplomats, including warnings about female agents who worked hand-in-glove with the UB, the Polish intelligence service.

"The UB agent, we learned, could be anyone, from . . . the seemingly dull and stupid waiter in the public restaurant, to the maid employed in our homes, to the ace mechanic at the embassy garage, or even our most efficient Polish aide or secretary in the embassy itself."

Nevertheless, Scarbeck saw her again the following day and took her for a ride in the country. Shortly thereafter, he became involved with her sexually. Then came the unmasking, when Polish agents smashed through the door of her apartment and ripped the blankets from their naked bodies.

As the agents dragged her away, three others held Scarbeck. She wrenched one hand free, swung around, and almost screamed, "What shall I do? What shall I tell them?"

When the Polish security service asked for classified documents, Scarbeck threatened to go to the ambassador. One of the officers commented blandly, "You can go to the ambassador if you like; we cannot stop you. But remember that the punishment of the Polish citizen involved in this with you will be carried out!"

Specifically, the police threatened to send Discher to a prison brothel, explaining that she would service the needs of male prisoners. It was a thought so disturbing to Scarbeck that he could not bear to talk about it. This was a threat the State Department had not warned him about, and he fell for it, agreeing to give the Poles classified documents from the embassy. At first he gave them personnel manuals. When the Poles were not satisfied, he gave them a classified appraisal by Beam, then the U.S. ambassa-dor to Poland, on Polish-U.S. relations.

When Scarbeck began making plans to meet Discher in Frankfurt, State Department security officers picked up their telephone conversations and closed in on him. Scarbeck admitted that he had given the UB three classified documents.

Scarbeck was tried in U.S. District Court in Washington. In a strange twist, Discher testified for the prosecution at his trial. Apparently, she thought she was helping him and would be reunited with him in Naples, Italy, which was to be his next assignment. Scarbeck could have instructed her not to come, but he did not.

"There was an element of masochism to it," Samuel C. Klein, his lawyer, said.[10] "He thought he could tell a sympathetic story and win the ear of the jury."

Weeping on the stand Discher said the Polish police told her they would brand her a prostitute and expel her from Warsaw if she did not cooperate.

"He was everything to me," she said.

Discher then returned to Poland, where Klein heard she entered a mental hospital. Other reports had her giving speeches about her experience.

Scarbeck was sentenced to ten years in prison but was released in 1966 after serving a term of four and a half years. After his wife divorced him, "Doc," as the bespectacled Scarbeck was called, worked as a wholesale book salesman in northern Virginia. In 1968 he petitioned to have his name changed to Irvin F. Chambers. According to his lawyer, he did not take care of his health and died two years later. Klein thinks he in effect committed suicide.

The fact that the Poles allowed Discher to leave the country, then allowed her to return, indicates their approval of her testifying against Scarbeck. Whether Scarbeck was set up from the beginning remains in dispute. Kenneth C. Knauf, the State Department's regional security officer in Germany, believed that Scarbeck and Discher had a genuine friendship, which the UB found out about later.[11] But Victor Dikeos, then the regional security officer in Warsaw, said, "She was set up to do it. It was a classic case."[12]

Nor is it clear why Discher agreed to testify and was allowed to travel to the U.S., then back to Poland.

"I don't know why she agreed to come here, or why they agreed to let her come here," Paul C. Vincent, the Justice Department lawyer who prosecuted the case, said.[13] "I was surprised when she agreed to come."

"She didn't seem to understand that he had really been arrested and that they would not be reunited," Klein said.

It was the only time a diplomat had been convicted of espionage involving the Soviet bloc, but it was not the last time an American embassy employee would succumb to such tactics.

# CHAPTER 5

## Guard School

GIVEN the well-documented tactics of the KGB, the last thing anyone would want to do is send a young, immature, single man to Moscow. Yet, almost perversely, that is what the State Department and the Marine Corps had been doing since 1934. And of all the candidates to be sent there, it would be difficult to imagine anyone less qualified than Clayton J. Lonetree.

Lonetree was the prototypical loser, a young man who could not make it even if he were given all the advantages in the world. At once self-pitying, naive, and impudent, he had unrealistic expectations of himself and the people around him, an almost all-consuming need to be loved, and barely enough intelligence to fire a weapon, let alone defend himself against the sophisticated onslaught of the KGB.

Almost from the day he was born, there was a curse on Clayton Lonetree. Not that he did not come from a distinguished family. His grandfather was Alexander Lonetree, who had been chief of the Winnebago Indians of Wisconsin. His great-uncle, Mitchell Red Cloud, was a descendant of Chief Fighting Bull and had been a Marine. During the Korean War he won the Congressional Medal of Honor.

But somehow the noble lineage had taken a detour around Clayton. His father, Spencer G. Lonetree, was a Winnebago and Sioux Indian. He was active in Indian affairs and had gained the respect of a number of local politicians. But he was also a stubborn, vain man, and Clayton felt he had a drinking problem.[1]

Like his son, Spencer Lonetree talked slowly and thought slowly, and he had an insolent streak that could turn people off.

Spencer never married Clayton's mother, Sally F. Tsotie, who is part white and part Navajo. She met him at the Chicago American Indian Center, where he was youth director and she was an aide. Clayton was born on November 6, 1961. Tsotie was sixteen and Spencer nineteen. She would later refer to Spencer as a "womanizer."[2]

When Clayton was eight, his mother took him and his younger brother, Craig T. Lonetree, to Farmington, New Mexico, where she began working as a cook for Navajo Missions Inc. Clayton would later refer to it as a kidnapping.[3] After four months she quit her job, returned to the Navajo reservation, and left the children at the mission. Clayton, who was then eight, never recovered from the hurt of being rejected.[4]

Lonetree later recalled that his mother visited him "very little" during that time and that he talked with his father "six or seven times" during the five years he was at the orphanage.[5] Lonetree's father, meanwhile, had married another woman and moved to the Wisconsin Dells in 1966. He eventually decided to reclaim his sons, an effort that took three years. Tsotie had instructed the orphanage not to let their father have the children.

Asked why she left the children at the mission, Tsotie said, "He didn't give me money to pay rent or buy food. Men never pay."

After three years of legal wrangling, Spencer Lonetree took the children to Minnesota, where he was then living. Clayton finished grade school on St. Paul's east side, a dingy, forgotten area of factories and a brewery. When locals refer to people who have an "east-side mentality," they mean people who are naive, don't take things seriously, and don't plan for the future.

Clayton attended Cleveland Junior High School, where the most notable local landmark was a strip joint called the Pain Reliever. In class, Lonetree spoke very little, kept to himself, and spent most of his time drawing.

"He was really good at drawing. He would draw instead of doing English," Virginia Broich, his eighth-grade English teacher, recalled.[6]

At Johnson Senior High School, Lonetree handed his American history teacher a notebook with a swastika and the inscription "Hitler Lives" on the cover. His teacher, June W. Dahl, returned the notebook to Lonetree without grading it.[7] After doing another assignment, Lonetree handed in the notebook again. This time, he added the inscriptions "Holocaust is a lie" and "Adolf Hitler." Inside, he wrote, "Jews are our misfortune" and "Hitler had the right idea." Dahl asked Lonetree to see her after class.

"Clayton," she said, "I'm sure a swastika doesn't mean to you what it means to me, because I'm old enough. Many of my friends went through agony because they would get word that Grandma and Grandpa had disappeared, cousin so-and-so had been shot, so-and-so had been sent to a work camp, and then they never heard anything else."

"Well," Lonetree responded, "you just believe all of those Jew lies."[8]

The teacher persisted. "I'm just sure that a swastika doesn't mean to you what it means to me."

Looking her straight in the eye, Lonetree said, "I know what a swastika means."

"Well, if you do, I would appreciate it if you would get another notebook, because I don't want to look at that one," she said.

It was lunchtime, and the conversation was over. But Lonetree would submit the notebook a third time. This time, it listed telephone numbers and addresses of members of the Socialist Workers Party. Another page appealed to blacks to fight "white savages" who kill "niggers."

Dahl took the notebook to the principal, saying she refused to correct it. Dahl did not return the notebook to Lonetree, and he never asked for it. It was the kind of pointless defiance that defined Lonetree's personality.

In his junior year, Lonetree got a job as a busboy at the Radisson Hotel coffee shop. If the hotel asked him to work extra hours, he always obliged. As a result, he was working up to eight hours a day in addition to going to school. His father would find him slumped over his books late at night, fast asleep.

"He finds it difficult to say no," his father told me.[9]

Spencer Lonetree discouraged his children from becoming

too involved in Indian culture, and Clayton saw himself as more white than Indian. Both father and son would describe themselves as being like an apple—red on the outside and white on the inside.

His father pushed Clayton to be number one in each of his pursuits. If he was number two, he was a loser.

"I used to push them pretty hard," he said. "I would impress upon them the need to excel. I would offer them money for A's."

But there was always an edge to his father's advice, an implication that Clayton was not up to his standards and never would be. Clayton never did live up to his father's expectations, which were hopelessly unrealistic. His father wanted Clayton to get A's, but Clayton was lucky to get C's. In an interview, his father said he had hoped his son would go to Georgetown University and obtain a degree in political science. At another point in the interview, his father said he had talked to his son about going to Harvard and obtaining a degree in law, then becoming a congressman from Minnesota. Yet Clayton is incapable of writing a grammatical sentence.

In Clayton's view, his father alternately was tough with him and let him go without any guidance.[10]

"Seemed every time I done anything he criticized me," Clayton would later recall.[11] "He was, himself, an alcoholic. We never—the only time we spoke was when he was drunk."

If he had it to do over again, his father told me, "I would have spent more time with them doing things. I was a workaholic."[12]

After graduating from high school in May 1980, Lonetree visited his mother and a half sister in Farmington, New Mexico.[13] There, he dropped in on the Navajo mission where his mother had left him. Nancy Snyder, then fifteen, was visiting her sister, who worked at the mission.

Snyder was an effervescent, wholesome, innocent young girl with long blond hair, a high forehead, and light blue eyes. She thought Lonetree was the cutest guy she had ever seen. She was impressed that he displayed a tender side with the children at the mission. Without speaking to him, she followed him as they helped Snyder's sister herd cows that had strayed onto the highway near the mission.[14]

Several days later, Lonetree asked Snyder to go for a walk with him along the nearby river. He told her he liked what he called her "Aryan features." He said he admired Hitler because he, too, was an unwanted child who had risen to be somebody. When he discovered her birthday was April 20, he became excited because it was Hitler's birthday.

Lonetree told Snyder he did not like being an Indian.

"He said to me, 'I was raised white, but I'm not,' and I told him he should be proud of his heritage," Snyder told me.

On the way back from their walk, Lonetree pretended to get lost. They sat down to rest, and Lonetree suggested Snyder lie down.

"Very funny. I'm not lying down," she said. "I know what happens to people who do that."

"What? Don't you trust me?" he asked.

"No, I don't trust me," she said.

After she returned to her home in Florida, she wrote to him almost daily. A devout Christian, Snyder chastised Lonetree for the way he talked about Jews. She told him they were God's chosen people, and it went against common sense to say Hitler was right to have slaughtered 6 million of them. She told him she was probably Jewish, since her grandfather's name originally was spelled Schneider. She thought that would change his opinion. The romance would continue, mostly by long distance, for more than three years.

The same summer he met Snyder, Lonetree enlisted in the Marines, in part to get away from his father. When asked on his application to list his ethnic group, he wrote "None."[15] In a military aptitude test, Lonetree scored in the lowest third when compared with other youths.[16] He was also one of the smaller recruits. Lonetree weighed 121 pounds and was five feet seven and a half inches tall.

After nearly three months of boot training in San Diego, Lonetree was supposed to have learned self-discipline and self-reliance, along with proficiency in military skills.[17] He was now one of the legendary "few good men." A grunt in the infantry, he was assigned to Guantánamo Bay in Cuba. There, he would get drunk in bars and call Snyder. Snyder passed up going to her senior prom because she was "going steady" with Lonetree. Yet if he found she was not home when he called, Lonetree would accuse her of being on a date.

"No, Clayton, I was at a girlfriend's house!" she would say.

"Do you still love me?"

"Yes, I do."

"Are you sure you weren't on a date?"

When Lonetree would call from Cuba, Snyder would notice he was slurring his words, and she would ask if he had been drinking.

"Oh, yeah, I've had a few," he would say.

At the same time, he castigated Snyder if she had a drink.

"I don't believe you'd put that stuff to your mouth. I can't believe you," he told her once when she said she had tried a piña colada.

When Snyder later saw Lonetree in the U.S., he would down two Big Macs, a Quarter Pounder with cheese, a fish sandwich, a root beer, a milk shake, french fries, and apple pie for lunch. Yet he became angry if they ordered a pizza and Snyder ate more than one slice.

Snyder thought Lonetree's apparent slowness and his monotone delivery hid great intelligence. In fact, Lonetree had the kind of brain that retains unimportant details but overlooks significant facts.

Snyder had done a school project on the military and decided to see what it was like for herself. Against Lonetree's advice, she joined the Marines. So they could be together when he transferred there, she became a trainee at Camp Pendleton in California. Snyder and Lonetree would run together on the base, and they talked of marriage and having children. They even chose names for their children—Winona, an Indian name meaning "firstborn daughter," and Hans because Lonetree was infatuated with German names.

Like Snyder, Lonetree was religious, and they attended church together on Sundays. One day in Farmington, they drove to a cliff and read the Bible in a van.[18]

Neither had had sex before, and Lonetree was proud that he was a virgin. On a date with Snyder, he upbraided her for playfully pinching his behind.

"If people see you do that in public, what will they think we do in private?" he said.

While at Camp Pendleton, they had sex for the first time, and both felt guilty about it. Yet Lonetree never overcame his jealousy. On the beach one day, Lonetree became agitated after several Marines whistled at her.

"What is it with you?" she said. "You are so jealous, and you have nothing to be jealous of. There are a million men on this base, and I've chosen to be with you. Doesn't that say something?"

Lonetree broke down and started sobbing.

"I just don't want you to leave me like my mother did," he said.

It seemed to Snyder that he had gone all his life looking for love that he never got as a child.

Snyder began having second thoughts about Lonetree when he started showing up at her barracks at 9:00 A.M. on Saturdays with the smell of beer on his breath, an odor barely disguised by rigorous tooth brushing. Lonetree's attitude about women had started to bother her, too. She was raised to be submissive to men, but Lonetree's macho tendencies were too bizarre even for her. He refused, for example, to salute female officers. Nor had Lonetree's Nazi fantasies diminished. Besides spy books, he loved books on the Luftwaffe and the SS.

As the two began to drift apart, Snyder began seeing someone else. Had it been love or pity? She was not sure. The last time they saw each other, she said, "*Adios.*"

He did not seem to care.


Lonetree managed to do well at Camp Pendleton, becoming a corporal and a squad leader. Flush with success, he decided to become a Marine security guard and see the world.

While Marines had been used sporadically to guard embassies over the years, most embassies employed civilian guards until 1949, when the Marines and State Department established the Marine guard security program. The main motive for the arrangement was cost-cutting. Ever the poor cousin, the State Department estimated it could hire three times more guards for the same cost if it switched to Marines.[19] Very little thought was given to the quality of the guards.

In any field, the way to get the best people is to hire professionals committed to their line of work. Marines had no particular interest in performing guard duty or even in remaining Marines. Most of them left for other occupations. Moreover, there was a natural conflict between being a good soldier and being a good guard. Soldiers are bred for action; guards must endure inaction. Using Marines as embassy guards was like hiring accountants to be musicians.

The Marines and State Department drew up a memorandum of understanding to set forth how the program would be run. Operationally the State Department would run it, while administratively the Marines would run it. On paper it looked good. In practice no one knew who was in charge, and the Marines and State Department constantly bickered over turf.

If the Marines were good at anything, it was public relations. None of the services had managed to project such an image of patriotism and enthusiasm as the Marine Corps. So it was in the Marine guard program. It is described in Marine literature as an "elite force" that serves in "every place and clime." Only volunteers recommended by their commanders were allowed to apply to Marine guard school. They had to be "mature and qualified Marines in the grade of corporal or above."

It was mostly hype. Many excellent Marines had served in the program, but by the time Lonetree came along the guard program was known as a dumping ground where less qualified Marines ended up. The corps needed the best Marines for fighting units.

"The Marine Corps was fighting to raise their manpower level but Congress wasn't giving it to them," Master Gunnery Sergeant Joey E. Wingate, who was in charge of the Moscow Marine detachment, told me.[20] "It made the grunt units short," he said, referring to the number of men assigned to combat forces. "They didn't want to give them up. The guards need top-quality people. If I'm on an [artillery] unit, I don't want to send them. Who do I let go? I let go the mediocre people to fill the quota."

If the Marines were sending unqualified candidates to be guards, they were also encumbering them with rules that cried out to be broken. The Marine Corps required applicants to the guard program to be single and to remain single for the duration of their tours as guards.

The Marines would claim the rule was needed because there would be no time to relocate dependents in the event of a hostile attack.[21] Presumably, the spouses of diplomats assigned to embassies would be killed in such an assault.

The real reason for the prohibition was money. Neither the Marines nor the State Department wanted to put up with the extra expense and fuss of housing dependents. Yet the entire worldwide cost of the Marine guard program—$36 million a year—was a twelfth the cost of one Stealth bomber. No other embassy in Moscow insisted on using unmarried guards.[22]

The U.S. could spend $3.6 billion a year on research for the Strategic Defense Initiative or "Star Wars" program—which most scientists said would never work—but could not afford to send wives of Marines to Moscow, whose embassy was the most sensitive appendage of the CIA and the focal point of the KGB's efforts to get its hands on U.S. intelligence secrets. Given the KGB's techniques, sending sex-starved Marines into such an environment was almost as bad as sending them into battle without guns.

The Marine's attitude toward married couples was as outmoded as its approach to using women guards. In what is now called a "noble experiment," the Marine Corps sent fifteen female guards in 1979 to places like Amman, Jordan; Bamaka, Mali; and Belgrade, Yugoslavia. But several embassies were attacked in 1979. One guard was killed in Islamabad, and thirteen were captured in Teheran. Fearing that women would be killed, the Marines stopped the program. The Marines later whispered among themselves that many of the women had become pregnant.

Like the State Department, the Marines had operated for years in Moscow in a certain way. By repeating the reasons to themselves over the years, the Marines had convinced themselves it was the only way. If they changed the way they operated, it meant they had been wrong all along. No one wanted to face up to that. The fact that the policy played into the hands of the KGB was no reason to change.

Lonetree applied to the guard program in May 1984. Then twenty-two, he admitted on the application that he was "very apprehensive" about starting guard school. Ironically, he said he wanted to become a guard because he was "looking for a little adventure."

Lonetree's first choice of posts was the Eastern bloc or "either of the two Germanys." In his ungrammatical English, he explained, "I'd like to observe how the oppressed people and political conditions are."

In response to another question on the application, Lonetree said that with men his favorite topics of conversation are "women, football, sports, weapons, politics." The application did not ask what he liked to talk about with women. His definition of integrity was "honesty." With typical bravado, he said he was not sure if he planned to make a career of the Marines, since he was interested in "pursuing to be a foreign service officer."[23]

On an aptitude test, Lonetree scored below the minimum required to get into Marine security guard school, and his application was rejected. After his father wrote to Senator Rudy Boschwitz, a Minnesota Republican, he was allowed to take the test again. His father cited the fact that Lonetree came from a family of distinguished military men.[24]

The second time he took the test, Lonetree passed. In August 1984 he began attending guard school at Quantico Marine base. Known as the "crossroads of the Marine Corps," Quantico consists of 60,000 sprawling, wooded acres thirty-five miles south of Washington. A replica of the statue of the Marines trying to raise the American flag at Iwo Jima stands at the base entrance off Interstate Route 95.

The guard school is in Marshall Hall, named for James Marshall, a twenty-two-year-old guard from Monroeville, Alabama, who was killed when the Vietcong attacked the American embassy in Saigon on January 21, 1968.[25] The school is outfitted like the ideal American embassy. Made of brick, the $23 million building has wide corridors and spotless vinyl floors. A security guard stands behind bulletproof glass and checks in visitors just as in a real embassy. The signs over the offices serve a dual purpose: they announce Marine battalion office names and also replicate titles that would be found in an embassy. The sign over the battalion commander's office, for example, also says it is the "ambassador's office."

Besides being in charge of the school, the commander directs the guard program, which stations 1,400 guards at 140 posts in 127 countries. Each post has six to thirty-seven Marines.[26] The battalion is divided into companies that supervise the guard program in different parts of the world. Company A, based in Frankfurt, covers the Soviet Union, the Soviet bloc, and Europe. On the organization charts, the Marine detachment at each embassy is headed by a detachment commander who reports jointly to the company commander and to the State Department regional security officer, or RSO. Smaller embassies or consulates have a post security officer who has other duties besides security.

The guard school conducts five classes a year and graduates 125 students in each class. Roughly a third of the Marines flunk out before graduating, an astonishing rate that suggests the candidates are not chosen properly or are not properly taught, or that Marines should not be guarding embassies.

Little in the training program had much relation to what guards need to know in a post like Moscow. While embassies in Nicaragua or Lebanon need guards who can repel a physical attack, guards in Soviet territory needed to be able to repel the KGB's much more sophisticated approach. Yet during the six weeks of training, the total amount of time spent on the entrapment threat was two hours, or about the same time devoted to instruction on how to wear civilian clothes.[27] In addition, guards about to be sent to the Eastern bloc sometimes received a one-hour briefing at the State Department, a talk that Marines would describe as perfunctory and generally uninformative.

The guard school also devoted an hour to the history of the guard program; an hour to the security program in the foreign service; two hours to the dress-blue uniform; an hour and a half to health, sanitation, and hygiene; three hours to social etiquette; five hours on preventive medicine; and two hours on detachment supply procedures.

Why would Marines need two hours to learn about civilian dress? To learn to match the color of their ties with their shirts and suits, for one thing. Then there was a three-hour course on answering critics of the United States, a class that could be summarized with the instruction "respond politely."[28]

To be sure, a substantial portion of the curriculum dealt with security threats—hostile intelligence subversion (one hour), fighting fires (four and a half hours), handcuff procedures (eight hours), and surviving a hostage situation (six hours). But the total time spent on counterintelligence—the area of instruction needed in Moscow—was eight hours, equal to one workday. The fact that the Marines and State Department were sending people to Moscow who had to be taught etiquette, hygiene, and how to wear their clothes said a lot about what was wrong with the entire program, through no fault of the guards themselves.

Lonetree had trouble passing even these primitive requirements. "Found small amount of soap film on shower wall. Two small spots of mildew in corners of shower stall," a gunnery sergeant, known as a "gunny," wrote of Lonetree's performance on August 10, 1984.[29] "Need to wash his belt. Had improper creases on trousers," he said.

On August 15 the gunny wrote, "Was told just prior to inspection to dust off his shoes but did not do so. Does not seem to have his undivided attention on his work."

On August 18 he wrote, "I have been watching you perform during the past week and have noticed a bad habit you seem to have. That is forgetfulness."

By September 3, Lonetree had been put on probation. But he pulled himself together and graduated eighty-seventh out of 127 in the class.

"Congratulations on making it," the gunny wrote.

Logically, the most experienced Marine guards should be sent to Moscow, where the greatest threat of a penetration exists. But the Marines did not see it that way. For the Marine Corps, running the guard program was a headache. Besides the chore of dealing with the State Department, transferring 1,400 Marines around the world was a logistical nightmare. The basement of Marshall Hall was filled with Monopoly sets and baseball bats supplied to the embassies just to keep the Marines happy at their posts. The Marines wanted to treat all posts the same, as if they were all work stations on an assembly line. Taking into consideration special requirements for Moscow would mean adding an extra procedure to make sure the right Marines were sent. For the Marines, that was one procedure too many.

The Marine Corps was not averse to distinguishing among posts to give the Marines something to look forward to. All the posts were graded according to their living and working conditions. The battalion usually sent guards to hardship posts at the start of their tours. Near the end of their thirty-month tours, they often got to go to nice places like Paris, Rome, or Geneva. Because of the Third World conditions in the Soviet Union, Moscow and Leningrad were considered hardship posts. As a result, the greenest, most inexperienced guards usually went to the two Soviet cities.

If anyone questioned the practice, the Marines had a ready answer. They said the newest guards had the latest, by-the-book training. The more experienced guards might have become less scrupulous. It was good to mix the inexperienced with the experienced.

The argument said a lot about the program. If more experienced guards were less conscientious, why were they trusted with guarding embassies? But that question did not concern the Marines as much as protecting their turf. The Marines spent far more time fending off the State Department, which it saw as a marauding predator, than worrying about the KGB.

After completing two years as commander of the guard battalion in 1984, David R. Mabry wrote to his superiors that some embassies were misusing Marine guards as servants, not providing them with vehicles for transportation and requiring them to stand post in civilian clothes.[30]

"Some post officials have insisted that our Marines purchase their own cleaning supplies and toilet paper," he wrote.

"Marines should no longer be misused, not supported, mismanaged, and shuffled around as they have in the past," he said.

"I am not suggesting that we throw down the gauntlet. However, I am suggesting that we stand fast and take care of our Marines."

Yet the Marines had much to hide. According to State Department records, 545 Marine guards had been removed from posts between 1980 and 1987 for infractions ranging from blackmarketeering, rape, fraternizing with Soviet nationals, and drug use to sleeping with State Department wives and failing to perform assigned duties.[31] A total of 100 of these were removed for substance abuse, 153 for criminal charges, 24 for fraternization, 58 for sexual misconduct, 6 for currency violations, and the rest for miscellaneous misconduct.

If there ever were a case for dropping Marines as embassy guards, it was contained in those records. Shocking though these findings were, the Marines tried to cover them up and explain them all away.

When the Naval Investigative Service finally obtained the list from the State Department, there was talk within Marine headquarters of classifying the document. When NIS subsequently included references to the list of infractions in briefings to congressional committees, the Marine Corps hit the roof.

Questioning its connection with the cases being investigated by NIS, Marine Major John R. Cohn of the NIS said in a memo, "The USMC will be furious if we draw attention to this [the infractions list] again, and I recommend that it be stricken from the chronology."[32]

Trying to minimize the damage, Major General Carl E. Mundy, in a letter to the State Department, said 9 of the 195 removals from January 1985 to April 1987 were transfers for medical reasons, 3 were accelerated promotions, and 35 of the removals stemmed from charges that were either dismissed or later dropped.[33]

But one does not have to be convicted under the Uniform Code of Military Justice to be adjudged in dereliction of duty. In any case, that still left 148 incidents of misconduct in the period chosen by Mundy that were justified. Since 1980 the number of Marines removed represents an astounding 10 percent of the total Marines on duty during that time.[34]

A Marine spokesman said many of the 545 cases were "extremely minor" and "could not have conceivably had any tie to spying or vulnerability." But nearly all of the Marines sent home from Moscow had engaged in conduct that could have made them vulnerable to compromise by the Soviets. If anything, the State Department tended to be too lenient in deciding whether Marines should be removed from their posts.

Clearly, there was something seriously wrong with the Marine guard program long before Lonetree entered it. But the biggest infraction was yet to come. After barely making it through guard school, Lonetree's first assignment, in line with Marine Corps policy, was a hardship post—Moscow.

# CHAPTER 6

## Snapping In

FOR LONETREE, as for the other Marines stationed there, arriving in the Soviet Union was like stepping onto another planet. Driving in a van from Sheremetyevo International Airport at night, he was impressed by how shabby and dark everything seemed to be. The few fluorescent signs that framed storefronts flickered like ghostly images on television screens. Inexplicably, the cars drove with only their parking lights on.

The embassy was even more of a shock. Located on a broad boulevard, it rose several stories above the surrounding buildings and was painted a ghastly yellow. To American eyes, it looked more like a grubby warehouse than an office building.

Lonetree entered the embassy through post number one, which controls access to the building. To the left of the entrance, just inside the door, was the guard post itself, enclosed in bulletproof glass. Carpeted with a rust-colored rug, it was the size of a toll booth on an interstate highway. Video monitors and light and alarm switches lined the cubicle. Keys dangled like icicles from hooks on the walls. An aluminum frame door separated the cramped cubicle from the inner hallway, which was almost as inviting as the foyer of a mortuary. The size of a large walk-in closet, the hallway was decorated with stock color photographs of Ronald Reagan and George Bush. Nearby languished a tired-looking plant made of green paper. On the floor lay a rubber mat with the seal of the U.S. on a blue background. For guests who had to wait, the embassy provided three dusty, gray chairs. They looked as if they had been there since the embassy was first occupied in 1953.

This was the central wing of the embassy that included offices and some residences. To the left and right were the south and north wings, mostly residences. Including the Marines, roughly a hundred Americans lived within the embassy.

In the back was a courtyard cluttered with wooden shacks that looked like construction site trailers. Besides being used for overflow offices, one of the shacks was called Uncle Sam's, a snack bar by day and a disco at night.

As one faced the embassy, the south wing was to the left. Inside, a corridor as narrow as a hallway in a small home ran parallel to the street. On the wall were prints of horse-and-buggy scenes from New England. Off the southern end of the corridor and to the left were the offices of the Marine detachment commander and the embassy employees who ran the travel, administrative, and personnel operations. Another labyrinthine corridor to the right led to the telephone room. Next to the telephone room was another miniature office for employees who worked with Soviet customs officials. Many of the employees in these areas were Soviets.

In the basement of the south wing worked "Radio Sasha." He was a Soviet who fixed the Americans' personal radios, TVs, and appliances. They realized Sasha most likely placed bugs in the equipment, but they didn't care. It was more important to have their TVs running, and they employed the usual rationalizations to explain the bizarre practice: Always assuming they were bugged, they never said anything secret in their own apartments. Or the KGB might find a way to bug them anyway. Using the same rationale, no houses would have locks: Burglars can always find a way to get in.

The basement of the north wing contained a tiny combination beauty parlor and barber shop run by another Soviet known as Valentina. Everyone from Ambassador Hartman to CIA Station Chief Natirboff was used to her probing questions, and the Americans for twenty-three years had let her continue to spy for the Soviets.

Malcolm Toon, when he was ambassador, read a copy of *Pravda* while Valentina cut his hair.[1] But others had not been so discreet. The embassy at one point traced a specific effort to recruit an American back to information the hairdresser had picked up from him.[2]

On the first floor of the north wing was the embassy's consular section, which issued visas and helped Americans with problems in dealing with the Soviet bureaucracy. On the second floor of the north wing was a bar, pool table, and kitchen for the Marines. On a wall near the lounge area two *Playboy* centerfolds had been hung wistfully.

Like the quarters for other embassy employees, the Marine House, as it was known, was depressing. Yellow, peeling linoleum barely covered the kitchen floor. The wallpaper was a black-and-gold design that nobody else wanted. One never knew when it would rain inside the embassy. The temperature in the building was so uneven that weather systems developed within it. Leaks from hot water pipes would create clouds of vapor that floated through the building. When the vapor reached an unheated room, it would condense, forming rain.[3]

The rest of the Marine House was on the second, third, and fourth floors of the central wing, where the Marines lived. The seventh floors of the central wing and above were the embassy's secure areas. Here, embassy employees worked on sensitive matters and stored classified documents. The CIA was on the seventh floor, along with the State Department's political section, which analyzed and reported on current political developments and represented American points of view on political issues. The eighth floor housed the State Department's economic section that analyzed and reported on economic issues. Also on this floor was the science section that handled scientific and medical issues and exchanges of information. The rest of the State Department's offices were in a commercial office in a separate building. Headed by a Commerce Department official, this office worked on issues affecting American business.

The ninth floor of the embassy housed the CPU, which encompassed more than half the floor. On the rest of the floor were the offices of the ambassador, the deputy chief of mission, and the regional security officer, or RSO. The tenth floor had the offices of NSA employees, who eavesdropped on Soviet communications, and the offices of the military attachés, who gathered information overtly and covertly on Soviet military strength. An attic contained sending and receiving equipment and a shredder and incinerator for destroying classified documents.

To get to the secure floors, the Americans had to take the main elevator to the ninth floor. There, in a small anteroom, a Marine stood post number three, the most critical guard post in the embassy. The guard post consisted of a raised platform surrounded by a high, horseshoe-shaped Formica counter. Anyone who wanted to enter the CPU or the ambassador's office, or walk to the other three secure floors, had to pass by the Marine at post number three. The other floors were accessible only from the ninth floor.

A door to the right off the anteroom led to the ambassador's office in the northwest corner of the embassy. To the left of post number three was the guard safe. At night, it contained the codes for opening the CPU in case of emergency. Straight ahead was a door leading to a small hallway and another maze of halls. To the left were stairways leading to the other secure floors above and below. To the right was another door that led to the vault enclosing the CPU. Besides housing the CIA, State Department, and NSA code rooms, the CPU enclosed separate rooms filled with secure photocopying machines and secure telephones.

At the rear of the embassy, approachable from the same hallway that led to the CPU, was a secure conference room. Known as the "bubble," it was made of clear plastic and raised off the floor so each of its sides could be examined for bugs. Three of the four secure floors in the embassy had their own "bubbles."

The Soviet employees were allowed to take a separate elevator to the ninth floor to drop off or pick up papers. The elevator was known as the "Soviet elevator" because it was of Soviet manufacture; the other elevators in the building were made by Otis. However, the Soviet employees were not allowed past the Marine who was standing post number three.

Master Gunnery Sergeant Joey E. Wingate, the Marine detachment commander, had picked up Lonetree at the airport. Wingate was known as "Top" because he was the top noncommissioned officer. The Marine Corps did not consider embassy posts to be important enough to be headed by a commissioned officer.

With a slight paunch, a cleft chin, a ruddy complexion, and a profusion of hair on his chest, Wingate was an old-line Marine who was respected by his men for being firm but fair. He had startling blue eyes that fixed on Marines like socket wrenches grasping a bolt. Most of his sentences were punctuated by "you see."

Wingate was born in Sarasota, Florida, in 1940. After graduating from high school, he spent much of his time sunning himself on the lovely beaches. After becoming embroiled in several arguments with his father, he decided to join the military. Because the Air Force had a six-month waiting list, he joined the Marines instead.

There wasn't much Wingate hadn't done or seen in his Marine career. At one point or another, he had been a marksmanship instructor, platoon commander, Marine security guard, and a public affairs officer. He had served on a helicopter squadron, a helicopter carrier, and in a jet transport detachment.

Wingate knew before he got there that Moscow was a problem post. When he arrived in Moscow on January 30, 1984, he carried a letter from the company commander ordering an investigation into alleged black-marketeering.[4] In Soviet bloc countries, currency may be exchanged only at the official rate, which is higher than the going market rate. On the street, Americans could buy four or five times more rubles for American dollars than they could at official Soviet banks. If Marines fell for the offers, they were subject to prosecution and could be compromised. Even selling a copy of *Playboy* was illegal. It would fetch thirty dollars, considerably higher than what it would cost if newsstands sold it at the official rate.

The commander of Company A had become suspicious when a Marine from Moscow arrived in Frankfurt to take some college-entrance tests. The Marine mentioned casually that the plane trip had cost him $200. Knowing that the trip should have cost $800 based on official rates, the commander decided the Marine must have engaged in black-marketeering.

Eventually, Wingate and the then regional security officer, Richard H. Klingenmaier, determined that, for the three previous years, nineteen Marines—almost half the detachment—had been buying black-market rubles from an African diplomat. They sent several of the ringleaders home.

The other major problem Wingate encountered in Moscow was a shortage of Marines. The detachment was supposed to have thirty-five, a larger contingent than normal because of the need to guard the new embassy construction site and warehouse. This was a constant source of friction between the Marine Corps and State Department. Under the memorandum of understanding between the two agencies, the Marines were to guard classified documents, not construction sites. The Marines considered the duty to be a waste of resources.

Because the guard program was not as important to the Marine Corps as its combat role, it was neglecting to send enough candidates through guard school. The guard program was chronically short of Marines. When Wingate got there, the detachment had only twenty guards, known as watchstanders, which was fifteen short of the required complement. That meant each guard had to work longer hours to make up the difference.

"Somebody's got to make up the forty hours per man per week that you're short," Wingate would explain. "So multiply that by fifteen people and you've got six hundred hours a week to make up. That's miserable. We had five or six posts and we shouldn't have even been standing them," Wingate said, referring to the construction site and the warehouse.

As the supply of guards dwindled, Wingate saw their quality deteriorate. The Marines claimed the better soldiers for fighting units. The twin factors led to more disciplinary problems, and Wingate came to consider Lonetree a prime example.

After Lonetree checked in, Wingate gave him the standard packet of regulations that dealt with everything from grooming standards to use of alcoholic beverages. According to the rules, his room was to be cleaned by seven each morning. His stereo was to be played at low volume. He could have female guests in the lounge area only.

"At no time will a female be allowed in any individual Marine's room," the rules stated.

Lonetree was to exchange money only at the official rate, either at a Soviet bank or through the embassy cashier. Another rule dealt with contacts with Soviet bloc nationals. It said Marines "will not fraternize with foreign nationals of either sex from any of the following countries: Bulgaria, Rumania, Hungary, Czechoslovakia, Poland, the U.S.S.R., Yugoslavia, or East Germany." Any contact with a national of one of these countries was to be reported to the noncommissioned officer in charge. The only exception was a contact at an embassy function. At the same time, a Navy rule said any "form of contact, intentional or otherwise, with any citizen of a Communist-controlled country . . . must be reported to the Naval Investigative Service."

This placed the Marines in a somewhat ambiguous position. On the one hand they were prohibited from fraternizing with Soviets. On the other hand they were supposed to report any contacts with them. The difference between a "contact" and "fraternizing" could be fine indeed, and many Marines felt they could get in trouble for reporting contacts because they might be considered fraternizing, which was prohibited. To make matters more confusing, the rule requiring reporting of contacts to the Naval Investigative Service could not be obeyed because NIS had no representative in Moscow. But a State Department rule said contacts should be reported to the RSO—the regional security officer—rather than to NIS.

Back in the States, the contact rules worked well. A Pentagon official might find himself sitting next to an amiable fellow at a bar in northern Virginia. They strike up a conversation, and the Pentagon official learns his bar companion is a Soviet embassy official. Since about a third of Soviet diplomats in the U.S. are estimated by the FBI to be KGB or GRU officers, chances are good that the Soviet diplomat will be an intelligence officer.

The Soviet, doing his job, tries to befriend the Pentagon official, perhaps inviting him to dinner. Eventually, by offering money, for instance, or compromising him, the Soviet may ensnare the Pentagon official in a spying operation, just as Soviets have corrupted dozens of American military men. Northern Virginia is so heavily populated with Pentagon officials that the FBI asks bartenders to report any contacts between military men and Soviets. If the Pentagon official reports the contact as required, the FBI assumes he is clean. Being aware that he will have to report such a contact helps to keep him honest. If the military man doesn't report the contact as required, he warrants closer scrutiny.

While there was a good principle behind the contact rule, it had not been written with the Soviet Union in mind. After all, Moscow was a city of 9 million Soviets, and the Marines were constantly in their company. In the course of a day, a Marine could chat with a Soviet sitting next to him on a bus, discuss the weather with a waiter serving him at a restaurant, or commiserate with a Soviet while they waited in line at a store. Because Soviet maître d's sit strangers together at the same table at restaurants, Marines often feel obliged to make conversation with Soviets throughout an entire meal. If Marines reported each conversation, they would have little time for anything else. Moreover, the RSO at the embassy was a busy man who had other things to do besides taking reports on conversations with sixty-five-year-old *babushkas*.

As a result, each Marine had his personal interpretation of what should or should not be reported. Some thought only a "suspicious" contact should be reported. Others thought only contacts with Soviets who asked questions about the embassy should be reported. The Marine rule prohibiting fraternization made them wary of reporting any contacts.

A more experienced and sophisticated hand might think he could see through this thicket and tell the difference between a casual, everyday contact and the beginning of a recruitment attempt. But as Lonetree would soon find out, there was no discernible difference between the two. A casual talk in a subway could be the prelude to a well-orchestrated KGB recruitment effort.

It took three days for Lonetree to be "snapped in"—taught by other Marines how to stand each post. Besides post number one on the first floor and number three on the ninth, he learned to stand posts four, five, and six at the new embassy construction site, and posts seven and seven-A at the warehouse. On posts one and three Lonetree wore his high-necked dress-blue uniform with red piping and brass buttons, matched with sky-blue trousers. On the other posts he wore "utilities," called fatigues by the Army. Because he was never considered responsible enough, he never stood post number two, that of the roving sergeant-of-the-guard who checks up on the other Marines and wears civilian attire.[5]

Almost from the beginning, Lonetree was in trouble, not only with Wingate but with his fellow Marines. One night early in his tour an alarm in the building went off, causing a "react"—Marine lingo for an emergency response. As required, each of the Marines in the detachment rushed to assigned posts wearing gas masks, flak jackets, helmets, and side-handle batons. All of them, that is, except Lonetree.

As usual, it had been a false alarm. Sergeant Todd M. Roen, a Marine from Minnesota, returned to post number one and saw Lonetree outside the building with the Soviet militiamen. He was dressed in react gear but appeared to be daydreaming. Roen was flabbergasted.[6] At the time, Roen was a corporal, while Lonetree was a sergeant. But Roen lashed into him anyway, telling him he would turn him in if he ever caught him doing that again.

One evening after having a few drinks, Lonetree came into the Marine lounge while several Marines were watching TV. Whooping and hollering, he turned on the lights and kicked the VCR, denting it.[7] Most of the Marines left in disgust, but Sergeant Donald S. Cooke from Fredericksburg, Virginia, lit into him.

Referring to Lonetree by his nickname, Sharkey, he said, "Why do you do these stupid things, Sharkey? You're not a bad guy. You do these things without thinking."

Lonetree broke down and began crying.

Cooke took pity on him and suggested they go for a walk outside. Lonetree began recounting his childhood—how he had been abandoned at the orphanage and been moved around. After that, Cooke stayed away from Lonetree. He realized Lonetree could not handle it if he got mad at him.[8]

One night Lonetree had a few drinks at the British embassy. Usually, it only took a few drinks for him to become drunk and unruly. This time he became sick as well, and the Marines had to carry him home.⁹ Reports of Lonetree's drinking filtered back to Wingate, who came to assume that if Lonetree had been involved, the job would not be done right.

The Marines had a midnight curfew on weeknights, but it was not unusual for them to cover for each other if they came in later. One night Cooke, Roen, and another Marine came back fifteen minutes after curfew.

"Okay, Sharkey, sign us in for 11:45 P.M.," Cooke told Lonetree, who was on duty that night.¹⁰

"Okay, I'll do it," Lonetree said.

The next day during inspection, Wingate looked at Cooke and Roen.

"Okay, how come you guys didn't sign in?" he asked.

"We did," Cooke said.

"Who was on duty?" Wingate said.

"Lonetree," Cooke said.

"Oh," Wingate said.

Wingate's look said it all. "That explains it," it meant. Even more puzzling, Lonetree had signed the other Marine in but not Roen and Cooke. It seemed to Wingate that everytime he turned around, Lonetree was in another jam.

One night while standing guard at the new embassy site, known as the NOB site, Lonetree called Wingate.

"Top, I've got a problem," Lonetree said.

"What's that, Lonetree?" Wingate said.

"Well, I lost my nightstick," he said.

"Well, don't come up here until you find it," Wingate said.

Lonetree was at the site until eight the next morning looking for his nightstick. Wingate knew he would never find it.

"Once he dropped it, the Soviets had it, you see," Wingate explained.¹¹ "It was gone. But I was trying to make a point with him, see."

The next day, Wingate gave Lonetree a special counseling sheet, which records any special criticism or praise given to a subordinate. He talked to him about the need to take care of his guard gear.

"You're right, Top. I'll do better," Lonetree said.

Two weeks passed, and Lonetree was in trouble again. He locked himself out of his room, passed out on the floor, and showed up for guard duty at 3:00 P.M. when he was supposed to begin at 7:30 A.M. The next day during inspection Wingate bellowed at Lonetree. Mentioning an American Indian who had distinguished himself as a Marine, Wingate said, "You know, he died a drunk in the gutter. If you are one of those Indians who can't drink, don't drink."

Several of the Marines cringed at the gratuitous racial reference.[12] Wingate insisted he had meant well. He said he had read in a medical magazine that Indians have a low tolerance for alcohol. He wanted to impress that fact upon Lonetree. Wingate ordered him off alcohol for sixty days.

It was a mystery to Wingate how Lonetree had ever gotten into the guard program. "He had all the traits he was not supposed to have to be in the program. He was a loner, not very articulate, borderline in the mental category," he would say later.[13]

Yet within several months of his arrival, the Marine Corps promoted Lonetree to sergeant. Unless there are major marks against a candidate, such promotions are virtually automatic. Wingate called the company commander, Major Allen Kris, in Frankfurt to recommend against it.

"Look, this guy is just not qualified to be a sergeant," Wingate said.

Kris promoted him anyway.

"If there's nothing in his record book showing disciplinary action, there's nothing you can do," according to Wingate. "Kris said our hands are tied. He had a good record." But he said Kris did have some discretion. "He could have said no. He didn't," he said.[14]

In the summer of 1985 a Navy officer found Lonetree asleep at 9:00 A.M. while guarding the warehouse. The officer reported him, and when Wingate looked into it he found that Lonetree had been wearing civilian clothes as well. Wingate did not always hear about Lonetree's infractions, but now he had two documented charges against him.

Lonetree explained to Wingate that he was wearing civilian clothes because he had broken an ankle playing soccer.

"Instead of saying, 'I couldn't get my utilities on with my cast,' he wears civilian clothes without permission," Wingate said.

Wingate recommended that he be returned to Quantico for

nonjudicial punishment, known as "office hours," and reduced in rank from sergeant to corporal. He wanted him removed from the guard program.

If Wingate's recommendation had been accepted, later events would never have happened. But the Marines were more interested in filling their quotas than in guarding the embassy properly. Kris disapproved Wingate's request.[15] Having made the mistake of sending Lonetree to Moscow in the first place, the Marine Corps now compounded the error by refusing to relieve him, despite documentation that he was unfit to guard a grocery store, let alone the CIA station in Moscow.

# CHAPTER 7

## Swiss Cheese

EVERY FRIDAY the Marines held guard school. Conducted in a secure "bubble" or in the Marine recreation area on the second floor, it was a chance for Wingate to discuss the latest rules, for Marines to get up to date on the latest procedures, and for everyone to let off steam. No week went by without extensive complaints about the lax security at the embassy.

The Marines complained that the alarms either didn't work or went off for no reason. The new embassy site was so poorly lighted the Marines could barely see anything. In one year, the Marines counted more than 200 false alarms in the old embassy. They could see very little on the video cameras. Guarding the warehouse was a joke because the cameras did not scan the entire area. If the Marines spotted an intruder, there was little they could do about it anyway. On Hartman's orders, they could not wear guns.

Frequently Richard H. Klingenmaier, the RSO, would attend. A former Marine guard whose last post as RSO was in Poland, Klingenmaier was well aware of the threat. But if he could find a reason for not taking action, he would grab at it like a drowning man grasping at a life preserver. With blue eyes, thinning hair, and an angular face, Klingenmaier smiled patronizingly when security problems were mentioned—as if the Marines were young kids who had once again seen hobgoblins in a nightmare.

Klingenmaier realized the Marines were taught by the book at Marine security guard school. But he knew better. He had been a

Marine himself. They came out of Quantico full of gung-ho spirit and enthusiasm. He admired that. But this was the real world. Things didn't operate in Moscow the way they did in Marshall Hall. Every post has problems with alarms, he would say. Of course, you try to get them fixed, but that takes time. There is only so much an RSO can do. If he insists on too much security, diplomats can get their backs up, and then the RSO loses all cooperation. Klingenmaier was not about to let that happen.[1]

As for Soviet nationals working in the embassy, he was all for it. Like the majority of the diplomats, he viewed proposals to replace the Soviet workers with American blue-collar workers as a threat. At least the Soviets were a known entity. The diplomats knew they were spies. The Americans, being lower in the pecking order than diplomats, might be more susceptible to recruitment than the seasoned, more worldly, more committed State Department officers. Or so Klingenmaier thought.

One was tempted to ask Klingenmaier if he thought Soviets should replace all Americans back home. Wouldn't it be a lot safer to have Soviets rather than Americans, who could be compromised, run the country? But one hesitated to ask him such a question. He might say yes.

Klingenmaier's cavalier attitude toward security infuriated the Marines. One of their most important functions was to write up embassy employees who violated the rules governing safekeeping of classified documents. A violation could lead to a suspension or dismissal. Yet very often when the Marines issued violations, Klingenmaier would refuse to ratify them.

To be sure, not every violation notice was justified. Sometimes, Marines wrote up violations when they found documents stamped "Confidential." But quite often Klingenmaier found other reasons to put aside violations that involved leaving classified documents out—"The violations did not lead directly to a compromise," "Let's give him another chance," or "Boys will be boys." His attitude was best illustrated by his reaction when someone pointed out the letters "C.C.C.P."—the Cyrillic initials for the Soviet Union—that the Soviets had formed in a wall of the new embassy by selecting bricks of the same shade of red.

"Yeah, I guess you're right," he said, laughing as if it had been a harmless Halloween prank.[2]

Among the biggest sources of complaints were the video cameras, which either produced blurry pictures, froze up, or simply didn't turn on at all. The Marines were supposed to peer at the video monitors from post number one or—at night—post number three to determine whether they should let cars enter the courtyard. If they did not recognize the drivers, they were not supposed to let them in.

"We complained and complained because you could not see who was there [through the video cameras]," Sergeant Roen, the Minnesota native, said. "You could barely make out if it was a car or if it was a Soviet or an American. We would write incident reports and complain to Klingenmaier, [who] would tell us our requests had been put in and how long it took to process. We felt we were being gaffed off."

Said Roen, "This is supposed to be the most important embassy in the world."[3]

The embassy ran a nursery school in the south wing. To get to it, parents, drivers, or nannies entered post number one and walked into the courtyard behind the embassy, where they met the children. If Soviet nannies or drivers motioned with their hands to show they were picking up a child, the Marines were told to let them in without issuing identification badges required of the Soviets. Thus anyone who knew how to motion with his hand was allowed in.

Another area of concern was Hartman's insistence that the Marines allow Soviets, Libyans, or Iranians into Uncle Sam's in the courtyard to attend Sunday church services without first checking them for bombs or guns. In the past, there had been at least two incidents involving Soviets who had forced their way into the embassy armed with guns or explosives. Anyone entering a government building in Washington—including the State Department—has to walk through a metal detector that uncovers weapons or explosives. But Hartman would not allow similar precautions in the Soviet Union.

"They could have blown the embassy sky high," Wingate said.

The same attitude applied to thefts of material and supplies from the new embassy. In general, anything that was not nailed down was taken.

"We were reporting theft after theft and couldn't apprehend

anyone. They [the Soviets] would take equipment, doors, motors, windows, tools. One time they stole a pallet full of building materials and put it on a truck," Wingate said.

When the Marines reported hearing footsteps at night in the new embassy, Klingenmaier would tell them they were probably hearing things. When they found a tunnel in the basement covered up with plasterboard, the RSO said that was to be expected; Moscow is full of utility tunnels.

If security at the new embassy was as porous as Swiss cheese, security at the old embassy was so lax that it would have been a miracle if the Soviets had not penetrated it.

Sergeant Donald S. Cooke, a Marine from Fredericksburg, Virginia, tested the alarms by walking around the embassy at night. He found he could walk the hallways on the seventh floor, where the CIA was located, and the eighth floor, where the State Department had offices, without tripping any alarms. On the other hand, the alarms on the tenth floor, where NSA was located, went off regularly for no reason. Eventually, many of the Marines ceased to take the alarms seriously.

"You'd have days when you had to get up at 6:30 A.M., and you'd been up three times," Cooke said.[4] "You'd get to where you'd just sleep through. There were twenty-eight other guys. I'd just pretend I didn't hear the alarm."

"Sometimes the alarms went off three or four times a night, night after night. You couldn't get any sleep. I still dream about them," Sergeant Richard W. Mataitis said.

Even the most trifling requests involving security were ignored. Realizing they would never get the video cameras replaced, the Marines suggested that the embassy paint a white line on the driveway leading to the courtyard. They wanted a sign that would instruct drivers to stop at the line, making it easier for the Marines to identify the occupants.

But that was too much to ask. After months passed, the Marines bought the paint and did it themselves.

The Marines perceived that there were two standards at the embassy—one for them and one for everyone else. They were expected to follow the rules, to wake up four times a night, to obey curfews, to avoid the tempting black-market deals, and to do without wives. Yet many of the rules were waived to avoid inconveniencing diplomats.

A symbol of the double standard was the "flea market" that Hartman and Klingenmaier permitted. These were sales of used goods to diplomats from other countries at rates that differed considerably from the official exchange rates. Because the sales were held on embassy territory, the Soviets could not take any action against the diplomats. Many diplomats made tens of thousands of dollars by selling cars and other expensive items. The Marines, because they did not have many goods to sell, generally did not participate. In effect, it was a way of circumventing, for those who could afford it, the prohibitions on black-marketeering.

Other examples were more blatant.

"If the embassy would treat the Marines as fellow humans instead of the bottom of the barrel, it would do much better," Wingate said. "The RSO [Klingenmaier] when I got there didn't give a shit about the Marines. He only cared about himself, things that made him look good. He didn't want to hear about problems—about alarms, for instance. He didn't really want to hear those things. 'Yeah, we'll look into it.'"

In fairness to Klingenmaier, many of the problems had been present for years. They were exacerbated by the fact that the State Department was not eager to pour money into improving security in the old embassy when a new embassy was being built. Yet it was Ambassador Hartman who was in charge, and it was Hartman's peculiar approach to security that was most to blame for the state of affairs.

Hartman insisted that he was concerned about security and that his deep involvement in the subject demonstrated that fact. His only desire was to help, he would say.

"If I say [security officers] should prove each [security] step is important, it doesn't mean I was against it," he said.[5] "My concern was what do you do to improve security? There are a lot of things you can do that look better. You can get rid of the embassy."

This was vintage Hartman, using outrageous exaggeration to make a point. The claim that simple self-protection would impair relations with the Soviets was as preposterous as the claim by

right-wing zealots that signing an arms-control treaty with the
Soviets meant the Soviets would drop nuclear weapons on the U.S.

The truth was Hartman knew little about security, nor was he
supposed to. That was the job of the bureau of diplomatic security
and the CIA and FBI experts who sometimes came calling on the
embassy. But Hartman was convinced he knew more than they
did. Arrogantly, he set himself up as more expert than the
experts. Inexorably, most of his suggestions were in the direction
of less rather than more security, and his attitude was not lost on
subordinates. If Klingenmaier had no backbone, Hartman actively undercut security measures.

Something as elementary as a metal detector was too great an
inconvenience for Hartman. Keys and belt buckles set off the
metal detector installed at post number one, so Hartman ordered
it out of the embassy.[6] He preferred taking his chances with
Soviets carrying guns or explosives rather than inconveniencing
diplomats by having them walk through the metal detector a
second time. Inexplicably, he saw the most trifling security
measure as preventing normal activities. Thus he would claim
that using a metal detector at church services meant the services
could not be held.

When Wingate arrived in Moscow, he was shocked to learn
that Hartman did not allow the Marines to wear weapons,
contrary to the agreement between State and the Marine Corps.

"One of the things you're there for is to make contact with
[Soviet] society, not to cut yourself off," Hartman would say when
asked why the Marines could not wear guns.[7] "If the idea is to
build a bunker you might as well close it down, listen to the radio
broadcasts here [in the U.S.], and let the professors go over."

Of course, it was possible to have both—a secure embassy and
daily contact with Soviets. But Hartman's style was to blow issues
out of proportion so all meaning was lost. The same crabbed
reasoning led Hartman to say he preferred Soviets over Americans for certain tasks.

"I'd rather have a sort of basic number of them doing things
like running my car and a few other jobs, and they would find out
no more than the guys watching us from the windows all the
time," he said. He maintained he wanted the Soviets to hear most

of what he was saying anyway. "I wanted them to know my view of what was going on. I hoped their facilities were good enough to hear it. We would go in the [secure] room on sensitive stuff."

There was always a reason for letting the Soviets have their way—they would learn the information anyway, they should know certain information. But rarely was there a reason for tightening security. Wingate went round and round with Hartman on the issue of wearing guns.

"He said, 'I just don't want an incident where we shoot a Soviet,'" Wingate said. "I felt he'd rather have a Marine killed."[8]

With Klingenmaier backing him, Wingate finally got Hartman to agree to let the Marines wear guns in the embassy—so long as they were not loaded. The ammunition was to be kept at their guard posts in a drawer. The Marines still could not wear guns at the new embassy site or at the warehouse.

If gentlemen did not read one another's mail, they certainly did not carry loaded weapons. Better to let an armed intruder get a bead on a Marine, watch him fumble for his ammunition in a drawer, then fire. In the diplomatic world, that was preferable to the unpleasantness that would ensue if a Marine killed a Soviet intruder.


In May, Staff Sergeant Robert S. Stufflebeam arrived at the post. A hard-charging Marine, he would soon become assistant to Wingate. With blond hair, green eyes, and ramrod straight posture, Stufflebeam stood six feet one inch tall and weighed 191 pounds. His gold-rimmed glasses gave him a bookish appearance. He was everything a Marine was supposed to be: tough, proud, confident. Like many Marines, he came from humble beginnings. Born in Bloomington, Illinois, he attended Bloomington High School and graduated from Normal Community High School in 1980.[9]

When he was growing up, Stufflebeam's father was in jail much of the time for armed robbery and other offenses. When Stufflebeam was eleven, his father stopped seeing him. Before his father died, he saw his father only one other time.

Stufflebeam is not an easy name to forget, and he had to suffer the humiliation of seeing his father's name plastered all over the local newspapers, causing snickers among his friends. His grandfather substituted for his father. He was a high school history teacher, a man who loved books and the outdoors, and Stufflebeam revered him. They would go canoeing together, and Stufflebeam would help his grandfather tend the hawks that he raised. The rest of the time Stufflebeam helped support his mother, who was divorced from his father and worked at a General Electric factory. They lived in a trailer.

Stufflebeam wanted to make something of himself, to show the world that he was not cut from the same cloth as his father. The way to do that, he felt, was through the Marines, an elite fighting force that had the reputation of being the best.[10] Stufflebeam went on active duty on June 9, 1980, in St. Louis. Promotions and awards came quickly. In boot camp, he became a squad leader. Then he was meritoriously promoted to private first class. Eventually, he was promoted to corporal, sergeant, and staff sergeant. He made Rifle and Pistol Expert and got the Navy Achievement Medal, the Good Conduct Medal, and a Meritorious Unit commendation.

After two years in the infantry, Stufflebeam applied to the Marine security guard program. He graduated third in his class of eighty-three at Marine security guard school. He was thus an exception to the wave of mediocre candidates being sent to guard embassies.

Stufflebeam was sent to Dakar in Senegal, then Harare in Zimbabwe. He transferred to Mogadishu, Somalia, where he was promoted to assistant detachment commander. He was interested in learning a language and had applied to become an interrogator and translator. He was turned down because the corps at the time needed more Marines with his specialty, which was antitank assault. He figured it would help his application if he gained experience in an Eastern bloc country. So, for his last assignment in the guard program, he applied for Moscow or other Soviet bloc posts. In May 1985 he reported to Moscow.[11]

Stufflebeam was aghast when he saw the level of security at the embassy. It was far worse than anything he had seen at his posts in Africa. The most glaring example was the embassy's practice of waiving the rules that required diplomats to put away classified documents when they were not using them. By long-standing agreement, the diplomats in Moscow were allowed to keep classified documents out on their desks or in open safes so long as a member of the staff was on the floor. Since the embassy was a massive building with dozens of offices on each floor, the waiver was tantamount to rescinding the security rules that applied everywhere else in the world.

Stufflebeam never forgot the first day he stood guard. It was lunchtime, and he was checking to make sure all classified documents were put away. He found classified documents laid out on desktops like fallen leaves. Safes containing top-secret data were unlocked.

"I couldn't believe it. I had hit a gold mine," he recalled later. "Anytime you leave the office area you put classified documents away."

As required by State Department's regulations, he confiscated the documents and locked them away in the guard safe on the ninth floor. He then wrote out violation notices, a form known as OF 117. Following the rules, he left one copy where he had found the documents, one copy with the documents in the safe, and one copy with the RSO.

To his astonishment, Klingenmaier called him in and said he was tearing up the notices.

"He said as long as there is one person on the floor, we do not write a violation," Stufflebeam recalled. After that, he rarely wrote security violations.[12]

Despite the policy, roughly 200 security violations were written each year in Moscow. In addition, there were 1,400 incident reports each year on everything from intrusions or alarms going off to light bulbs that needed replacing.

Within a few weeks of arriving in Moscow, Stufflebeam asked Wingate when he could become a squad leader. Wingate told him he would have to be an ordinary watchstander first.

"Just because you're the senior man doesn't automatically make you a squad leader," he told him. "I want you to earn it, and I want you to stand watch. I run the show. You do as I say."[13]

After two months Wingate made Stufflebeam assistant detachment commander. He had noticed that Stufflebeam caught on to paper work quickly. He was sharp with the computer. He did not have to be told things twice. Wingate thought he was as straight-up a Marine as he had ever seen. In fact, he was the best in the detachment.

Stufflebeam became the whip—the operational man who carried out the commander's orders.[14] If that did not always endear him to the other Marines, Stufflebeam was not concerned. He took his job seriously, working far into the night and on weekends preparing reports and guard schedules. Some of the Marines thought he was too uptight. When one drew a mustache on his photograph in the Marine House, he called a formation in the recreation room and had them stand at attention until the culprit confessed. But most of the Marines respected him because he was fair and did not play favorites.

Stufflebeam had had a stormy relationship with a woman in Zimbabwe, and one day she wrote him a "Dear John" letter. Stufflebeam lost his temper, smacking the wall with his hand and breaking a finger. So Wingate called him into his office and dressed him down.

"That's it," Wingate said. "No more of that stuff. If you can't control yourself emotionally, I don't need you here. Either straighten out or you're gone."

Still upset about his girlfriend, Stufflebeam decided in late July 1985 to let off steam with two other Marines at the Mezhdu-narodnaya Hotel, Moscow's nicest and newest hotel about a mile from the embassy. The Mezj, as the Marines called it, was the closest thing to a Western hotel in Moscow. Built in 1980 as part of the International Trade Center, it was bisected by an atrium complete with Hyatt-like elevators. Atop a clock at the center of the atrium, a rooster crowed on the hour. Fountains played onto white marble, and ice cream parlors, souvenir shops, a Japanese restaurant, and a German restaurant called the Bier-Stube lined a mall within the extended hotel lobby. Next to the Japanese restaurant was a magnificent bar paneled in dark wood.

The bar was off-limits to Marines because it was one of the few "dollar bars" in the city that took only foreign or "hard" currency and catered to tourists. The Soviets used currency to segregate foreigners. Since most Soviets did not have hard currency, they could not go to dollar bars and mingle with foreigners.

The Marines were not allowed to go to dollar bars either because the KGB often ran prostitutes out of them. The policy was never put in writing, and there seemed to be as many exceptions to the rule as there were Marines in the detachment. For example, the disco at the Kosmos Hotel, also a dollar bar, was not off-limits. No one knew just why one bar was off-limits and another was not. Sometimes it had to do with a long-forgotten fistfight that may or may not have taken place there. Often the question of what was or was not off-limits had more to do with which Marine was giving the briefing than anything else.

"The policy was very ambiguous," said Roen. "We were told you can't go to dollar bars but you can go to the Bier-Stube [which took foreign currency and served drinks] or to the disco at the Kosmos Hotel. I never had a clear idea in my mind whether this [the bar at the Mezj] was a bar you could go to or not."[15]

The Marines resented the rule because they had no place else to go. Beyond beer halls, Soviet bars did not exist. Moreover, State Department officers and Seabees were allowed to go anywhere they pleased. Navy construction personnel, the Seabees supervised the construction of the new embassy and helped maintain the old embassy. In the Marines' view, the rule was but another manifestation of the double standard that placed them at the bottom of the embassy's hierarchy.

Despite the rule, Stufflebeam went with Corporal Duane B. Parks and Corporal Roland L. Paquette to the dollar bar at the Mezj. There they struck up a conversation with an American contractor. The man introduced them to two attractive, shapely twenty-two-year-old women. The women—one with long brunette hair and the other with short blond hair—said they were models from Italy.

It was impossible to tell who was a Soviet and who was not. Many of the Soviets spoke flawless English, even better than many Americans. If they walked down a street in Indiana, no one would guess where they were from. At first, Stufflebeam assumed the two young women were telling the truth when they said they were Italian. After the other Marines left and the bar closed up, he accepted their invitation to go home with them.

Stufflebeam and the two women arrived at one of the young women's apartments at 1:30 A.M. It was a studio with a kitchen and a bathroom. After they offered him food, the two women spoke in Russian to each other. Stufflebeam began to suspect they were Soviets after all.[16]

The blonde changed into a nightgown and lay down on a cot in the kitchen. Meanwhile, the brunette invited Stufflebeam into the bedroom, where they had sex. At 4:30 A.M., Stufflebeam left. Because he was an assistant detachment commander, Stufflebeam had no curfew.

The next day, he reported to the RSO that he had shared a cab with some Soviet women and had gone to the bar at Mezj. He did not mention having sex with one of the young ladies, an admission that would have subjected him to punishment.[17]

That would soon be his undoing.

# CHAPTER 8

## Finding Bugs

IN AUGUST 1985, Klingenmaier was rotated out of the embassy and Frederick A. Mecke replaced him as RSO. Mecke was Klingenmaier's opposite in almost every way.

Like most people in the State Department's bureau of diplomatic security, Mecke did not start out as a security expert. Born in New York, he majored in history at the University of Maine. Having graduated magna cum laude, he enlisted in the Marines and became a sergeant. In 1970 he moved to Portland, Maine, where he joined the local police force. After five years as a policeman and a brief stint with the Treasury Department's Bureau of Alcohol, Tobacco and Firearms, Mecke joined the State Department's bureau of diplomatic security in 1976.

Mecke investigated passport fraud and helped train other security officers. He then volunteered to guard the U.S. ambassador to El Salvador, becoming an assistant RSO. After two more posts, he was assigned to Moscow as regional security officer.

A slight man with a neatly trimmed beard and large brown eyes, Mecke was forceful and decisive, with a mind that was the equal of any diplomat's in Moscow. At the same time, he knew how to deal in the murky world of the State Department, where impolitic remarks were not appreciated and decisiveness could be interpreted as a sign of bad breeding. Mecke was not intimidated by Hartman, and Hartman knew it. Hartman could run rings around Klingenmaier with his philosophical arguments against security measures, but Mecke had the intellectual prowess to counter anything Hartman could come up with.

Mecke had another thing going for him. A year earlier, bugs had been found in the embassy typewriters and in the structure of the new embassy. Until then, any concerns about security seemed theoretical. Because of those breaches, members of Congress had been expressing increasing frustration with the amount of attention paid to security by the State Department.

Because of these pressures, the State Department was becoming more concerned about security. Mecke came to Moscow with a new deputy chief of mission, Richard E. Combs, and a new administrative counselor, David R. Beall. All three had been instructed to tighten security.

Periodically, NSA had checked the typewriters and printers in the embassy and found nothing amiss. But in 1984 a defector told the French General Direction of External Security (DGSE), the French intelligence service, that the Soviets had bugged typewriters in the French embassy in Moscow. After the French uncovered the bugs, NSA, in an operation known as Gunman, began shipping typewriters from the Soviet Union back to Washington.

First in typewriters coming from the American embassy in Moscow, then in ones from the consulate in Leningrad, NSA found tiny, highly sophisticated bugging devices.

In most ways the Leningrad consulate was a carbon copy of the embassy in Moscow, only smaller. The organization of the staff was almost identical, and the consul general reported to Hartman. But instead of 191 Americans, the consulate had 26.

There is a softness to Leningrad that makes it more inviting than Moscow, a pastel quality that is more Western European than Russian. Located on the Baltic Sea, Leningrad has broad, tree-lined boulevards and picturesque arched bridges that span the Neva River. It was the setting for the stories of Pushkin and Dostoevsky, and the audience for Tchaikovsky and Rachmaninoff, who are both buried there. Leningrad has one of the world's great museums, unknown to many Westerners: the Hermitage, with forty Rubenses, twenty-five Rembrandts, thirty-five Matisses, twenty-six Renoirs, twenty-five Picassos, and two Leonardos.

Because it is not the capital, Leningrad is far more relaxed than Moscow, symbolized by the way the militia outside the missions greet visitors. In Moscow they stare tensely ahead and ask gruffly for identification. In Leningrad they say, "Good morning, sir," and smile.

In other ways Leningrad is more depressing than Moscow. The sun shines just 152 days a year, and then only for a short time. During the winter, it rises at 10:00 A.M. and sets by 4:00 P.M. Because it is not the capital, Leningrad is not high on the priority list to get consumer goods. If lines for chocolate or shoes filled the stores in Moscow, in Leningrad they snaked outside into the bitter cold.

The U.S. opened the Leningrad consulate in 1973 as part of a reciprocal agreement that permitted the Soviets to open a consulate in San Francisco. Located on Petra Lavrova Street, less than a mile from the Hermitage and the Neva River, the consulate is a four-story, red-stucco building that was formerly an apartment house.

The Leningrad consulate was even less secure than the embassy in Moscow. Attached on both sides to Soviet apartment houses, the building is U-shaped with a courtyard inside it. A single Marine guard on the third floor controlled access to the entire building, including the secure area—the fourth floor, where the CPU was located. A sergeant-of-the-guard checked up on him twice a night. In Leningrad, the thirty-four Soviet workers outnumbered the twenty-six Americans.[1]

The first person a visitor encountered was a Soviet receptionist who also answered the consulate's phones. When he was consul general in 1980, Thompson R. Buchanan considered replacing the receptionist with an American but was told an American would cost too much money.[2]

As in Moscow, the Marines were not supposed to fraternize with Soviet-bloc women, take women to their rooms, or engage in black-marketeering. But there was an even greater disparity in Leningrad than in Moscow between what the rule book said and the reality.

When Sergeant Rodney Pope arrived in Leningrad for his tour as a Marine security guard in December 1981, he was met by the detachment commander and three British girls who announced they lived in the Marine House.[3]

The night before he was to stand guard for the first time, Pope went to a dollar bar with Sergeant John J. Weirick. Unlike the Marines in Moscow, those in Leningrad could go to dollar bars. Pope and Weirick met some Finnish girls, and Pope—not used to the high-proof vodka—got drunk. The next day, Pope was to stand guard at 8:00 A.M. but couldn't get up. At 3:00 P.M. Weirick called him in his room.

"Are you ready to stand guard duty now?" Weirick asked.

"Yeah, I'm ready," Pope said groggily.

"Good," Weirick said. "I stood your post, now you can stand mine."[4]

In Leningrad, as in Moscow, the alarms went off for no reason at all hours of the night. The Marines felt shunned by the State Department officers and ignored by Marine Corps headquarters. They would run down the street in forty-degree weather wearing boots, gym shorts, and T-shirts just to act out their frustrations. "The Few, the Proud, and the Forgotten" was the motto they dreamed up for themselves.

As in Moscow, the Marines were unarmed by order of Hartman. They kept their weapons locked in drawers and wore empty holsters, making them look absurd. Christopher A. Squire, the consul general at the time, disagreed with the policy and questioned it through his regional security officer. "If you have the need for guns, you wear them and you use them," he said. But he could not get Hartman to budge.[5]

Because the city had more dissidents than Moscow, its police tended to be more brutal. Every year there were reports of Marines being beaten up by the militia, but it was not always clear what had happened. Very often, the Marines got drunk and were unruly.

In September 1981, Sergeant Joseph Goddard received a severe brain injury while in Leningrad, and there were reports that the KGB had beaten him up and left him on the steps of the consulate because he resisted recruitment attempts. But Goddard said he recalls falling backwards on a marble staircase within the consulate while returning a charcoal broiler to an American employee.[6]

The Marines also passed along the story of a couple they dubbed "Mork and Mindy" who undressed in front of an open window in a Soviet apartment at the rear of the consulate. The Marines claimed it was a KGB effort to distract them while they were making their rounds in the rear of the consulate, but that was more speculation than anything else.

Pope found that women not only lived in the Marine House, which was on the second and third floors of the consulate near the rear, but stood guard with them. Pope was as patriotic as they come, a Marine who would have given his life to defend the mission without giving it a second thought. But he never understood why he could not see Soviet girls. He began going with one and later married her.[7] Weirick, meanwhile, had sex twice with a Soviet girl.[8]

It seemed to Pope that the worst punishment he could get was being relieved from post—which was what he wanted. Another Marine brought a Soviet prostitute into the Marine House and was sent to Hawaii.

"I mean, punish me," Pope thought to himself.


For NSA technicians, finding the bugs in the typewriters was a nearly impossible task. Even though they knew they were there because of information received from the French, X-rays at first turned up nothing. Nor did the bugs emit any signals. Using more sophisticated X-ray techniques, NSA finally found the bugs secreted in a horizontal aluminum bar in the typewriter casing. The bar had been sliced in half and then resealed so the seam was barely visible. In all, NSA found bugs in thirteen IBM Selectrics, including one from the Leningrad consulate.

The bugs transmitted each movement of the typing balls to nearby antennas. The antennas, in turn, relayed the signals to a Soviet apartment house attached to the south wing of the Moscow embassy, the one filled with KGB officers.

In May 1978 a Navy Seabee had discovered one of the

antennas snaked through a chimney.[9] Apparently, the Soviets had installed the antenna when the embassy was renovated after a fire on August 27, 1977. The fire demolished the roof, gutted the eighth floor, and severely damaged the ninth and tenth floors. During the eighteen-hour fire, Soviet firefighters had the run of the embassy. Hammer marks were later found on a safe containing top-secret documents. The Seabee who discovered the antenna traced the wire. It went down the chimney, into the basement, and through a tunnel leading to the Soviet apartment house. The Soviets on the other end began frantically rolling up the wire, but the Seabee recovered enough of it to preserve as evidence.[10]

NSA found that it could not detect any signals from the typewriter bugs because they stored data and transmitted it only intermittently. The Soviets controlled when the bugs dumped their information. Moreover, the coded signals used the same frequency as a Moscow broadcaster. When the bugs transmitted, they created momentary static during the broadcasts. Since the signals were on the same wavelength as the broadcaster, routine electronic sweeps of the embassy had detected nothing.

Checking records, the State Department found that the typewriters had been shipped to Moscow in three stages going back to 1976. Typewriters from two of the shipments were being used in secure areas of the embassy to type a variety of top-secret documents. The Soviet nationals working in the embassy were using typewriters from a third shipment.

By the time NSA found them, the batteries on the older versions of the typewriters had gone dead. Until 1979, the typewriters in the embassy were serviced by a Soviet IBM repairman, who worked while a Seabee watched. But he had apparently not replaced any batteries. More recent versions of the bugs ran off the typewriters' power.

When NSA engineers examined the bugs more closely, they were amazed at how ingenious the circuitry was.

"I think people tend to fall into the trap of being disdainful too often of their adversaries," said Lieutenant General Lincoln D. Faurer, who headed NSA at the time.[11] "Until recently we tended to think that in technical matters we were ahead of the Soviet Union—for example, in computers, aircraft engines, cars. In recent years we have encountered surprise after surprise and are more respectful. Most folks would now concede they have enormously narrowed the gap and have caught us in a number of places."

In its investigation, the State Department found that the typewriters had not been handled according to government rules for shipping equipment to be used in secure areas. Most of the typewriters had been left overnight in a Soviet customs warehouse. The typewriter in Leningrad, part of a fourth shipment, was most likely bugged when it was shipped by train to Helsinki for repairs.

In contrast, when the Soviets ship equipment to their embassy in Washington, they use Aeroflot—their own airline—and pick up shipments immediately at the airport. If the items are not called for within an hour, they are shipped back to the Soviet Union.[12]

For some time, NSA and the CIA had been concerned about the increasing number of roll-ups—intelligence jargon for the expulsion of spies. Some of those expelled were CIA officers, while others were attachés or diplomats. Some were expelled in retaliation for an expulsion of a Soviet in Washington and had nothing to do with spying. But there were enough terminations of productive CIA operations in the Soviet Union to cause grave concern that the Soviets either were reading CIA communications or had a mole within the agency.

The wave of expulsions began in March 1983, when the Soviets declared Richard W. Osborne, a first secretary of the embassy, persona non grata. The Soviets claimed to have caught him with spy equipment, including radio equipment for "transmitting espionage information via the U.S. Marisat communication satellites."[13] Marisat is the Maritime Communications Satellite system, which is used for commercial and Navy transmissions. The Soviets said they also seized Osborne's "own notes which were written in a pad made of paper that quickly dissolved in water."

In June 1983 the Soviets expelled Lewis C. Thomas, an attaché and electronics expert, saying they caught him red-handed in a spying operation. In March 1985 they expelled Michael C. Sellers, a second secretary of the embassy. *Izvestia* ran a photo of him disguised as a Ukrainian, wearing a false mustache and a wig.[14]

Next came Paul M. Stombaugh, a second secretary, who was expelled in June 1985. The Soviets said he had been caught taking documents from Adolf G. Tolkachev, who was later executed by a firing squad.[15] According to Tass, U.S. intelligence agencies had given Tolkachev miniature cameras for photographing secret documents, two-way radios, encoding devices, and special poisons.[16] Tolkachev, who worked for a Soviet research institute, was accused of passing on details of Soviet research and development on electronic guidance and countermeasures, advanced radar, and Stealth technology for evading radar detection.

The diplomats liked to think there were unwritten rules about expulsions: that one side would not retaliate against the other if a spy were caught red-handed. The problem was the definition of what constituted spying could vary. What was legitimate information gathering in the U.S. might be considered espionage under Soviet laws.

"There have been a number of cases where people are expelled, and the other side retaliated even though the argument was this was a case of being caught red-handed," a State Department official said. "Usually, the expulsion is based on something unless it's retaliatory. Then it's very transparent, and they say it's for conduct unbecoming diplomatic status. The issue always arises of whether they did or did not have a [legitimate] basis."[17]

Even more sinister than the expulsions were the number of Soviet citizens working as CIA agents who were being exposed and executed. While some could have been given up by former CIA officer Edward Lee Howard, the executions predated Howard's interviews with the KGB in Vienna in September 1984 and his defection to the Soviet Union more than a year later.

Had the Soviets learned about CIA operations through the bugs in the typewriters? Or were they getting even more information by bugging the CPU itself? Beyond the physical evidence, the executions, and the expulsions, the intelligence agencies had other reasons for suspecting that the Soviets might be reading U.S. intelligence traffic. The Soviets seemed to know too much about American negotiating positions and strategies.[18]

After discovering the bugs in the typewriters, NSA sent an officer to the embassy to see if the secure floors could be entered at night without alerting any Marines. The officer reported that it was possible for intruders to enter several of the secure floors. NSA decided that the CPU at the embassy should be replaced.

After obtaining President Reagan's approval, NSA officers arrived in Moscow with a letter from the State Department authorizing NSA to cart away the CPU. Signed by Robert E. Lamb, then assistant secretary of state for administration, the letter instructed the communicators in charge of the CPU not to tell anyone of the secret mission. If NSA could remove the CPU without letting the Soviets know about it, the agency could introduce disinformation on the circuits to mislead the Soviets. Confirming the State Department's reputation for being a sieve, one of the communicators immediately sent a message to Washington questioning the authority of the NSA officers and asking for further guidance.

That weekend, as 20,000 pounds of equipment were being removed, the embassy's power went off. NSA suspected that it was a Soviet move to erase any data stored in the bugs. Because they transmitted information in occasional bursts, the bugs stored data before it was sent.

Meanwhile, the State Department and the CIA were finding equally shocking evidence that the new embassy had been penetrated. Security in the new embassy had been handled in the same cavalier fashion as in the old. Nominally, the State Department's Office of Foreign Buildings was in charge of constructing the new embassy. But SECOM, an interagency committee headed by the CIA, was in charge of security.

The committee decided that the best way to handle security during construction of the new embassy was, in effect, to do nothing. The strategy—if it can be called that—was to let the Soviets install whatever bugs they pleased. That way, the CIA and NSA could find the bugs and determine what kind of technology they were using. Moreover, the theory went, if the Americans prevented the Soviets from installing bugs in the new embassy, it could make it harder for the FBI to install bugs in the Soviets' new embassy in Washington.[19] The committee figured the bugs could always be removed or burned off later with electrical charges. As a result, any examination of the building during the early stages of construction was perfunctory.

The Soviets, meanwhile, were not so dumb. During construction of their new embassy in Washington, they had thirty personnel supervise the work of a hundred American construction workers. In contrast, the Americans had twenty to thirty Seabees watch 600 to 800 Soviet construction workers in Moscow.[20] At night, the Soviets maintained tight security behind the embassy's high fences with roving armed guards, video cameras, and alarms. The Americans had an unarmed Marine sit in a shack at the new embassy site and watch four video monitors that usually didn't work. The fences had alarms, but they often didn't work either. Two other Marines patrolled the site. Later, the Americans moved all three Marines into the new embassy itself, where they were to patrol the corridors. Most of the time, they watched one another in the guard room.

In Washington, the Soviets paid $50,000 in delay costs to have Whiting-Turner Construction Company leave the girders for their new embassy overnight so they could examine them thoroughly before they were installed. Instead of a standard X-ray machine, the Soviets used one that bombards material with neutrons. The method penetrates thick construction materials far better than X-rays and provides clearer resolution. The Soviets even took windows and doors apart before they were installed. If they had the slightest question about a component, they halted construction until the issue could be resolved.[21]

The Americans, meanwhile, were in a hurry to get out of their cramped quarters and move into the new embassy in Moscow. They let the Soviets install girders immediately without examining them. They did not take components apart. And they let the Soviets install precast concrete panels manufactured in Soviet plants. The Soviets, back in Washington, allowed no precast materials. All concrete had to be poured on-site while the KGB watched.

The result was predictable. Since 1982 the State Department had been noticing that some of the steel in the new building was not configured according to the plans. The CIA proposed examining the building with neutron-bombarding X-rays. After six months of wrangling over the health effects and the Soviet reaction, Hartman approved the plan. Even using neutron bombardment, taking X-rays of a building already constructed is considerably harder than examining each component before it is installed. It is akin to trying to X-ray the leg of a football player when he is making a touchdown.

To do the job, the technicians had to tear out the existing walls to reach the girders and other reinforcements behind the red-brick exterior. Then they had to try to maneuver the equipment to get to the inaccessible areas where the girders were joined. Some of the areas still could not be examined. But what the technicians were able to see sent shivers down their backs.

There were literally thousands of bugs.

Like those in the embassy typewriters, the bugs in the new embassy had been designed so that it was nearly impossible to detect them. Made of materials that were the same density as the surrounding steel, they were secreted in hollow areas where the I-beams were welded together. Since X-rays can only detect variations in the density of materials, the bugs usually did not show up with ordinary X-ray techniques.

Other bugs had been mixed into the precast concrete along with thousands of electronic diodes meant to confuse the Americans. With ordinary detection methods, it was impossible to distinguish between a bug and junk. Moreover, the rebar or steel reinforcing rods embedded in the concrete had been cut to particular lengths so they would serve as antennas. All the steel in the building had been welded together so the signals could be transmitted easily. Finally, steel components of the building had been shaped so they would act as cavity resonators that responded to microwaves—just like the bug in the Great Seal found by George Kennan thirty years earlier.[22]

The job was so massive, so ingenious, and so varied that no one claimed to understand fully how it all worked.[23] Like the Greeks who left a wooden horse full of soldiers to fool their Trojan enemies, the Soviets had given the Americans a magnificent new building that was nothing more than a gigantic eavesdropping device.

"We didn't have good security on the construction site," said Lamb, now assistant secretary of state for diplomatic security. "We knew it. We were proud of the techniques we had developed to find it [electronic eavesdropping devices]. The trouble is they knew what we were going to do and hid it fairly cleverly. . . . They put it in places so it would be difficult for us to take it out because it affects the structure."

Ultimately, said Lamb, security was not coordinated.

"The people with the political balls to say "This is what ought to be done' didn't have the technical knowledge to formulate a good position. The bridge between the engineers on the building and those who make the political decisions didn't exist," he said.

"The amazing thing is that everyone in the government knew what the Soviets were doing at Mount Alto to make it secure, and yet our own State Department didn't think enough to do the same thing in Moscow," said John Carl Warnecke, Jr., vice president of W. Carl Warnecke and Associates, the architect for the Mount Alto embassy. "It's like leaving yourself open and saying, 'Kick me.' "[24]

Just as the Americans had let the Soviets put Soviet workers in the old embassy, they had let them put bugs in the new embassy. By the time the Americans figured it out, the building was nearly finished. As the State Department frantically tore out walls at night so the building could be examined, the Soviets speeded up work so they could cover up what they had done with bricks.[25]

Slowly it began to dawn on policymakers in Washington that the bugs could not be removed. Removing the bugs would require demolishing the building. The Soviets had pulled a perfect scam.

Realizing they had screwed up, the CIA and NSA tried to hide the findings by referring to the bugs as "anomalies" or "spurious devices." To this day, the intelligence community will not openly admit that the new embassy is full of bugs. The agencies insist that doing so would let the Soviets know what methods the Americans have for finding such devices. This is the same argument the intelligence agencies use to try to thwart prosecutions of spies.

Invariably, when a spy is apprehended, the CIA and NSA complain to the Justice Department that a prosecution would reveal too much. According to this argument, the other side would learn what the U.S. knows about what the other side did. If the other side finds that out, it might change its methods and make it harder for the U.S. to detect what the other side is doing. Beyond that, even if it seems the other side learned a particular fact, it is best to keep the fact a secret from the American public. The other side may have failed to report the fact or may not have appreciated its significance.

If the argument sounds like gobbledygook, it is. The concept of keeping secret what the other side already knows because the other side did it is absurd on its face. If prosecutions of bank robbers, murderers, or con artists were handled in the same Alice-in-Wonderland fashion, no one would be sent to jail for fear other criminals might learn their methods.

"The intelligence community often believes that nothing is known unless it originates with them, and that revealing anything previously kept secret helps the other side," said John L. Martin, chief of the internal security section of the Justice Department. "That ignores the reality that our adversaries know much more than we publicly admit and that the national interest will inevitably be better served by a public trial revealing and re-creating precisely what took place. Not only does it expose and punish the defendant, it is a way of impressing upon the bureaucracy the ultimate consequences of its oversights, if any. The purpose should be to deter the American who is tempted to spy and to correct within the government the reasons why things have gone wrong."[26]

Behind the intelligence community's contorted reasoning is the fact that the intelligence agencies are insulated from public scrutiny, making it easier to fashion illogical rationales to justify their own actions. Why publicize the failings of the intelligence community when it is much easier to stamp everything "top secret" and file it away in the archives? When all else fails, it is always possible to cover up mistakes by whispering that the "national security" is at stake. What truly endangers the national security is bureaucrats who are so unaccountable that they permit Soviets to bug U.S. embassies and work in them.

A new form of congressional oversight only preserves the chummy atmosphere. Obviously, much about intelligence matters must remain hidden. But an occasional public hearing on intelligence failures or abuses is a good antidote to the unreal atmosphere that pervades the intelligence world. Today, congressional committees tend to get their information in secret briefings or secret testimony by intelligence officials. If they seem reasonably forthcoming, the officials are often allowed wide latitude. The method only serves to further insulate the intelligence agencies from any form of accountability.

By August 1985 it was clear to the intelligence community that no countermeasures could ensure that the new embassy was free of bugs. With 65 percent of the work done, the State Department halted work on the project and removed the Soviet workers from the site.

As in any bureaucratic bungle, it was difficult to find a face in the crowd to take responsibility. The CIA, the NSA, and the State Department were all represented on the committee that dictated security policy. But as director of central intelligence, William J. Casey, the czar of the intelligence community, was the man in charge.

Ironically, Casey came to office as CIA director in 1981 with a conservative mandate to strengthen intelligence and win the silent war with the Soviets. The same lack of focus that led him to support an exchange of arms for hostages in Iran enabled him to preside over one of the greatest counterintelligence disasters in U.S. history.

# CHAPTER 9

## The Hairdresser

As soon as he got to Moscow, Frederick Mecke, the new regional security officer, began trying to improve security. For the first time, the Marines felt they were being supported and listened to. Already under pressure from visiting intelligence officials and from the State Department's bureau of diplomatic security, Hartman realized he had to bow to many of Mecke's concerns.

With Hartman's approval, Mecke added another guard to the roster of Marine posts. Known as post number two-A, it provided a roving guard for the secure floors only. Mecke ordered an entirely new alarm system, new video cameras at all the sites, and a new courtyard vehicle gate to replace the one that froze in the "up" position.

But the State Department continued to regard security as a distant priority. Two years later, when Mecke was gone, some of the equipment he had ordered still had not arrived.

As a former Marine and policeman, Mecke was appalled when he saw that the Marines carried unloaded weapons. In his view, an unloaded weapon was worse than none. As soon as an intruder saw that a Marine was armed, he would assume the gun was loaded and react accordingly; the Marine would be left standing helplessly with an empty weapon. Finally, Mecke convinced Hartman to allow loaded weapons.

While Hartman accepted most of his changes, Mecke knew there was only so far he could go. He drew up a shopping list of improvements and ranked them by order of priority. Back in

Washington, the Defense Department was buying toilet seats for $640 and Allen wrenches for $9,606, but security for Moscow was judged on an entirely different scale. Mecke knew he could not get everything he wanted, nor could he come across too strongly. To be accepted by the diplomats, he had to be seen as flexible— someone who could deal and trade. A case in point, involving Valentina, the Soviet hairdresser, occurred a month after he arrived.[1]

Valentina was a short, bouncy lady who kept track of the comings and goings of the embassy staff from her perch in the beauty shop in the embassy's basement. When he returned as an adult, Carl A. Provencher, who had lived in the embassy as a child of ten, was amazed to find that Valentina remembered everything about him and his family from twenty years earlier.

"She recalled who my father was. She said she was sorry to hear about the death of my mother—in 1976. She asked about my puppy. In 1963 it was a puppy. She asked how I enjoyed the Naval Academy [he attended West Point]. She wanted to know where I learned Russian. She asked a lot of questions as if she were verifying information she had heard," he said.[2]

Before Mecke got there, Valentina had finally gone too far even for his predecessor. Information she had picked up while questioning an embassy employee had been used by the KGB to try to recruit the employee.[3] Klingenmaier recommended to Hartman that Valentina be fired. Hartman, who had been annoyed by her questioning while she cut his hair, agreed. But they neglected to prevent her from continuing to enter the embassy to do the hair of diplomats' wives. Instead of working out of the beauty shop, she now saw the ladies in their apartments in the embassy. Thus she continued to keep up to date on the latest gossip.[4]

Hearing this, Mecke ordered the Marine guards to bar her from the embassy. Two of Valentina's customers, E. Charlene Kurth and Shirley Benson, decided to give her a farewell luncheon with their husbands. Raymond E. Benson was the press and cultural attaché; Rear Admiral Ronald J. Kurth was the defense attaché. Mrs. Kurth thought Valentina had been let go as a reciprocal measure when the Soviets withdrew Hartman's favorite receptionist. In fact, the two events were unrelated.

Mrs. Kurth asked Hartman for permission to bring Valentina into the embassy one last time, and he agreed.[5] Hartman told Mecke, but Mecke did not pass the order along to the Marines. Mecke thought it was a bad idea, and when he discussed it with Beall, the administrative counselor agreed with him.[6]

On a crisp September day, Corporal John S. Hlatky, Jr., was standing post number one when Mrs. Kurth showed up with Valentina to attend the luncheon. Hlatky told Mrs. Kurth that Valentina was not allowed in. Infuriated that the exception had not been conveyed to the Marines, she asked to talk with Mecke. Hlatky said Mecke was out. She then demanded to talk with Hartman. She recalled that Hlatky refused. He recalled that she asked for the ambassador's extension. Because he was juggling other calls at the time, he did not immediately give it to her.[7]

When she got through to Hartman's office, the ambassador was tied up in a meeting. But what could be more important than letting a fired Soviet employee who worked for the KGB into the embassy? Mrs. Kurth got Hartman's secretary to interrupt Hartman, who granted permission for Valentina to enter. The secretary called post number one, where Stufflebeam answered the phone.

After being told to let her in, Stufflebeam insisted that she fill out a temporary identification badge, since all Soviets were required to wear identification badges in the embassy. This was too much for Mrs. Kurth, who burst into tears.[8]

As planned, Valentina had lunch with the Kurths and the Bensons in the admiral's apartment on the sixth floor of the north wing. During the lunch, Valentina cried in the admiral's arms.[9] Valentina's performance was so magnificent that the next day the admiral walked down to the first floor and gave Stufflebeam a dressing down. He said he had been discourteous to his wife and should have let Valentina in, since his wife was accompanying her.

"I'm sorry," Stufflebeam said. "The RSO said explicitly she wasn't allowed in."

"Well, since she's the wife of the defense attaché, you knew where she was going. You should have made a judgment call to let her in," he said.

"I was specifically told this woman was not allowed in. The RSO must have had a good reason for not allowing her in. No one was discourteous to your wife," Stufflebeam said.[10]

"Everybody was warned about Valentina," Charlene Kurth said. "She was finding out as much as she could. We knew that. They all went to a meeting once a month to report on their employers." But she said Valentina was a friend.

"You may not be able to fathom this, but she had worked for the embassy for almost twenty-three years," she said. "It was a terrible way to treat faithful employees."

What Mrs. Kurth did not fathom was that Valentina worked for the KGB, not for the Americans. While it was not her job to understand that, it was the ambassador's.

Because Admiral Kurth reported to the Defense Intelligence Agency, he was not in Stufflebeam's chain of command and theoretically could take no direct action against him. Nevertheless, the incident became widely known among the Marines, who took it as another sign that the embassy did not support them. Influential members of the embassy community could get security rules waived when they inconvenienced them. Apparently the best course for the Marines was to ignore violations rather than face humiliation.

When I related this incident to Lieutenant General Faurer, who served as vice director of the DIA before he became head of NSA in 1981, he said he did not believe the story because no defense attaché would have done such a thing.[11]

"First, an attaché's wife, I would think, wouldn't have that much clout," Faurer said. "Second, an attaché is far better prepared to be suspicious of the environment. He undergoes enormous scrutiny and pressure by the Soviets. For an attaché to evidence that attitude about a Soviet who has been expelled strikes me as absolutely unlikely."

There were many unlikely occurrences at Moscow station.

Wingate meanwhile was trying to relieve Lonetree from the security guard program with little success. Company A had just rated the detachment in a semiannual inspection. As a whole, the detachment was adjudged "outstanding."[12] Stufflebeam was rated the best Marine in the unit and called an "impressive NCO." Lonetree came in last.[13]

Based on Lonetree's previous infractions, Wingate held non-judicial punishment or "office hours" over the phone with Major Allen Kris, the commander of Company A in Frankfurt. Wingate read the charges and Lonetree responded. The proceeding was tape-recorded. At one point, Lonetree referred to another Marine by his first name instead of his rank and last name. That brought another reprimand. Kris found Lonetree guilty as charged but decided the infractions were not serious enough to warrant his removal.

"Well, sir, he has a long record of doing these minor things," Wingate said. "He's just not doing well in the detachment. He's not liked by the other Marines, and we need to get him out of here."

"Well, Top, you're in a hardship post. You're just going to have to work with him," Kris said.[14]

Removing an unfit Marine in Moscow should have been done with no questions asked. But at the time, the detachment was still short four to six people. Under those circumstances, Wingate felt Kris was concerned that a removal would make him look bad because it would mean he had not taken steps to shape up the Marines and keep him on post.

Relieving a Marine "shows you're not using leadership traits and principles to bring these people around," Wingate said. If Wingate had known about another infraction that occurred several months earlier, there would never have been a question about relieving Lonetree.

In the earlier incident, Lonetree was about to teach a class in firearms at Friday guard school. As a joke, in front of several Marines, he put a .38-caliber revolver to his head. Beyond stepping on the American flag, nothing is considered so heinous by Marines as playing with a weapon.[15]

When he learned of the incident later, Wingate was not surprised. It was what he had come to expect of Lonetree. The fact that it was not brought to his attention did not surprise him either. He knew that Marines cover for one another. If Lonetree had been removed, it would have meant more work for them. Besides, Wingate didn't want to be known as a hard-ass, pursuing every minor infraction to the exclusion of everything else. Then the Marines would say he wasn't looking out for them. In the Marine Corps, that was not a good reputation to have.

If he could, Wingate would try to save a Marine, and he was proud to say he had saved many good Marines in his career. But Lonetree was not his idea of a good Marine.[16]

What did shock Wingate was the number of Marines who were seeing Soviet women. Unbeknownst to him, Hlatky had been going with a curly-haired, well-built Soviet girl for six months, eventually leaving her pregnant. She was the daughter of a GRU officer formerly stationed in Washington. Several Marines knew about the affair but said nothing.[17]

The fact that Hartman allowed the Marines to dance with Yugoslavian girls at Uncle Sam's did little to discourage such liaisons. If Hartman thought he was trying to make some obscure political point by distinguishing Yugoslavians from other Communists, it was lost on the Marines, who only knew the girls were extremely pretty. Predictably, at least one Marine began going with a Yugoslavian girl.

Not that barring Yugoslavians would have kept the embassy free of Soviet-bloc women. Besides those working in the embassy and those knowingly invited to parties, the KGB sent sexy female officers to the embassy undercover.

One evening a good-looking woman with an Italian passport showed up for the Marines' "Thank God It's Friday" party, usually held once a month. The woman wore black leather pants and no bra under her blouse. Every Marine was after her. She finally wound up with one member of the detachment. Later that night he decided she knew more about him than she should have. Like the Americans, the Soviets could screw up.

At 2:00 A.M., the Marine called Wingate at his apartment two miles from the embassy.

"Top, I think I have a problem," he said.[18]

Wingate drove to the embassy, and while the woman talked with other Marines, Wingate and the Marine checked photographs of known KGB officers filed in the guard safe on the ninth floor. Sure enough, she was on the list, under a different name. The Marine escorted her out of the embassy.

Between checking up on attractive KGB officers and discouraging Marines from taking home Yugoslavians from Uncle Sam's, Wingate had enough to do without playing nursemaid to Lonetree. Yet that was what Kris wanted him to do. To try to improve his behavior, Wingate and Stufflebeam gave him extra duties and talked to him and to his squad leader. The fact that a Marine could not be relieved for misbehaving in the most sensitive diplomatic post in the world demonstrates how lightly the Marine Corps took the job of guarding the embassy.

Wingate and Stufflebeam thought they noticed an improvement in Lonetree. In fact, he had found another interest.

# CHAPTER 10

## The Swallow

FOR MONTHS, Lonetree had had his eye on a foxy twenty-five-year-old Soviet woman who worked in the embassy's customs office on the first floor of the central wing. To Lonetree, it seemed she had everything. Five feet nine inches tall and weighing 130 pounds, she had fair skin, high cheekbones, a good figure, large gray eyes, and sandy brown hair cut to her neck. She dressed stylishly, wore makeup well, and spoke almost perfect English.

Lonetree thought she was the most beautiful woman he had ever seen. UPDK, the Soviet agency that supplied the embassy with Soviet workers, had sent her to the embassy in May 1985. She told the embassy she was last employed at the Institute for Foreign Languages and had no family.[1]

Initially, the embassy employed Violetta A. Seina at Spaso House as a receptionist. She replaced one of Hartman's favorite employees, a Soviet who knew how to send Hartman's invitations to home addresses so the KGB wouldn't intercept them all. Hartman knew that if a Soviet worker performed his job for the embassy too well, UPDK would yank him. This was one of many ways the Soviets used the Soviet nationals to manipulate the Americans.

Hartman tried to make the receptionist more valuable to the KGB by leaking her information about coming events. Perhaps a senator would soon be coming to town, and he would let her know it a few weeks early. He thought the KGB would appreciate her more if it looked as if she were getting inside information. It didn't work. Ultimately, UPDK withdrew her.[2]

In contrast to her predecessor, Seina didn't seem to care much about her work for the embassy. She made a lot of mistakes in addressing invitations. Was it purposeful, or was she just bad at writing English?[3] Hartman never knew. But his wife, Donna, took an immediate dislike to her.

"She was one of those cool ladies who watch very closely what is going on," she said. "She was like a pussy cat, always waiting and watching."[4]

Because of his wife's dissatisfaction with her, Hartman had Seina reassigned to the customs area on the first floor of the central wing.[5] There she worked no more than ten feet from post number one, where Lonetree could not help but notice her.

Lonetree loved to ride Moscow's subways, which cost five kopeks—less than three cents—and were literally works of art. With mahogany-paneled walls surrounding the escalators, bas-reliefs of Lenin, marble floors, and crystal chandeliers hung over the platforms, the subways were an enchanting place to meet anyone, particularly a comely young lady like Seina.

In September 1985, Lonetree saw her in a subway station.[6] Lonetree thought the meeting was a chance encounter, but most likely the KGB had set it up. From listening in on phone conversations and picking up office gossip, it would have been easy for the KGB to learn that Lonetree had just gone through disciplinary proceedings and that the other Marines did not hold him in high esteem. The fact that he usually became a loud, boisterous drunk after only a few drinks was perfectly obvious. He was thus a ripe target for KGB recruitment.

After Lonetree and Seina chatted for a few minutes in the subway, he continued on to a diplomat's house. Thereafter, he would try to find ways to run into her at the embassy. He saw her again on a subway train in October. Moscow's extensive subway system crisscrosses the city like a spider web. The chances of running into someone twice by accident were as remote as running into the same person twice on New York City's subway system. Yet Lonetree again thought it was a chance encounter. Slyly, she let him see her first.

As Lonetree and Seina chatted over the noise of the train, she missed her subway stop. He was flattered. This was too good to be true. Her soft, gray eyes seemed to hold the promise of all the love he had missed as a child. They got off together at the next stop and took a walk, chatting animatedly about American books, movies, and food. She asked him about his family background and how he liked living in Moscow.

Common as it is, asking about family is a standard part of the recruitment process. It enables a KGB informer to report details back to Moscow center to demonstrate that he or she has talked with the target of the recruitment effort.

After two hours they parted. But Lonetree would see her again in the embassy over the next few days. The KGB had to be chuckling at how smoothly the plan was working. Hartman's preference for Soviet employees over American ones played nicely into the KGB's hands.

"That was really smart, having Soviets," commented Stanislav Levchenko, a former KGB major who defected from Tokyo in 1979. "I suspect to this day the State Department perceives there was nothing wrong with that. It was very naive."[7]

Lonetree and Seina agreed to meet again at the Chertanovskaya subway stop in the southern part of the city. This time, because she had to go home, they talked for only a few minutes. Most likely, she had been instructed to play coy so Lonetree would think he was chasing her.

They next met at the Marine Corps ball on November 10. The ball celebrates the founding of the Marine Corps in 1775. As in the past, Hartman allowed the Marines to invite Soviet workers from the embassy. Looking stunning, Seina showed up for the dance at Spaso House with Galya and Natasha, two Soviet nationals who worked at the embassy. Seina introduced them as her friends. The CIA later identified them as KGB officers.[8] That evening, Lonetree danced with Seina several times. He was taken by her grace. By now he was firmly hooked. Seina was far more beautiful and enchanting than any girl he had ever been able to attract.

The next month, Lonetree saw Seina at a Marine House party. Another Marine had invited Seina and several other Soviet employees to the party. Lonetree wound up talking to Seina all night, and they agreed to meet a few days later at a metro stop.

Lonetree was soon scheduled to be transferred. But because of his infatuation with Seina, he asked for an extension of his tour. Had the Marines been sensitive to counterintelligence matters, they would have prohibited any extensions. But Company A was only too happy to have any extra Marine in Moscow. In short order it granted Lonetree's request.

Lonetree met Seina at a subway station again in December, and she invited him to her home at 31–1–6 Volzhskiy Boulevard.[9] Contrary to her claim to the embassy that she had no family, she introduced Lonetree to a woman she said was her mother. She also introduced him to a young girl she said was a younger sister. Neither appeared to speak English, and they seemed shy. Most likely they were KGB officers.

Seina showed Lonetree some books and records, along with photos of her when she was small. They discussed the fact that the embassy had just fired her, and UPDK had assigned her to work at the Irish embassy. Beall, the administrative officer, had given her a warning, saying she was not doing enough work. In addition, she seemed to be asking too many questions. When she did not improve, he terminated her.[10]

But that did not matter to the KGB. She was now needed for other, more important duties. Unknown to the embassy, Seina had performed her work exceedingly well.

Stufflebeam visited the bar at the Mezj again in late September, this time with Sergeant Richard W. Mataitis.[11] He ran into the blonde and brunette he had met there before. By now he knew the routine, and he suggested that they go back to the apartment together.

"This time you have to help me out," the brunette said.[12]

"How much do you need?" Stufflebeam asked.

"We can talk about it later," she said.

The blonde left with some other friends, and the brunette went with Stufflebeam to her apartment at 10:00 P.M. After having sex they sat on the living room sofa.

"You have beautiful eyes. Would you mind if I put makeup on them?" she asked.

Almost certainly, it was a KGB effort to compromise him. If

the KGB could get pictures of him made up like a woman, the photos could be used as blackmail to try to get him to spy for the Soviets. Having already violated the regulations about fraternizing with Soviets, Stufflebeam would be hard put to explain that the photos were innocent.

"You don't think I'm KGB, do you?" she asked.

She was laughing, but Stufflebeam thought of the warnings he had been given about Soviet prostitutes. If they're operating in Moscow, it was most likely under the direction of the KGB. But Stufflebeam couldn't be sure. When he looked at her he saw a fresh-faced, innocent-looking young woman who was very good in bed. It was difficult to believe she might be an informant. The offer to make him up seemed so whimsical, as if it were a prank. It was hard to imagine that there was anything sinister attached to something that had felt so good. Yet Stufflebeam was offended that anyone would ask such a thing. Who did she think he was? He said he had to go and asked how much money she needed.

"Don't worry about it," she said.

Stufflebeam did not report this contact, nor a third one in October with another attractive brunette. Stufflebeam met her with several other women at the bowling alley at the Mezj. Even though it served drinks, the bowling alley was not off-limits. Along with Mataitis and Hlatky, Stufflebeam and the young ladies left to go to a bar at the Kosmos Hotel that was off-limits. Stufflebeam knew that this brunette was a prostitute because she immediately said he would have to help her out. He also realized she was probably a Soviet.[13] They had sex at her apartment and he paid her thirty rubles.

Meanwhile, Stufflebeam's extracurricular activities were not going unnoticed in the Marine detachment.

When Corporal Duane B. Parks arrived in Moscow in March 1985, he seemed to be a well-disciplined, straight-up Marine who worked out daily and obeyed the rules. By October he had undergone what seemed to be a personality change. He smoked, drank, went out with Soviet-bloc girls, and bought black-market rubles. Parks bought the rubles from another Marine who apparently bought them from an African diplomat. When a ruble cost $1.70, he would get four or five rubles for one dollar. He spent the money on champagne and caviar that he enjoyed with Soviet women in Russian restaurants.[14]

Like the other Marines, Parks had trouble understanding the rationale behind the rules that restricted his life in Moscow. The Marines were entrusted with top-secret material but were not trusted to have girls in their rooms. The fact that the Navy Seabees could have girls in their rooms in the embassy only underscored the unfairness of the rule. Moreover, it was sometimes difficult to understand what exactly was wrong with having sex with Soviet women. If they were such a threat, why did Hartman let Soviets answer the embassy's telephones, enabling them to listen in on conversations at will?

Most of the Marines in the detachment had women in their rooms anyway. Some attributed this to Wingate's less-than-firm stance on the subject. If Wingate felt strongly about something, everyone knew it. Thus when Wingate came to Moscow he put a stop to the practice of stealing Soviet flags. He let the detachment know that the first Marine caught stealing a flag would be sent home. That was the end of the practice. But Wingate disagreed with the rule about women. While he insisted he enforced all the rules, several Marines thought they detected a glimmer of a smile when he told them they could not have women in their rooms.[15]

One night Parks brought two buxom Polish women back to his room at the Marine House. He had met them at the Bier-Stube, the German restaurant in Moscow that was not off-limits to Marines. They had wine and cheese together and listened to his Led Zeppelin records.

The girls undressed, and he tried to have sex with one of them. Because of the amount of liquor he had consumed, he could not perform. He took the other girl to the room of a friend, Corporal Roland L. Paquette. Normally, Paquette became enraged when he was awakened unnecessarily. He opened his mouth to yell but caught himself as Parks shoved the naked blonde into his room.

"Have a good time!" Parks said as Paquette peered dumbfounded at the girl.[16] The young lady stayed with Paquette until 4:00 A.M., when Parks escorted both women out of the embassy.[17]

When Parks first came to Moscow, he had lifted weights with Stufflebeam next to the Marine recreation room. Now that Stufflebeam was assistant detachment commander, their relationship changed. In December, Parks showed up eight hours late for guard duty, and Wingate initiated nonjudicial punishment, or "office hours." "Office hours" can result in reduction in rank, removal from post, fines, extra duties, or restriction to the Marine House. Company A gave him a fine.[18]

Parks decided to get even. He reported to Mecke that Stufflebeam was seeing Soviet prostitutes.[19] Sure, he had done some things, but so had his assistant detachment commander. Why should he be punished? Parks wanted to know.[20] Stufflebeam denied the allegations to Wingate.

In February 1986, Stufflebeam and his date, Lisa L. Villalobos, an embassy employee, strolled into the embassy at 10:20 P.M. to find Parks fast asleep at post number one. Besides the fact that Parks was sleeping with his chin on his chest, Stufflebeam noticed that Parks had left the vehicle gate to the courtyard in the "up" position.

Parks would later complain that the ever-changing watch-stander schedules—not to mention the incessant false alarms—made it impossible to get a good night's sleep.

Asked how often he slept on post, he said, "I hate to answer a question like that. It happened. It wasn't just me. It was everyone."[21]

A few days after getting back from Frankfurt for his nonjudicial punishment, Parks dropped off two students at Pushkin University after a Marine party. He came back after the curfew, and Wingate and Mecke had Parks relieved from the security guard program.

Before being sent home, Parks complained to Major Kris about the lax security at the embassy. To Parks, it seemed Kris didn't want to hear about it. Kris felt he already knew what Parks was complaining about and was trying to get the problems corrected.[22]

Parks was glad he had been relieved. He didn't want to be in Moscow anyway.

Lonetree began having sex with Seina in January 1986. He fancied himself a character out of James Bond and read up on countersurveillance techniques in books by John Barron. Before he would meet her, he would try to throw off KGB surveillance by changing from subways to buses, wearing different coats, and altering routes to her apartment.[23]

Undoubtedly, the KGB set up each meeting, so there was no need for the cloak-and-dagger stuff. Even if the KGB had not orchestrated the affair, it was virtually impossible for an American embassy employee to engage in such activities with a Soviet woman without the KGB knowing about it.

Now the KGB began stepping up the pressure. First, Seina introduced Lonetree to a man she said was her father. She explained that her mother and father were divorced, accounting for the fact that her father was not living at her apartment. This got Lonetree ready for the next introduction, which came a few weeks later. While she and Lonetree were riding the subway, Seina said her uncle wanted to meet him. Lonetree asked why.

"He wants to meet you," she said simply.

Seina asked Lonetree not to mention to her uncle that he had met her father. She claimed the uncle was from her mother's side, and the two men did not get along. The tale of family strife lent more credibility to her story. After taking a bus to the uncle's apartment, Seina introduced Lonetree to a man she said was her Uncle Sasha. Thirty-three years old, Sasha was six feet four inches tall and had a large frame. He had a clear complexion and graying brown hair combed back. According to CIA files, Sasha in fact was Aleksei G. Yefimov, a KGB officer.

Yefimov was well-known to the CIA and the State Department. Since 1983 he had served as a back channel communicator to the embassy, passing along information and positions that the Soviet government did not want to articulate officially. Yefimov dealt with Sean M. Byrnes, the head of the embassy's internal political unit.[24] In that job, Byrnes obtained information about political developments within the Soviet Union and explained U.S. policies to the Soviets. Jeffrey Chapman, Byrnes's predecessor, had introduced Yefimov to him at a luncheon at the embassy in July 1985. In turn, Kent Brown, Chapman's predecessor, had introduced Yefimov to him.[25]

Yefimov did not say he was with the KGB. He said he worked for the State Committee for Science and Technology. But he did say his approach to the embassy had been ordered by the Central Committee of the Communist Party with the approval of the KGB.

About once a month, Yefimov and Byrnes met to exchange information. Yefimov would fill Byrnes in on the latest moves within the Communist Party hierarchy or underscore how strenuously the Soviets opposed U.S. development of the Strategic Defense Initiative, or "Star Wars." Byrnes would discuss political developments in the U.S. and ask about rumors he had picked up concerning Soviet dissidents, one of Hartman's major interests.

With Lonetree, Yefimov wore a different mask. Pretending he did not speak English well, Yefimov asked Lonetree how he liked life in America and how much Americans are paid. With Seina translating, Lonetree told him his salary. Yefimov commented that it was more than he made. Yefimov never said what he did for a living. But as they watched television together, he mentioned that he was a member of the "upper class" with friends in the Communist Party. Yefimov said he did not have any children. It seemed to Lonetree that Yefimov treated Seina as if she were his daughter.

Yefimov played his role well, but then his audience was not very discerning. Lonetree did not suspect that Yefimov was anything other than Seina's Uncle Sasha.

He would soon find out otherwise.

# CHAPTER 11

# A Defector's Information

As THE AMERICANS were debating the fine points of having Soviet workers in the embassy, Vitaly S. Yurchenko strode out of the Soviet embassy in Rome. Telling Soviet officials he was going to visit the Vatican museum, the blond, swaggering KGB officer darted instead into the American embassy and announced he wanted to defect.

Very often, in the intelligence world, the best information comes from defectors. Then the problem becomes what to do with it. So it was with Yurchenko.

Whisked off to the U.S. and then to a CIA safe house in Virginia, Yurchenko began telling the CIA and the FBI about KGB operations targeted at the West. In all, he gave up twelve spies, including Howard, the former CIA officer, and Pelton, the former NSA employee. The insight he gave into KGB operations was invaluable. Almost immediately, Yurchenko's revelations began hitting the press. But his most sensational disclosure never appeared: that the KGB could read all the embassy's secure communications.[1]

As the highest-ranking KGB officer ever to defect to the U.S., Yurchenko's credentials for making such a claim were impeccable. From 1975 to 1980 he had been the Soviet equivalent of an RSO at the Soviet embassy in Washington. In the Soviet system, the security officer has far more stature and authority than a State Department RSO. After that, he was chief of the Fifth Department of Directorate K in the First Chief Directorate. Known as

Line KR, Directorate K has a range of counterintelligence functions, including penetration of foreign intelligence services, maintenance of Soviet embassy security, and investigation of espionage within the ranks of the First Chief Directorate.[2]

More recently, Yurchenko had been deputy chief of the First Department of the First Chief Directorate. In that capacity, he supervised KGB residences in Washington, New York, San Francisco, and Ottawa; assisted other KGB officers to recruit Americans anywhere in the world; and coordinated Eastern European and Cuban intelligence efforts directed against the U.S.

In keeping with KGB compartmentation* practices, Yurchenko had not been told of the embassy penetration as part of his official duties. That information was supposed to be tightly held within the KGB's Sixteenth Chief Directorate, the new department charged with compromising the secure communications of the U.S. and its allies. But KGB officers, like CIA officers, pass a lot of information around at lunch and in the corridors. Yurchenko said he learned the information in this fashion.

While Yurchenko said the KGB had been allowed to enter the embassy, he was not sure who had let the officers in. He said the KGB could read communications not only at Moscow but at the consulate in Leningrad and the embassy in Vienna.

Meanwhile, another defector told a Western intelligence service that the KGB had successfully recruited Marine security guards at American embassies in the Soviet Union.

Now the pieces were starting to come together. The roll-ups, the executions, the bugged typewriters, and the bugs in the new embassy were all part of a concerted and successful KGB effort to penetrate Moscow station.

Yurchenko said he thought he had heard something about who had helped the KGB penetrate CIA communications. He mentioned two names. But before he could reveal more, he was gone.

Any defector feels a tremendous sense of loss upon giving up his homeland, not to mention his family, friends, and culture.

---

* For a definition of this and other intelligence terms, see the Selected Glossary beginning on page 290.

Yurchenko had particular reasons for feeling despondent. He had hoped to be reunited with a woman he had had an affair with when he was stationed in Washington. She was the wife of a Soviet diplomat now stationed in Toronto. To his chagrin, she spurned him.

Then there was the fact that almost everything he said seemed to wind up in the press. Trying to overcome the embarrassment of mishandling Edward Lee Howard, CIA Director Casey had been leaking stories to show that the CIA had scored a coup in Yurchenko. At the same time, he called for prosecution of journalists whose stories he did not like. If the CIA could not keep a secret, Yurchenko wondered, how could it protect his life?

But there was much more to Yurchenko's melancholy than that. Unlikely as it seems, the CIA does not know how to handle defectors well. By their very nature, defectors are difficult, strong, independent characters who may have trouble fitting into a bureaucracy. Aside from the trauma of giving up their country, they are sometimes so plagued with personal problems that they may be unable to function in either country. On top of that, they are haunted by the fear that the KGB will one day catch up with them. Although there has been no known case of a KGB assassination attempt in the U.S., several defectors have been killed in Europe. Harassing phone calls late at night sometimes add to their dread.

Nor is every defector genuine. Sporadically, the KGB slips phony defectors into the U.S. to try to learn what the CIA knows. Other defectors may make up stories to enhance their own importance. Defectors with intelligence value may get a stipend from the CIA, and this usually increases with the importance of the information.

These are problems the FBI handles all the time when dealing with Mafia informants. As in dealing with any source, it is important to evaluate credibility and try to obtain corroboration. Handled professionally, this can be done without causing alienation or sowing mistrust—a lesson the CIA has yet to learn.

Since its founding, the CIA has had a deeply rooted fear of being hoodwinked by defectors. In the 1950s the Soviet Union was sending dozens of phony defectors to the U.S. In addition, many CIA officers deeply mistrust any Soviets. Yet a high-level defector can provide more intelligence about the Soviet Union than Moscow station can acquire in three years of spying. Instead of taking risks to suck a few drops of information from Moscow, the CIA can swim in a river of information in one of its safe houses in the U.S.

The trick is to treat a defector with dignity, honesty, and understanding even though he may turn out to be a phony. The fact that most defectors are genuine and risk their lives to enjoy American freedoms is even more reason to accord them respect.

The CIA has yet to grasp this.

Alexandra Costa is still bitter about Barbara. Barbara is the CIA case officer initially assigned to her after she defected from the Soviet embassy in Washington in August 1978. Costa was not an intelligence officer, but as the wife of a Soviet diplomat she could provide an inside account of life in the Soviet compound in Washington. An intense, curly-haired woman of forty-three, she is the first person in forty years to defect from the Soviet embassy in Washington.

FBI agents initially coaxed Costa into defecting. They got a salesman at her car dealership to strike up a friendship with her. Since she felt alienated from her husband, she welcomed the male attention. The FBI agents watched her and protected her, anticipated her needs, and kept her happy. Because the CIA has jurisdiction over defectors, they then turned her over to the CIA and Barbara, a former CIA secretary who had never handled a defector before.

Costa says she would have preferred a man, but she had many female friends and feels she could have hit it off with Barbara if she hadn't been such a cold fish. She felt Barbara was more interested in planning her forthcoming wedding than in helping her.

Every morning Barbara visited Costa at a CIA safe house and gave her forms to fill out. During the day, CIA officials with various specialties would interview her and prepare reports. Without identifying her, the CIA let others in the intelligence community know that they could send in questions for Costa. The answers then went back to the officials.

One day Barbara took Costa to her optometrist, where the saleslady called her "Judy."

"Why did she call you 'Judy'?" Costa asked.[3]

Instead of explaining that CIA case officers routinely use aliases, Barbara said, "She got me mixed up with my twin sister. We look very much alike."

During the Labor Day weekend, Barbara left Costa alone in the safe house with her two young children and no car. By Sunday afternoon she was running low on milk and diapers. She felt lonely and depressed. As it happened, one of the FBI agents who had helped her to defect called her. When the agent learned that Costa was feeling blue, she came over within a half hour and stayed for the evening.

On another occasion, Barbara told Costa she would be bringing along a couple of social scientists to ask about Soviet psychological research. The next day, Barbara arrived with one man.

"Where is the other person?" Costa asked.

"Oh, yes," she said. "The other person is not coming." And she left them alone. The man began asking personal questions: Did she love her mother? Did she feel a need to compete with her?

"I don't understand what my feelings about my parents have to do with the state of Soviet psychology," Costa protested. "Whose business is it whether I ever tried to compete with my mother?"

"It is my business," he said. "I am a psychiatrist."

"But Barbara told me that you were interested in Soviet psychological research."

"I don't know what she told you," he said. "I met her for the first time outside of the door. But a psychiatric evaluation of defectors is a standard agency procedure, and that's what I was sent to do."

Costa has an IQ of 153. She graduated from the University of Leningrad and holds a master's degree from the Moscow Institute of Sociology. Subsequently, she taught Marxism and Leninism at an institute for foreign students in Moscow. Yet Barbara advised her to get a job as a secretary.

Other defectors have had similar experiences. After promising him a good job when he defected in 1971, the CIA arranged for Vladimir Sakharov, a former prominent Soviet diplomat with several advanced degrees, to receive training as a hotel manager. When the hotel school went bankrupt, the CIA suggested that he become a salesman. Instead, he obtained a Ph.D. from the University of California and is a lecturer in Soviet affairs. Other defectors have wound up washing dishes or driving taxicabs.

While Costa found some CIA officers to be professional and personable, Barbara's suggestion that she become a secretary made her furious. She elected instead to obtain an M.B.A. degree from the Wharton School. She cut her ties to the CIA, preferring the uncertainties of the job market to the umbilical cord of her $12,000-a-year stipend. She opened a computer consulting firm in Reston and wrote a book, *Stepping Down from the Star*, about her experiences. Yet Costa continues to be plagued by problems that are chronic to most Soviet defectors.[4]

Americans do not quite know what to make of defectors. In a sense, they are like any immigrant group that tries to make it in America. Yet they have special disadvantages. No one is sure they should be trusted. Defectors who have worked in intelligence can never work in that field again. Logically, Soviet defectors should teach about life in the Soviet Union, but many who have tried have found the academic establishment resents them.

Then there are the problems of adapting to freedom and to leaving one's family behind. Costa was already on the verge of divorcing her husband and she was able to bring her children with her, so the strain was lessened. Lately, she has been dating Levchenko, the KGB major who defected from Tokyo in 1979. In contrast to Costa, Levchenko left his family behind and has had trouble dealing with the competitive atmosphere in the U.S.

"People who escape from the Soviet Union bring with them a slave complex," Levchenko said.[5] "Everything is prescribed there—what you read, where you live and work. There is practically no unemployment, they have free education there, the health care is disastrous but it's free. You never feel happy at all but there are guarantees that you grow accustomed to."

Donald F. B. Jameson maneuvers his scooter to the bar of his sprawling home in Great Falls, Virginia. A polio victim, he can zip along at five miles an hour on the battery-powered chair. Jameson pours a drink for Costa. In the living room, Jameson's wife, Lisa, chats with Victor Belenko. After a buffet dinner, Costa, Lisa Jameson, and Aleksandr A. Ushakov take out their guitars. They play "Borodino," a Russian song celebrating Napoleon's defeat in his march toward Moscow. The other guests sing along in Russian.

After being charged with writing anti-Communist literature, Ushakov escaped from the U.S.S.R. in 1984 by crossing two mountain ranges and swimming across icy rivers at night. Belenko flew a Soviet MIG-25 plane to the U.S. a decade ago.

This is the defector underground—an unofficial support group that tries to fill the vacuum left by the CIA. The underground consists of private individuals and voluntary organizations contributing their own time and money to help defectors adjust to America.

Jameson began his career with the CIA by handling defectors in West Germany in 1951. Later, as a high-ranking official in the CIA's Soviet section, he continued to supervise defector handling until he retired in 1973. Since then he has counseled defectors, referred them to jobs, introduced them to one another, and served as a refuge of last resort. With the exception of Yurchenko, Jameson has known nearly every major defector, including Yuri I. Nosenko (who claimed the KGB did not send Lee Harvey Oswald to kill President Kennedy) and Svetlana Alliluyeva, Stalin's daughter.

Lisa Jameson joined the CIA in 1967. She was a case officer whose responsibilities included defector handling. She quit in 1982 and went to work for the Voice of America. Over the years, Lisa Jameson has known twenty-five defectors.

While neither Jameson had anything to do with the Yurchenko case, they say from what they learned about it that his handling is symptomatic of the problems experienced by defectors and the way those problems are dealt with by the CIA.

"It's hard enough for us to envisage death in a family or a divorce, which causes a major upheaval in your life," Lisa Jameson said.[6] "But try to imagine a complete rift with everything you knew since you were born—your wife, children, family, neighbors, friends, culture, language, the food. A more cataclysmic trauma I cannot imagine. If you're a Soviet defector, you have committed an act of treason. An act of treason is punishable by death. In anything but a Communist country you simply decide to change your place of residence. For a defector, it's like going to another planet."

First, there is exhilaration: the escape is successful and the defector becomes the center of attention within the CIA.

"Some of the senior people from the agency come and talk to him," she said. "For a period of time, he is 'it.' Everybody can't get there fast enough. Then it begins to wind down. The euphoria usually leads to a period of depression. 'Did I do the right thing?' Even if he is always convinced he did, it's still depressing. The case officer has to be able to identify the depression. If he doesn't, then they wind up like a Yurchenko."

"There is a general attitude [within the CIA] that you can never fully trust defectors," Jameson said.[7] "Of course you always have to be on the lookout that the defector may be a plant, that the person was sent. Of course you don't want to say anything that would reveal intelligence sources or methods or information. So you can't be totally open and straightforward."

But, he said, that doesn't mean CIA officers cannot be intellectually honest with defectors.

"You don't tell them what the task force on them discussed, about other cases, or what other people said about them, or information that corroborates or doesn't corroborate what they said. Being intellectually honest with them and straightforward are completely different things.

"There have been a lot of cases where promises were made about future careers or money matters that were not kept," he said. "If you can't fulfill a request, say it. I'm sure the truth is not always on the defector's side. They'll say, 'We'll take care of you.' To Americans that means nothing. To a Russian, it means, 'I'm obligated to make sure you survive.' A lot of this comes from people in senior positions who don't understand how you talk to a person in this kind of situation. Sometimes they say things that just aren't so to avoid an argument. The defectors know *Pravda* is all lies but they think they've come from a society that is all black to one that is all white."

"I would always speak in Russian even if I felt a defector's English was very good," Lisa Jameson said. "Often it was even better than my Russian. But they had enough stress. Why put additional stress on them? I knew how much stress it was for me to speak Russian. I felt it put them more at ease. I also tried to find out what they wanted to do and tried to acclimate them and told them the good and the bad side of our society. I tried to have some humor in the relationship," she said.

Both Jamesons said the most important element in good defector handling is assigning one case officer to remain with a defector throughout the debriefing and resettlement process. Yet, like a faceless bureaucracy, the CIA insists on using an ever-changing crew.

"New faces appear and they are frequently rotated," said F. Mark Wyatt, a former CIA official who has been involved with helping defectors since he retired from the agency in 1978.[8] "The new contact personnel are simply not of a sufficiently high caliber to deal with the traumas of a person who is leaving all behind for an unknown future. . . . They lack the motivation and skill to do their delicate jobs properly."

Over the years, handling defectors has not been considered one of the more prestigious jobs within the CIA.

"Some of the people who have run that operation were inappropriate," Jameson said. "One individual was callous and exploitative. He came from Eastern Europe and remembers how his grandparents sweated to make it in America. Then these guys come over and are given everything. He wanted to know, why are they better than my grandfather or me? He used defectors as a foil for his own problems.

"Another reason [for the way the CIA handles defectors] is they are a lot of trouble," Jameson said, noting that some defectors have been handled properly despite that attitude. "You have to pull off people from working on something else. The handling and resettlement are difficult. There's a feeling of 'We're not going to take the time and trouble. They're a pain in the ass.' "

On the night of November 2, 1985, Yurchenko was dining with a CIA escort at Au Pied de Cochon, an inexpensive French café in Washington. In his three months in the U.S., Yurchenko had been constantly in the company of a CIA employee. He felt he was a virtual prisoner.

The CIA escort this night was in his twenties, spoke no Russian, and knew next to nothing about the Soviet Union. He was hardly fitting company for one of the highest-ranking KGB officers ever to defect to the U.S.

Over dinner, Yurchenko asked if the young man knew a good haberdasher. The escort mentioned Hecht's, a local department store like Macy's. Similarly, when Yurchenko suggested they dine at a French restaurant that night, the escort took him to this crowded bistro that was not even on the map of fine French restaurants in Washington.

Yurchenko was homesick, and the fact that the CIA seemed to care so little about him and was leaking stories to the press only added to his despair. Yurchenko told the young man that if he was not back in fifteen minutes, it was not his fault. He hurried up Wisconsin Avenue to the new Soviet embassy complex at Mount Alto, conveniently only a few blocks away. Two days later, the Soviet embassy held a press conference in Washington starring Yurchenko. He charged that the CIA had drugged and kidnapped him.

Yurchenko's redefection ignited an immediate debate within the U.S. intelligence community: Was Yurchenko's original defection a ruse? Since he had said the KGB has no mole in the CIA, were his statements devised to lull the CIA into thinking it had not been penetrated by the Soviets? Or was Yurchenko a genuine defector, who had had a change of heart?

To those familiar with the way the CIA handles defectors, there was never any question that he had fallen victim to the peculiar malaise that grips Soviet defectors and the unfeeling way in which the CIA treats them.

Yurchenko's redefection was the U.S. intelligence community's equivalent of letting a civilian plane enter Soviet airspace and land in Red Square. Yet no heads rolled. President Reagan did not ask for Casey's resignation, nor did the CIA ever assign culpability within the agency.

Since William H. Webster took over the agency in 1987, more attention has been focused on defector handling. Webster's deputy, Robert M. Gates, regularly meets with defectors and listens to their problems.

"I used to tell Casey on a regular basis this was wrong or that was wrong. He would agree but not much happened," said lawyer William Geimer, the head of the Jamestown Foundation, the most prominent organization helping defectors.[9] Now, according to Geimer, the CIA assigns an official to take responsibility for each defector. However, the CIA still rotates case officers.

"There has been a substantial increase in numbers [assigned to defector handling] and a shift in attitude and emphasis," Webster testified at hearings held by the Senate Governmental Affairs' Permanent Subcommittee on Investigations in October 1987.

But it will take more than cosmetic changes to transform the way the CIA handles defectors. Institutions tend to perpetuate the values and outlook of their founders, regardless of who is in charge. It does not require advanced degrees to handle people with dignity. It does require the desire. Yet Clair E. George, until 1987 the CIA's chief of covert operations, is quoted by Wyatt as saying of defectors, "If they don't like it here, they can go back where they came from."

When Casey briefed President Reagan on what Yurchenko had said about the penetration of the embassy's communications, he presented it as a coup for the CIA.

"Look what we've done now. We've got a high-level defector, and he's told us this information," is the way Casey characterized the disclosure.[10]

In fact, the disclosure was hardly anything to boast about. It meant that the CIA had fallen down on one of its most basic responsibilities: countering KGB threats to American security interests overseas. As in the case of the bugs found in the new embassy in Moscow, the agency kept Yurchenko's information secret. Fewer than a dozen CIA, FBI, NSA, and National Security Council officials knew about it.

"The bureaucracy never admits a mistake or weakness," said a high-level intelligence officer with knowledge of the defector information.[11]

There was another factor at work as well. No one wanted to believe the worst. If anyone had asked Defense Department officials during the twenty years that Walker was spying, they would have said it was impossible to penetrate secure Navy communications. Similarly, Adolf Hitler most likely would have found it impossible to believe the Allies had compromised the German Enigma cipher machine during World War II.

Unlike bank robberies, there is usually no physical evidence to demonstrate espionage has occurred. But in the case of Moscow station, there would be.

# CHAPTER 12

## A Slide Show

RATHER THAN revealing what Yurchenko had said, the CIA stepped up pressure on the State Department to tighten security at the embassy. As usual, the agency did not want the KGB to know what it knew about KGB activities. In its own way, the CIA was just as passive as the State Department, preferring to carry on a silent dialogue with the KGB rather than bring embarrassment to itself by making public its own ineptitude. In any case, the State Department was the last place the CIA would tell any secrets. But Robert Lamb, the assistant secretary of state for security, got the message anyway.

Lamb knew his way around Washington, where the coin of the realm was not money but power. A former administrative counselor in Bonn, he became assistant secretary of state for administration in 1983, a post that then included security. In 1985 the job was split, and Lamb became assistant secretary for security.

With a poker face and soft blue eyes, Lamb was easygoing and self-effacing. He often compared himself to a cowboy riding herd on stampeding cattle. The best thing he could do was keep them headed in the right direction.[1]

Early on, Lamb agreed with the State Department's Soviet desk that having Soviet nationals in the embassy was the best thing since the invention of peanut butter. He had even argued the point forcefully before skeptical congressional committees. Lamb changed his mind after he saw a slide show put together by David G. Major, an FBI counterintelligence agent assigned temporarily to the National Security Council staff. Concerned about mounting indications that the embassy was being penetrated, the FBI had sent Major to Moscow to check on security there.

Major was appalled by what he saw. Burglar alarms at corner grocery stores worked better than those at Moscow station. The Soviet nationals had the run of the place. As in 1940, when Hoover sent an agent to Moscow to report on security at the embassy, Major came back with a devastating critique.

Instead of sending a memo to Reagan, as Hoover had done with Roosevelt, Major gave the President a twenty-minute slide show. Everyone knew the President responded better to pictures than to words. Narrated by Major, the slide show compared security at the embassy in Moscow with security at the Soviet embassy in Washington. As he flashed shots of Soviet nationals working in the Moscow embassy, Major said the FBI would give anything to have one American working in the Soviet embassy in Washington. As Major pointed out a female KGB officer in the embassy, Reagan agreed she should be let go.

Besides Reagan and Lamb, Major presented the show to Hartman and to the Senate Select Committee on Intelligence. Predictably, Hartman didn't understand the point and thought it was scandalous that Major had gone around him to the President. He thought the show only illustrated the differences between American society and the closed Soviet system.[2] But the message was not lost on Lamb, who not only had a keen mind but a politician's instincts. He recognized that momentum was building on the Hill to get rid of the Soviets, and he felt that defending the policy of employing them only undermined the State Department's credibility. In his view, continuing to employ Soviets in Moscow was not only foolish from a security standpoint but politically unwise.[3]

Lamb felt there was more to the State Department's love for the Soviets than met the eye. At the heart of it was a fear by the diplomats that "inferior" Americans would crowd them.

"I think there probably is a relationship between not wanting to replace Soviets with the fear of being overwhelmed by administrative [types]," Lamb said. "It's the 'yellow peril.' We're going to be swallowed up by these inferior people who are less patriotic."[4]

Beyond that disquieting thought, Lamb felt the diplomats

were afraid more Americans would overload the embassy's already overburdened facilities.

As a former key officer of the embassy said, "The more demand you put on them by adding more Americans, the more you depress overall morale because there are fewer goodies to go around." By that, the State Department officer explained, "We only have so many cars, the size of our medical facility is limited. So if everyone gets the runs and there are a lot of Americans, there will be relatively less medical attention for each person. The snack bar is small. The more Americans you have, the lower the quality of the food and service."

Thus the issue of getting rid of the Soviets had more to do with not standing in line at the snack bar than lofty arguments about Soviet recruitment. The same considerations were behind Hartman's objection to Lamb's plan to shield the secure areas of the new embassy. As originally planned, the new embassy was to have a CPU just like the one in the old embassy. Computers, typewriters, and copying machines in the secure areas were to be equipped with their own shielding, known as "tempest" protection, to prevent stray emissions from leaking out. As more and more embassy business was transacted on computers, it became more efficient and more secure to shield the entire top five stories of the new eight-story embassy. The steel shielding would also prevent the Soviets from picking up vibrations from the sounds of voices striking embassy windowpanes.

The new embassy was not supposed to be under Hartman's direct control. The interagency committee headed by the CIA was in charge of security; the Office of Foreign Buildings was doing the construction. But an ambassador is supposed to have the final say on any activities within his country, and Hartman elected vigorously to oppose shielding the building. In doing so, he marshaled an impressive array of arguments and even consulted manufacturers of CPUs in an effort to torpedo the plan. He said shielding the building would be prohibitively expensive and would not guarantee protection, since the Soviets might come up with something to counter the shielding.

At times, Hartman seemed to be spoofing himself, so outrageous and outlandish were some of his points.

"I said that we didn't know with certainty what their technology is, and how are you going to protect against future technology?" Hartman said. "I said as a taxpayer, I really object to this [shielding], since you cannot tell me you have technology that can stop in the future what they're trying to do now. If you can't, then let's not spend the money on that. Let's protect what needs protection."5

By this reasoning, the Defense Department should be closed down and production of all fighter planes, submarines, and missiles should cease because today's technology may be outmoded tomorrow.

What most concerned Hartman was the fact that the shielding would block the sun. Ever conscious of his own comforts, he said there was little enough sun in Moscow as it was without blocking all the windows. What Hartman overlooked is that employees in the old embassy had gotten along for years with no sun in the building. Because of the microwave bombardment, all the windows had been fitted with heavy curtains, drawn at all times. Moreover, many federal workers in the U.S.—including a large cross-section of State Department employees—worked in windowless inner rooms.

As he had with so many other security issues, Hartman had become intimately involved in a field he knew nothing about. As usual, his thrust was in the direction of less rather than more security. So adamant did he become that he appealed Lamb's decision to shield the building to Secretary of State George Shultz. After he and Lamb each presented their arguments, Shultz sided with Lamb, but Hartman said to Lamb as they left the secretary's office, "You haven't heard the end of this one."6

Even if Lamb won a few, he could only do so much. The foreign service had two classes. There were the diplomats, or "black dragons," who ran the show. They were the Arthur Hartmans of the world—clubby, extremely bright, and often arrogant. Then there were the administrative types like Lamb who supported them. They included the security officers who were thought by the diplomats to wear polyester sport coats and to be hostile to the Soviets. The diplomats looked down their noses at them, and it was the diplomats who ruled the department.

From George Kennan's days, the diplomats wanted as little to do with security as possible. They saw it as a threat to their own hegemony, an intrusion into their private hunting preserve. As it was, they felt their authority was constantly being threatened. With no visible results for their efforts, they had ho natural constituency. Layers of bureaucracy on top of them and other agencies on all sides of them constantly countermanded their decisions. While the defense and intelligence budgets kept growing, the State Department's kept shrinking in relation to the number of countries where the U.S. had representatives. In fiscal 1987 the State Department cut travel by 13 percent and furniture and equipment purchases by 45 percent.

The diplomats' paranoia was fed by the fierce competitiveness of the foreign service, where officers who were not promoted were required to leave. Increasingly, the field of diplomacy was inhabited not by the State Department's generalists but by specialists from other agencies with degrees in engineering, economics, or law. Worldwide, only 30 percent of embassy officers came from State.

While the diplomats had become a minority in their own house, they remained a powerful one. When it came to having the President's ear, the State Department had no peer. That was as it should be. In the long run, solutions to tensions between the U.S. and the Soviet Union would come from diplomacy, not arms. But meanwhile the U.S. had to remain strong.

In pursing that goal, no one looked at the overall picture, which was that the State Department's expenditure for protecting the intelligence community's secrets, as compared with the value of those secrets, was badly skewed. The entire budget for State Department security was $300 million, which compares with the CIA's budget of $6 billion a year and NSA's budget of $15 billion a year.[7] Yet much of the work of the intelligence agencies could be compromised by a penetration of the ten-story building in Moscow.

"We haven't found a way to measure the relative difference to security of one Stealth bomber versus communications security," said Faurer, who headed the NSA until 1985.[8] "If you look at the communications budget in the past ten years, there's been a wonderful increase. You'll find another slope for security for those communications. It stems from a desire to delude ourselves that we are not as vulnerable as we are."

One of the few government officials who saw the disparity was Kenneth B. deGraffenreid, a former staff member of the Senate Select Committee on Intelligence who directed à component of the National Security Council staff devoted to intelligence. He viewed the government's counterintelligence efforts as so much spaghetti. Each agency—State, the FBI, the CIA, and NSA—had a piece of it, and there was no real control or coordination. He spent much of his time trying to convince the CIA to focus more on learning about the KGB. In part because of his lobbying efforts, Congress established the Office of Foreign Missions within the State Department to better coordinate responses to Soviet provocations in Moscow. Now if the Soviets cut off power to the embassy in Moscow, the State Department could do the same to the Soviet embassy in Washington.

At the same time, the problem of embassy security was getting more attention because of the spurt in sensational spy arrests. During 1985, known as the "Year of the Spy," the government arrested an average of a spy a month.[9] Meanwhile, a committee headed by former CIA deputy director Bobby R. Inman recommended improved security at embassies to combat terrorist attempts. Responding to the report's recommendations, Congress authorized an additional $3.5 billion for security countermeasures at American embassies over five years, beginning in fiscal 1987.

Many in the State Department saw the increased emphasis on security literally as a plot by administration hard-liners to keep the Cold War going. According to this theory, deGraffenreid and other Reagan administration conservatives were soldiers in Reagan's "evil empire" approach to relations with the Soviet Union. They saw increased security as inimical to efforts to negotiate arms agreements.[10] Privately, the diplomats ridiculed the claims of some in the intelligence community that Soviets were creeping into the embassy in the dead of night. Did they think the Soviets were dwarfs or contortionists who could wiggle their way through the air ducts?

"Some people in Washington had the feeling people were

walking in and out of the building at will," Hartman said. "I said, 'I'd like to know if that's true.'" He said CIA and other officials responded that they couldn't say why they believed the embassy was being penetrated.

To be sure, there was reason to be suspicious of many Reagan administration strategists; some could be more belligerent than the Soviets. Nor was the intelligence community above exaggerating the Soviet threat to obtain more funding. The Defense Intelligence Agency, as one example, was notorious for overestimating Soviet military strength in order to win bigger budgets for its constituency, the military. But even a ten-year-old would know that employing the enemy, letting them place bugs in the new embassy, and relying on alarms that don't work are not good ideas. The instinct to protect oneself transcended liberalism or conservatism, but the State Department chose to politicize the issue by labeling advocates of better security "conservatives."

As pressure on him mounted, Hartman composed diatribes accusing his critics of seeking to cut off relations with the Soviets. Referring to proposals to remove the Soviets from the embassy, Hartman haughtily cabled Shultz on November 4, 1984:

Quite apart from the outrageous effort by ignorant people to instruct me on the way to staff this post, I object to these schemes on the simple ground that they run absolutely counter to our policy. First, they are not based on realism because they ignore the absolutely predictable Soviet reaction which will take the form of retaliation designed to hurt us most; this, after all, is the closed society. Second, they are not based on a premise of strength but of weakness. They assume that we are so inept that we cannot combat the threat of a few hundred resident Soviet citizens and a few hundred Soviet visitors each year, while the Soviets somehow manage to cope with over 200 American permanent employees, dozens of long-term construction specialists on our building site, and 50,000 American visitors each year.

The argument also neglects the fact that we are an open society that will not close for this purpose, and that agents of any nationality, including unfortunately a few Americans, can be bought by the Soviets and their third-country friends. And finally, most importantly, these proposals are guaranteed to sabotage the realistic dialogue we seek with the Soviets. You'll recall the deep personal anger of Gromyko when we placed limits on his airplane. The all-out assault (and that's what it is) on

Soviet official presence in the U.S., coupled with demands for an increase here, will lead to four years of Arctic solid-frozen relations. Is that what the President wants?[11]

Hartman's arguments were such an admixture of non sequiturs and misconceptions about security and counterintelligence that it was difficult to untangle them all. His argument that barring Soviets from the embassy would be an admission by the U.S. that it is too weak to counter Soviet recruitment efforts recalls the arguments of American car manufacturers in the 1960s over safety. They maintained that designing cars with padded dashboards and collapsible steering wheels condoned drinking and speeding. If drivers did not drink or speed, the companies maintained, there would be no accidents. Why make it easier for them by padding dashboards when they were to blame for causing the accidents?

This corporate version of original sin ignored the reality that human weaknesses will always exist. Changing the environment minimizes the damage caused by those weaknesses. In fact, since the auto manufacturers started designing safer cars, the number of fatalities per thousand miles traveled has dropped dramatically.

By citing the visits of American tourists and construction workers who can spy in the Soviet Union, Hartman was muddying the waters still more. The fact that both countries gather intelligence on each other in a variety of ways, from lofting spy satellites to reading newspapers, does not mean that the U.S. should lay bare its secrets from the embassy in Moscow.

By citing a temper tantrum by then Soviet foreign minister Andrei Gromyko, Hartman was demonstrating his own weakness. Gromyko's dislike of a U.S. policy was no reason to let the Soviets spy in the American embassy.

Perhaps the most bizarre argument of all was Hartman's claim that the Soviets would retaliate against the Americans for refusing to employ Soviet workers when the Soviets themselves refused to employ Americans in their own embassy in Washington. In effect, Hartman was saying that some Americans will always engage in spying, so why place obstacles in their way? Indeed, Hartman and the State Department went quite a bit further than that. They affirmatively placed temptations right alongside the Americans in the embassy.

Even as Hartman was arguing that the Soviet workers posed no threat, Violetta Seina was tightening the noose on Lonetree.

# CHAPTER 13

## A Promotion

Now that Lonetree and Seina were having sex regularly, the KGB moved in for the kill.

Seina told Lonetree that her Uncle Sasha would like to see him again. He thought that was strange. He could not understand why he had wanted to meet him in the first place. But having already become subject to blackmail by seeing Seina and eager to continue seeing her, he was in no position to argue. He agreed to meet him early in February 1986.[1]

This time, Yefimov's English was quite good. Indeed, it had improved so remarkably in the course of a few weeks that he no longer needed Seina as an interpreter.

Like the Mafia, which invites victims to dinner before they are eliminated, Yefimov offered Lonetree food and drink. Seina had previously told Lonetree the Soviets wanted peace, and Lonetree had empathized with that view, saying he was a friend of the Soviet Union. Now Yefimov recalled Lonetree's words and said he needed his help.

"You're a good guy," he told Lonetree. "If you are a friend of the Soviet Union, you will help me and Violetta," Yefimov said.

"How is helping you going to help her?" Lonetree asked naively.

"She's your friend, but you would also be helping the Soviet people," Yefimov said.

Removing the velvet gloves, Yefimov pulled out a list of questions he said had been prepared by a friend who was a

142

general in the KGB and a member of the Central Committee of the Communist Party. Almost all the questions had to do with the CIA's presence in the embassy.

Yefimov wanted to know if Michael C. Sellers, a second secretary of the embassy, was in the CIA.[2] Lonetree did not always know for sure who was in the CIA and who was not. But from the locations of their offices in the embassy, who they associated with, and their work habits, he could make a few deductions.

About a month later, on March 14, 1986, the Soviets would expel Sellers for allegedly engaging in spying.[3] Given the timing, it is likely the Soviets already knew enough about Sellers and were testing Lonetree to see if he would confirm Sellers's affiliation.

Yefimov next asked about Murat Natirboff, who was widely known to be the CIA station chief. Lonetree confirmed that he was. Natirboff openly disclosed his CIA affiliation to the Marines when he briefed them on how to handle Soviets who want to defect to the U.S.

Yefimov next asked Lonetree if he could plant bugs in the offices of Mecke, Natirboff, and Hartman. Lonetree said he would not do so.[4]

The fact that Yefimov did not ask Lonetree to place bugs in the CPU is significant. Indeed, nearly all of his questions had to do with the seventh floor, where the CIA was located, rather than the ninth floor, where the CPU was located. In retrospect, this raised the question of whether the Soviets already had bugs in the CPU.

"Are you in the KGB?" Lonetree asked innocently.

"No," Yefimov said.

But Lonetree realized from his questions that Yefimov was. Yefimov asked Lonetree if he could obtain the plans to the seventh floor, and he said he would try. From having an affair with a Soviet woman, Lonetree had passed over the line to espionage. It happened just as outlined in KGB training sessions.

"Starting with an ordinary, even innocent, friendly contact, the [KGB] case officer gradually finds the prospective agent's vulnerabilities, plays the agent much as a fisherman plays a fish until he can land it, and then pulls him in. He begins making suggestions, cautiously offers gifts, and begins to exact favors until his target is caught," said Levchenko, the former KGB major who defected to the U.S. in 1979.[5]

A few weeks later, Yefimov asked to see Lonetree again. Lonetree realized there was no way he could say no without losing Seina. He brought along the floor plans that he stole from the embassy. This time, Yefimov produced a folder containing photos of more than 300 permanent and temporary embassy personnel. Most of the pictures were visa photos, but some were family snapshots. Photos of many of the Marines, including Lonetree, were included.

Yefimov asked Lonetree to arrange the photos to show who was married to whom. Lonetree did as he was told. Meanwhile, Yefimov pulled out an embassy phone book and began asking Lonetree about the functions of each person, covert and overt. The phone book itself was not secret. Each Soviet worker in the embassy had one, and the Soviet telephone operators helped prepare it. But some of the information Lonetree gave Yefimov was secret. Besides Sellers and Natirboff, he disclosed the names of two other covert CIA employees who were never expelled.

Turning to the floor plans Lonetree had brought, Yefimov asked Lonetree to mark the locations of sensitive spaces, secret doors, and security devices on the seventh floor. He also asked him to identify the purpose of each room and each of the occupants and their functions. Yefimov asked about the rest of the embassy as well, and Lonetree told him how the alarm systems work and how the Marines react to them. He discussed each floor of the embassy and identified the offices and their occupants, mentioning where particular furniture was located. He gave Yefimov similar information about the attic where the NSA kept listening equipment and the secure warehouse where material for the new embassy was stored.[6]

Yefimov asked about the new embassy, but Lonetree had little to say about it. Yefimov was particularly interested in Hartman's desk. Several times he asked Lonetree to describe it, presumably so the KGB could design a listening device for it. Repeatedly, he asked if Lonetree would place listening devices in the embassy, and repeatedly Lonetree declined.[7]

Yefimov gave Lonetree a piece of paper to sign. It said, "I am a friend of the Soviet Union. I always will be a friend of the Soviet Union, and will continue to be their friend."[8] This is a common KGB tactic to ensure that an individual is compromised. It was used, for example, when the KGB recruited Leakh Bhoge, a Guyanese immigrant. He pretended to spy for the Soviets in New York while helping the FBI apprehend Gennadi Zakharov, a KGB officer working for the United Nations.[9] After his arrest, Zakharov was traded for journalist Nicholas Daniloff in the fall of 1986.

Lonetree did not tell Yefimov all he knew, and Yefimov did not press him. Now that he was recruited, there would be plenty of time for that. Lonetree could still tell himself that he had not given everything away. In his childish mind, he thought he was outfoxing Yefimov, telling him only enough to keep him happy.

Lonetree had not thought through the full implications of what he had done, nor did he want to. Gradually, the meetings had progressed from social visits to espionage debriefings. He tried to tell himself that the nature of the visits had not changed, that they were still social, and that Seina had no connection with the KGB. If he had admitted to himself that Seina was a KGB plant, he would have to face up to the fact that she did not love him after all. That he was not willing to do.

Between January and March, Lonetree had sex with Seina four times. After having wangled an extension, he was scheduled to be transferred to Vienna on March 10, 1986. The day before he was to leave, he had a last meeting with Yefimov. Saying he was going to be in Vienna that summer, Yefimov suggested they get together. Lonetree resented the idea. Now that he wasn't going to be seeing Seina, there was no reason to continue to see Yefimov, he thought. He began fantasizing about somehow exposing Yefimov as a KGB spy.[10]

Yefimov gave Lonetree a slip of paper with some dates in June and July when they were to meet. He also gave him an enameled wooden box as a gift.

"You're a good guy, even though you did not help out too much," he said.

Apparently the KGB thought otherwise. That month, Yefimov told Byrnes, his State Department contact at the American embassy, that he had just gotten a promotion and an award. It meant moving up from deputy chief of his department at the state committee to chief, he said. The new job brought a raise and a chauffeured car.[11]

"For what did you get this big promotion?" Byrnes asked him.

"For excellence in my work. I accomplished great things in the last year, and I was duly recognized," Yefimov said with a trace of a smile.

Back at the embassy, Mecke was going down the list of changes he wanted to make to improve security. Ever since he arrived, he had thought the system for checking employees' identities at the entrance to the building was a disgrace.

Essentially, there was no system. The Marines were supposed to recognize American employees and let them in. Soviet workers were supposed to wear pink photo badges. Visitors wore no badges unless they were Soviet-bloc citizens, who wore yellow badges.

Even at the end of their fifteen-month tours, the Marines had trouble remembering the faces of the nearly 200 Americans who were rotated in and out of the embassy. A newly arrived Marine was lucky if he recalled three or four faces. If the Marines had any question about an American's identity, they were supposed to consult photographs pasted to identification cards kept in a box at post number one. Even if the Marines had time to check, the diplomats would become impatient and sneer, "Don't you know who I am?" Their tone made it clear that the Marines were low-grade morons for not recognizing them.

Mecke thought the most bizarre aspect of the identification system was the requirement that Soviets wear pink badges. If they removed their badges, they identified themselves as non-Soviets who did not have to wear badges.

The same system prevailed at post number three, where the Marines controlled access to the secure areas and the CPU. In the morning, dozens of American employees would show up at one time to go to work. There was no way a newly arrived Marine could possibly know their faces or have time to look up their identities.

Mecke changed the system so that embassy employees had to wear a badge at all times, just as they did at the State Department in Washington. This was too much for the old guard, the diplomats who had spent ten to fifteen years of their lives within the confines of the yellow stucco building and considered it their home. Who was this thirty-eight-year-old newcomer to question what they had been doing for so long? The diplomats took it out on the Marines, who got flak from the diplomats as soon as the new system started in February 1986.

"They didn't want to wear their badges," said Roen. "They would get very upset when you wrote them up. Even on the ninth floor we'd get people giving us a hard time. They'd forget their badges at home. You'd have to issue a temporary badge. 'I've been here for this many years, and do you know who I am?' Or 'My husband is colonel so-and-so. You have no right to ask for my badge.'"

Some of the diplomats cut pictures of cute faces from magazines and pasted them over their identification photographs to see if the Marines would notice. Even the Soviets gave the Marines a hard time. When asked to show her badge, one Soviet worker picked up her dress and displayed her identification badge pinned to her panties.[12]

Two of the biggest complainers were Raymond E. Benson and Jaraslav Verner.[13] Then the counselor for press and cultural affairs, Benson had helped negotiate the 1985 cultural exchange agreement that brought the Bolshoi Ballet to the U.S. and sent Vladimir Horowitz to Moscow. Verner worked for the U.S. Information Agency and was in charge of press relations at the embassy.

Like Hartman, they thought an open embassy demonstrated the openness of American society. Mecke thought the argument was divorced from reality and let them know it.[14] But the two diplomats were a source of constant irritation to the Marines.

One day Cooke stopped a nineteen-year-old who did not have his badge. After asking him to open his bag for an inspection, Cooke asked where he was going.

"I'm the Bensons' son," he said.

"I'm sorry, sir, but you're going to have to wear a badge," Cooke said.

The next day, Benson's wife came down to post number one and took Cooke to task for searching the young man's bag.

"That's my son!" Shirley Benson said.[15]

Another time, the Bensons returned to the embassy in the evening. Shirley Benson held her badge up but was not wearing it. The Marine at post number one told her she had to wear it. The next morning, she called Mecke to complain. Realizing he could push the diplomats only so far, Mecke said she did not have to wear it at night so long as she was going to her apartment.[16]

Her husband, meanwhile, often forgot his badge altogether. "It took me awhile to get used to it [showing a badge]," Benson said.[17]

Explained Shirley Benson, "After all, this was our home. I don't know if you understand the situation. When you've lived in a place for six years—four in the seventies and two in the eighties—and all of a sudden you have to start conforming to these various things, which in some cases seem unreasonable . . . there were bound to be a lot of problems."[18]

On another occasion, Benson complained to Wingate that a Marine told Dusko Doder, then the Moscow bureau chief for the *Washington Post,* that he could not enter the embassy unescorted unless he wore credentials issued by the embassy to American journalists. Doder had showed up with only a Soviet press card.

That day, Benson was acting deputy chief of mission, and Wingate thought he was enjoying being in charge. He asked him to come to his office on the eighth floor.

"This guy Doder is a very good friend of mine, and he is quite powerful with the pen. We don't need to harass him," Benson told Wingate.

"What do you mean?" Wingate said.

"The Marines were harassing him because he didn't show his ID card," he said.

"They were just doing their job," Wingate said.

"We've got to make exceptions for this guy," Benson said.

Benson suggested posting Doder's photo in the sentry station at post number one so Marines would let him pass without showing a badge. But Wingate said the Marines wouldn't be able to see out the window of the guard station if they started posting photos of people exempt from the rule.

"Sir," Wingate said, "unless the ambassador or RSO tells me, there's no exception."[19]

Verner, meanwhile, made it clear he had no use for the badge system. One day, he displayed his irritation with the Marines when he had to wait on the first floor for an elevator that the Marines were using.

"What the f—— is going on up there?" he yelled up a stairwell. "Goddamn it, we've got work to do."[20]

Stufflebeam was on the first floor along with several other embassy employees. Turning to Verner, he said, "If you have anything to say, you should say it to me as the assistant detachment commander."

When Wingate heard about the incident, he reported Verner to Mecke for behaving rudely.

That same month, Mecke, Beall, and Combs put into effect Hartman's plan for cutting the size of the Soviet work force and moving the remaining Soviets to the shacks in back. Among them were Raya, a key Soviet employee thought to be a KGB colonel, and Galya, later identified by the CIA as a KGB officer.

The first to be fired were the telephone operators. Sensing that his tenure at the embassy was up, Radio Sasha had already left.

As part of the general firing, Mecke also dropped two Soviets who cooked for the Marines. Nina Sheriakovo was the senior cook who had been with the embassy for nine years. Blond and busty, she was forty years old. Even though she wore low-cut dresses and was seductive, the Marines did not think she was particularly attractive. The fact that she did not take baths as often as Americans did not help.[21]

Her helper, Galina N. Golotina, or Galya, had been with the embassy since January 1985. More petite than Nina, she was twenty-eight years old, weighed 115 pounds, and stood five feet three inches tall. She had green eyes and brown hair.

Neither woman knew how to cook American meals when she first got there, but the Marines gave them Betty Crocker cookbooks and soon they were turning out hamburgers, brownies, and apple pie. Still, the Marines thought they added too much grease to the recipes. When they got the runs every few months, the Marines would call it "Lenin's Revenge" and blame it on the Soviet cooks.

Since the kitchen and dining rooms were adjacent to the Marines' recreation room, the Marines spent a lot of time with the cooks. They made fun of Sheriakovo, claiming she made a habit of offering to show them her breasts. On the other hand, they liked Golotina, a divorcee with an eight-year-old son.

As the noncommissioned officer in charge of ordering food supplies, Corporal Arnold Bracy had the most contact with her. Several times a week, the six-foot one-inch Marine consulted with Golotina to find out what food the cooks needed. The two would watch television or videotapes together in the recreation area.[22]

After Mecke fired Golotina, Phillipe Duchateau, Verner's deputy as public information officer, hired her as the nanny for his young daughter.

Over the coming months, it would become clear that her relationship with Bracy went beyond watching television.

# CHAPTER 14

# Finding a Replacement

WITH LONETREE GONE, the KGB needed a replacement at the embassy. It chose Arnold Bracy.

Bracy was an unlikely candidate. A straight-up Marine, he was respected by the other Marines and by diplomats alike. Wingate considered Bracy, after Stufflebeam, the best Marine in the detachment. The fact that he did not drink or carouse with girls made him an even less likely candidate for recruitment. But Bracy had one weak spot: he had obviously developed a fondness for Golotina, the Soviet cook.

Certainly there was nothing in Bracy's background that would lead one to suspect that he could be compromised. Born on November 28, 1965, he grew up in a religious family in Queens. His father, Theodore R. Bracy, is a subway motorman and an evangelist deacon at Calvary Full Gospel Church in Woodside, New York. Both he and his wife, Frieda L. Bracy, have bachelor's degrees in theology. Besides Arnold Bracy, they have two daughters, one older and one younger than he.[1]

If Bracy was not going to church while he was growing up, he was studying. On Thursdays, he attended Bible school. On Fridays, it was Bible school and youth choir rehearsals, on Sunday church services.[2]

He was well-liked in school and got A's and B's. There was a modesty to him that was endearing. When he made the honor roll in high school, he did not tell his parents. His father found out anyway and asked his son why he had not told him.

"Papa, that's not a big deal," Bracy told his father.[3]

When he was sixteen, a friend asked Bracy to help him beat up a young man who had taken away his girlfriend. When Bracy's father found out about it, he advised Bracy that if he were a real friend, he would tell the jilted suitor to stay away from the other teenager. Bracy never forgot the advice. He lived in a housing project beset by crime. When several of his friends got into trouble with the law, he steered clear of them.

Bracy graduated in June 1983 from Thomas Edison Vocational Technical High School. He decided to join the military as a way of saving money. Of all the services, he felt, the Marines were the best. Later, he regretted that he had not enlisted instead in the Army, where pension benefits were better.[4]

Bracy completed boot-camp training at Parris Island in South Carolina. He spent a year and a half in an amphibious assault battalion at Camp Pendleton in California. Then he decided to see the world and signed up for Marine security guard school on May 22, 1985.[5] After sailing through guard school, Bracy chose Moscow as his first post. He figured it was safer than hardship posts in Africa or the Middle East. He thought Moscow also might have better medical facilities.

At the time, the guard school devoted roughly two hours to dealing with the threat of being entrapped or blackmailed—about the same amount of time devoted to instruction in wearing civilian clothes. Bracy also got a perfunctory half-hour briefing at the State Department on what he could expect in a Soviet-bloc country. Once he arrived in Moscow, he received a security briefing from embassy security officers. In addition, Mecke talked about the entrapment threat during Friday guard school.

Bracy thought security guard school did not emphasize entrapment because the Marine Corps never expected it to happen.[6] There was a lot of truth to that. The Marines held themselves out as the purest of the pure, the ones least likely to betray their country. That attitude was just as unrealistic as the CIA's approach to countering electronic eavesdropping in the new embassy—by letting the Soviets do what they wanted while pretending publicly there were no bugs.

Over the years, the Marines' ostrichlike attitude had hindered law-enforcement efforts to apprehend KGB spies. When the Naval Investigative Service or the FBI asked the Marines to cooperate in a double-agent operation, the Marine Corps usually refused, claiming no Soviet would ever believe that a Marine would turn on his country. In fact, aside from Lonetree, four Marines have been convicted since 1982 of engaging in espionage-related crimes.[7]

As a result of the Marine Corps' know-nothing, see-nothing policy, the Marines were less experienced in dealing with entrapment threats than the other services. Moreover, the attitude of headquarters rubbed off on the Marines, who thought the KGB was something they saw in the movies and had nothing to do with them.[8]

Like the Marines who went before him, Bracy was appalled when he arrived in Moscow in July 1985. The city was drab and dreary. The people seemed unenthusiastic unless they were drinking. Nor did they seem very friendly. When he first arrived at the embassy, pieces of the roof were falling down on the street below, and the area had been roped off.

"This is the U.S. embassy?" Bracy thought to himself.[9]

Bracy was astonished at the lax security. The diplomats left the windows to their offices open at night, an invitation to the KGB to take pictures of the embassy's interior with cameras equipped with telephoto lenses. Bracy wrote incident reports each time, and the diplomats would leave the windows open again the next night. The video cameras that monitored access to the courtyard were a joke. A Soviet could drive into the courtyard with a trunk full of other Soviets, and no one would know the difference.

It seemed to Bracy that a premium was placed on not ruffling diplomats' feathers. He learned that another Marine had tried to inspect a briefcase of a Middle Eastern diplomat who flew into a rage. Conscious that his tenure ultimately depended on the diplomats, Mecke told the Marines to check with him before asking to look in any diplomat's belongings.

As Bracy told me, it did not take him long to realize that the alarm system, like everything else about the embassy, had a fatal flaw, one that would make it relatively easy for the guard at post number three to let the KGB into the CPU at night. Because the detachment was undermanned, the Marine at post number one guarding the main entrance to the building went off duty at 11:30 P.M. At that point, through video cameras and intercoms, the Marine at post number three on the ninth floor controlled access to the entire embassy in the most hostile territory in the world. That Marine could not only let the KGB through the front door, he could also let the KGB into the secure areas and provide the combinations to the CPU vault doors.

Ultimately, this was the most scandalous fact of all: that the security of Moscow station and the protection of many of the CIA's and NSA's most important global secrets depended on the integrity of a single young Marine stationed on the KGB's home turf.

To be sure, letting in the KGB would have required more effort than opening the door. The combinations to the CPU were encased in plastic pouches like the bags that encase sauerkraut at grocery store deli cases. If a pouch were opened, it could not be resealed. After sealing it, a CPU communicator wrapped it in tape that he signed. The pouch remained in the guard safe overnight. The next morning, a communicator checked it to make sure it was intact.

But it would have been relatively easy for the KGB, whose bugs in the embassy typewriters made NSA sit up and take notice, to bring along a replacement pouch complete with tape and forged signatures.

The roving sergeant-of-the-guard occasionally checked up on the Marine at post number three, but his was not a full-time post either. Most of the time he was checking on guards at the new embassy or the warehouse across town. Because he called in on a walkie-talkie as he made his rounds, the Marine at post number three usually knew where the roving guard was. Later, after Mecke established the roving post known as two-A for the secure areas, it would have been harder to let someone in. But the Marine at post number three usually knew where he was, too. Because the roving guard set off alarms as he went, he had to ask the guard at post number three to shut them off for him as he made his rounds.

Occasionally, communicators entered the CPU at night to

work on special projects. But just as Ilya Dzhirkvelov, the former KGB officer who penetrated the Turkish embassy, had planned for such surprises, the KGB could come up with a way to escape. As a last resort, Dzhirkvelov said, the KGB officers would pretend to be ordinary thieves looking for currency in the embassy. They hoped to be arrested by the Soviet police.[10]

The one defense against a surreptitious entry—the CPU alarm system—was useless because the State Department did not want to spend the money to update it. When the alarms in the CPU were triggered, a buzzer and red light went off on a panel at post number three. By flipping a toggle switch, the Marine could silence the buzzer and turn off the red light. A yellow light then went on to show that the alarm had gone off. Only a communicator from the CPU could turn off the yellow light by resetting the alarms. But the alarm system created no permanent record to show when the alarms had been triggered. The Marine on post number three was supposed to log the time when they went off, but he could have easily entered a fictitious time. Thus the Marine on post number three could let the KGB into the CPU at 2:00 A.M. At 6:00 A.M., he could tell the CPU communicators the alarms had just gone off. No one would be any wiser.

Counters on the doors to the CPU showed how many times the CPU doors had been opened, but the communicators frequently neglected to reset them each morning, so no one knew for sure if an entry registered by them was real or not. Every bank in the U.S. had several video cameras recording everything on the premises twenty-four hours a day, yet not a single video camera recorded what took place at the entrance to the CPU in Moscow. The alarms for the other secure areas of the embassy could be turned on and off by the Marine at post number three without anyone knowing. Not even a yellow light showed that they had been triggered.

While Mecke was assigned to Moscow, the alarms in the CPU sounded five times.[11] He never knew if they were false alarms triggered by a piece of paper falling to the floor or if the KGB had entered the CPU with the connivance of the Marine at post number three.

The new alarms ordered by Mecke created a permanent

record showing the time when they had gone off. Yet the alarms did not arrive for more than a year.[12] In all, the equipment Mecke wanted cost a few hundred thousand dollars—less than a tenth of 1 percent of the State Department's annual security budget. It would have meant the difference between a relatively secure embassy and one that practically invited the KGB to come in. Still, the State Department dragged its feet.

Wingate soon placed Bracy in charge of a squad, which supplied the Marines for one shift. He later made him a roving sergeant-of-the-guard. Even though Lonetree was on his squad, Bracy had little to do with him. Bracy felt that Lonetree was always "zoning" —in the "Twilight Zone." The Marines passed stories about how Lonetree had gotten hammered or blitzed at some party. If someone had told Bracy that Lonetree had run naked down the street, he would not have been surprised. In any case, Lonetree remained in his own room much of the time, either because he had broken a rule or was getting over a hangover.

Occasionally, Lonetree tried to engage Bracy in conversation about political conditions in the Soviet Union. He claimed reforms were being made. Bracy wasn't interested. As far as he was concerned, the entire place could go down the tubes.[13]

Articulate and outgoing, Bracy was much in demand at diplomats' dinner parties. Young women from other embassies also found him attractive, the more so because he did not come on too strong. While he had dated a few girls in the past, Bracy had remained a virgin because of his religious convictions. He would not totally rule out sex before marriage. If the right opportunity came along, he might grab it. But so far no one in his life had been important enough for him to take that step.[14]

Changing before Marine parties, several women undressed in Bracy's room in front of him, hoping to attract his attention. He would walk out so he wouldn't see them naked.[15]

But Golotina, the Soviet cook, was different. She was not pushy and did not run around with other men. Bracy admired that. Her English was not good, and that made Bracy feel protective toward her. He helped her with her English, and she helped him with his Russian. Bracy danced with her at the Marine ball on November 10, 1985.

In the months before Mecke fired her, several of the Marines noticed that Golotina and Bracy seemed to have become quite close. Roen, one of Bracy's friends, put it to him one day.

"Is there anything going on?" he asked Bracy.

"No," Bracy said.[16]

Sensing the same thing, Wingate and Stufflebeam gave Bracy a warning about fraternizing with Galya. Bracy appeared to see her less after that.[17] But many of the Marines thought the relationship had not cooled.

At the main entrance to the new embassy, the Marines kept a two-by-four that they called the "Russian stabilizer." To pass the time, they would scribble the latest gossip on it—who was the "black-market king," for example, or which female embassy employee had taken on the most Marines. While the inscriptions were mere rumors, many of them tended to be true. On the stabilizer someone had written "Bracy and Galya [Golotina] are secret lovers."[18]

Mecke was reading in his apartment at the embassy on Sunday, June 29, 1986, when Bracy asked if he could talk with him. They went in the secure "bubble" on the ninth floor, and Bracy began unraveling a bizarre tale.

Bracy said he had gone for a walk in the Park for Economic Opportunity, a monument to Soviet industrial and technological progress near the Kosmos Hotel. As if by chance, he saw Golotina in the park, and they began chatting. She asked how the Marines were doing, and he asked her how she liked her new job as the Duchateaus' nanny. After a few minutes of pleasantries, she blurted out that someone, possibly from the KGB, had called her and asked her to meet him near the Kremlin. The man wanted her to bring Bracy to an apartment that would be provided. The idea was that the KGB wanted to entrap him sexually.[19]

Golotina said she refused to go along. The man said she could get into serious trouble if she did not coooperate. But she told Bracy the worst that could happen was that the UPDK would fire her. After ten minutes, Bracy said he had to go. He went straight back to the embassy. Or so he told Mecke.

The next day, Mecke reported the incident to the State Department's bureau of diplomatic security. He also briefed the Marines on what had happened. He wanted them to be alert to similar attempts. After consulting with the officers above him, he decided Golotina should not be fired as nanny to the Duchateaus. After all, she had reported the KGB attempt. Mecke let Bracy know that Golotina would not be fired but warned him, as he had before, that he should have nothing to do with her.[20]

Mecke was pleased Bracy had reported the incident. It was hard to get across to the Marines that nothing would happen to them if they reported contacts with Soviets. This would serve as an example of how things should be done.

Still, there was something troubling about Bracy's report. While every security service makes mistakes, the KGB usually was not so clumsy. While Soviet citizens sometimes refused to cooperate with the KGB, it was highly unlikely that someone who worked for UPDK would do so. So far as Mecke knew, UPDK only employed KGB officers or informants.[21]

During his meeting with Mecke, Bracy had seemed nervous and tense. Perhaps that was because he had just been the target of a KGB recruitment attempt. Then again, perhaps Bracy had something to hide.

It was not long before Mecke got some of the answers.

# CHAPTER 15

# The Duchateaus' Bedroom

MECKE was in his office on the afternoon of August 20, 1986, when Phillipe Duchateau, the embassy's deputy press secretary, came in with a strange tale.

Duchateau and his wife, Golnar, had been vacationing in Scandinavia for the past month. They let Stephen Wright, an ABC-TV soundman, and his wife stay in their apartment while they were away. When the Duchateaus got back, Wright said that a black Marine and the Duchateaus' nanny were having sex in the bedroom when they arrived at the apartment.[1] Flustered, the Marine told the Wrights he had been inspecting the place. He quickly left.

Bracy's report of nearly two months earlier flashed through the regional security officer's mind. He hurried down from the ninth floor to the Marine detachment commander's office and checked the liberty log for July 20, when Duchateau said the Wrights arrived at his apartment. Bracy had signed himself out to a softball game that day; he was the only black Marine who had signed out.[2]

Mecke immediately called him in. This time Bracy seemed even more nervous than when he had reported the earlier incident with Golotina in the park. Under questioning, he said he had been in the Duchateaus' apartment with the former embassy cook. However, he denied having sex with the Soviet. He said he went to the apartment because Golotina was pressuring him to cooperate with the KGB. He wanted to tell her he would have no further contact with her.[3]

Mecke did not a believe a word of it.[4] His story simply made no sense. Why would anyone visit someone to say he would not see her?

If Bracy had not already been recruited by the Soviets, he was well on his way to being recruited, Mecke thought.[5] He wondered, too, about Bracy's first reported contact with Golotina. Had it merely been a ruse to draw attention away from him? Very possibly he had thought an American had seen him and wanted to report the contact first. Alternately, Mecke thought, the KGB may have directed him to report it as a way of testing the waters in case he was already under suspicion.[6]

Beyond the possibility that Bracy had been recruited, he had clearly violated Marine Corps and State Department rules by seeing a Soviet and not reporting it. Mecke discussed the incident that day with Beall and Combs. The next day Mecke told Hartman about it.

"Given what Golotina told him and what has occurred, he is very vulnerable. It's in our best interests to get him out of the country immediately," Mecke told the ambassador.

Hartman agreed. Mecke next cabled Washington. "Irrespective of which scenario—romance or espionage—is closer to the truth, it appears that we will be seeing Bracy's early departure from post," Mecke said. "If proceedings under UCMJ [Uniform Code of Military Justice] are in order, we would prefer that they be done elsewhere."[7]

Bracy would later confess to the Naval Investigative Service to having sex with Golotina as early as January 1986, a month before the embassy fired her, and to helping Lonetree let the KGB into secure areas of the embassy, including the CPU.[8] Subsequently, Bracy retracted his statements, saying he had fabricated them because of pressure from the NIS. Lonetree later passed lie-detector tests showing he did not let the KGB into the embassy nor conspire with Bracy.

Putting that aside, there are enough conflicts between Bracy's story and the accounts of other witnesses to make it clear he has not told the truth about his relationship with the Soviet cook and the KGB. His own accounts of what happened vary so fundamentally from telling to telling that it appears even he cannot keep his cover story straight. These conflicts raise serious questions about what Bracy did do with the KGB.

My first interview with Bracy was in the coffee shop of the Quality Inn at the Quantico Marine base outside of Washington in November 1987. After giving an interview four months-earlier to *The New York Times,* Bracy had stopped talking to the press.⁹ At Stufflebeam's urging, Bracy agreed to talk to me.

It was a cold, rainy Sunday morning. The McDonald's and Burger King outside the base were doing a land-office business, but the coffee shop was virtually deserted. Bracy arrived promptly at 8:00 A.M. He ordered a Coke, and I drank coffee. He was a picture-book Marine—clean-cut, squared away, well-spoken, energetic and enthusiastic. Yet I got the feeling he was acting—that he knew how to create the right impression without revealing his true feelings.

By the time I interviewed him, I had seen enough evidence of improper NIS tactics to be wary of anything the NIS said. For that reason, I decided early on that nothing in this book would rely exclusively on an NIS statement. I would have to verify everything independently. I therefore came to the coffee shop fully prepared to believe Bracy's story that the NIS had coerced him into confessing.

As he talked, I became absorbed not in what he was saying but in the way he was saying it. With his right hand, he kept fiddling with the earpiece to his glasses as if he were swatting a mosquito. He seemed closed, contained. But what bothered me most was the fact that he never looked me in the eye. Indeed, he strenuously avoided it.

Beyond the physical manifestations of deception, listening to Bracy's story was like trying to grab hold of a bubble in a bath—as soon as I grabbed at one fact, it burst or slipped into the mass of other bubbles.

Bracy related to me how he had run into Golotina in the park that spring day in 1986. A week later, he saw her at the embassy. Although she had been fired, she still delivered the Duchateaus' four-year-old daughter to nursery school inside the embassy. Golotina told Bracy the KGB was pressuring her family. He cut Golotina short and said he would talk to her later.

Several weeks went by, and he saw her again.

"She said she wanted to meet me some place because they were pressuring her," he said.[10]

It would have been a simple matter to tell her to get lost. But Bracy said he was offended that the KGB could think he was such a pushover. In Bracy's view, Mecke had done nothing about his earlier report to him. Bracy decided to tell Golotina in person to leave him alone.

That Sunday at 9:00 A.M. he took a bus to the Duchateaus' apartment at 83 Lininsky Prospect, an apartment house reserved for diplomats.

Bracy did not say how he knew that Golotina would be there or how he thought he would explain his presence to the Duchateaus. Golotina only worked for the Duchateaus during the day; at night she lived at home. The Duchateaus knew that fraternizing with Soviets was prohibited. It did not make sense that Bracy would simply show up. But he said he had chosen to go there on Sunday because it was his first day off.

Like most Soviet apartments, the Duchateaus' residence was cramped. To the right as one walked in was a small living room. To the left was a small bedroom for the Duchateaus, another small bedroom for their daughter, and a kitchen. Because space was at a premium, the Duchateaus stored their vacuum cleaner in their bedroom.[11]

Bracy said he spent about thirty minutes with Golotina as she cleaned the living room of the apartment.

"She said she wanted me to meet her uncle and talk about politics or nuclear arm talks," he said. He told her to leave him alone. "You can tell your people to pick on some other Marine because I already reported it," he said he told her. Bracy said she looked shocked.[12]

Why did it take a half hour to tell her to leave him alone? I asked him.

"She hardly talked English, and it was hard to keep up with her anyway [as she was cleaning the apartment]," he said.

While they were talking, Wright and his wife walked in. He said he shook hands with the newsman and told him who he was and where he worked.

"I said if you have any questions, you can talk to Mecke," he said. "I figured he was a reporter and nosy. Everyone knows there was a nonfraternization policy." He said he did not report the contact because he knew he was not supposed to have gone to the apartment.

After hearing Bracy's story, I felt that I had just eaten a meal and was still hungry. It simply didn't hang together. Now I went to Duchateau, who had just returned to the U.S. from Moscow. Duchateau said that Wright had reported seeing Bracy and Golotina together in the bedroom, not the living room. Moreover, he said Wright heard "sexual noises" coming from the bedroom.

I later asked Bracy about that. Noting that the bed was "not put together," he said he was not in the bedroom.

Putting aside the question of how he knew the bed was not "put together," I told Duchateau what Bracy had said.

"The bed was put together. It definitely had a bed in it when I let it [to the Wrights] and when I came back, and of course Steve Wright stayed in it," he said.

I recalled Bracy's averted eyes. It was clear that more investigation would be required. Obviously, besides Golotina and Bracy, the key witness in this mystery was Wright. But interviewing him was easier said than done. Since the incident had occurred, he had steadfastly refused to talk to the press, embassy officials, or the NIS. He no longer worked for the television network. Apparently he feared that the Soviets would deny him a visa if he became embroiled in a controversy over Golotina.[13]

"I don't wish to make any comments, give any information, talk about it," he told me by phone from his home outside of London. "I gave what information I felt necessary at the time. I don't want to be involved in this kind of thing."[14]

But Wright had made an exception early on for his then-employer. In that interview, arranged by Helen Westwood, then ABC-TV's London bureau chief, Wright directly contradicted what Bracy told Mecke and me. Asked if he could describe the incident in the Duchateaus' apartment, he said, "Yes, I was going to 'flat-sit' the apartment [a British term for staying in an apartment while the occupant is away] for an American diplomat who had gone away for a month's holiday."

Arriving on a Sunday afternoon, Wright said he opened the

door and found a magazine stuffed under it to keep the door from opening. "As I entered the flat, I heard the sound of a vacuum cleaner starting up in the bedroom. Very quickly a young lady came out of the bedroom pushing the vacuum cleaner and looking very flustered and making a faint attempt to be cleaning the flat up," he said.[15]

"A couple of minutes later, a tall black man dressed in a baseball T-shirt and . . . boots came out of the bedroom and introduced himself as an American Marine who worked at the American embassy," Wright said. "He said that he was there to check the flat, and after a very brief conversation, he made his departure."

"What made you think that there was something going on?" the TV interviewer asked.

"Well," Wright said, "when I looked at the VCR machine that was in the corner of the lounge, there was still a cassette in the machine as though the machine had been in use that afternoon, and that the flat had been occupied for several hours. The fact that they both came out of the bedroom together suggested that they'd probably been having some sexual relations—obviously more than cleaning the flat and checking the flat, and that they'd been there for quite some time."

While Wright said he did not learn the Marine's name, he found out later the embassy shipped the man back to the U.S. after Duchateau reported the incident.

I asked Westwood if Wright had said anything else during her discussions with him. Yes, she said. Wright had told her he heard "sexual noises" coming from the bedroom.[16]

I went back to Bracy and asked him about this latest information. I began by going over what he had already told me.

"You were in the living room with Galya [Golotina], right?" I asked.

"That's right," Bracy said.[17]

"And the bed was taken down? What does that mean? That it wasn't put together?" I said.

"Yeah," Bracy said, "the bed wasn't put together."

I told him that Duchateau had said the bed was put together.

"When I say it wasn't put together, I mean it was not made

up," he said. "I'm not saying the bed was in pieces or anything." Rather, he said, the sheets and blankets were "folded on the bed."

Now Bracy had undermined his own story. First he said the bed was not put together to show that he could not have been in bed with Golotina. Now sheets and blankets were folded on it, which would not prevent him from having sex on it.

I was also interested in the conflicts over how long Bracy was in the apartment. In the ABC-TV interview, Wright said that he arrived at the apartment in the afternoon. Bracy told me he took a 9:00 A.M. bus, which should have gotten him to the apartment by 9:30 A.M. That suggests he was with Golotina most of the day. Yet he told me he was only with Golotina half an hour. Which version was correct?

I asked Bracy. He offered no explanation. Instead, he tried to explain why Wright had said Bracy was in the bedroom. He said that when he got there, Golotina was watching videotapes in the living room, and he followed her around.

"They [the tapes] were on and we were talking and walking around the house," he said.[18]

Now Golotina was watching videotapes. Before, she was cleaning the house.

When I told Bracy that Wright said a magazine was stuffed under the door to prevent it from being opened, he said, "I don't know why people say things like that. I'm glad people like yourself are writing a book, and maybe it will come out."

By now, I was used to Bracy's circumlocutions. Rather than answering a question directly, he would offer some irrelevant comment with a note of wonder in his voice, then change the subject.

I was still curious about why Bracy happened to show up on a Sunday, so I asked Duchateau about the timing of his trip to Scandinavia. He said he had left early Sunday morning. His wife told Golotina there would be no need for her to come in. She had not said anyone would be house-sitting.

That would suggest that Golotina had told Bracy to come to the apartment on Sunday. Bracy had claimed he happened to show up on Sunday because that was his first day off.

The fact that Golotina was not supposed to be there also

undercut Bracy's claim that he followed her around while she cleaned the house. It would take a very conscientious employee indeed to come in early on Sunday morning to clean house when she was not supposed to be there in the first place.

But those were only the first of the inconsistencies.

As one might expect, Golotina had never been interviewed about the incident, at least not by anyone from the West. Before leaving for Moscow in January 1988, I got her old telephone number from Duchateau. To my surprise, when I dialed the number from my hotel in Moscow one Friday night, she answered the phone.

Contrary to what Bracy had said, I found Golotina's English passable. Occasionally, I moved the conversation along with a few words learned in high school Russian courses. When she had trouble understanding me, she asked me to slow down. She was personable and not at all flustered by the unexpected call.

Golotina said she had read an American magazine article suggesting that she had had sex with Bracy.

"What they said in the magazine was not true," she said. "[There was] no sex. We were only good friends."[19]

She also denied they were in the bedroom together. Instead, she said, they were watching video films.

This was a new twist. Bracy had said he went to the apartment to tell her off and had stayed a half hour. Now Golotina said they were watching films. I asked her how often Bracy came over.

"He was there from time to time. He thought he would show me some films," she said.

When I asked her which films he brought, she said they were horror films. Trying to obtain colorful details, I pressed her on which film they watched that day. It was the wrong question. Her tone of voice changed. I pictured her wondering if I was a KGB officer trying to find out if she had been watching censored Western movies. She said she had to go, and I should call back on Monday.

When I called back, she was not home. After that, she was never home. The older woman who answered always said she was out. She showed no inclination to take a message.

But Golotina had said enough. There was reason for her to lie about having sex with an American Marine. There was no need for her to make up a story about Bracy coming to the apartment on occasion to watch films.

When I got back to the U.S., I told Bracy what she had said.

"Huh? Hmm. I hope she's doing okay," he said.[20]

I asked him which films he brought her. He sidestepped the question.

"She was into horror flicks but the Duchateaus had their own selection," he said. That was one thing Golotina liked about being a nanny, he said. "I didn't take any [films] over to the Duchateaus' house because they had their own videos."

Bracy simply could not keep his story straight. He had told Mecke and me he went to the apartment once to tell her to leave him alone. Now he knew there was no need to bring films because the Duchateaus had their own collection.

I asked him how many times he had been to the apartment.

"There was no reason to go over there or anything," he said.

Then why would she say he had?

"It could be they're trying to make it seem she was chasing me around," he said. "Our country threw her in a bad light. Maybe they're trying to change it around."

Quite the contrary, the Soviets have tried to minimize reports of spying, claiming they are part of a U.S. plot. They would have no reason to create more suspicion about the Marines' activities.

As if theorizing about his own actions, Bracy said, "I can't see myself just popping over there to watch movies."

Eventually, I interviewed Golnar Duchateau, Duchateau's wife. As the financial administrator of the ABC-TV bureau in Moscow, she knew Wright and had offered their apartment to him. She was the only one who had heard his story directly after it occurred.

Her recall was quite good, and her story made a lot more sense than Bracy's. Now it all seemed to come together.

After she got back from vacation, she said, she called Wright to see if there had been any problems.[21]

"No," he said. "However, there is something that happened. I'll tell you at work."

When she got to the ABC offices the next day, Wright wanted to know if Golotina knew that someone would be house-sitting. No, she had said. Golotina only knew she did not have to come in.

"That's what I thought," Wright said.

Then Wright told her how he and his wife had showed up that afternoon, opened the door to the apartment, and realized two people were in the bedroom. From the noises and other circumstances, it was clear to him that the people in the bedroom were having sex.[22] Hearing someone in the apartment, the people in the bedroom slammed the bedroom door shut.

Wright and his wife looked at each other. They could have sworn that Golnar Duchateau had not said anything about someone else being in the apartment.

A few minutes later, Wright heard the vacuum cleaner start up in the bedroom. Then the bedroom door opened, and a man emerged, still buttoning his clothes. Although he was black, Wright said his face was red from embarrassment. He identified himself as an American Marine checking the apartment. Finally Golotina emerged, wielding the vacuum cleaner. She said she was cleaning up the apartment.

"Steve asked if this was a common practice [for Marines to check apartments] when people from the embassy leave. I said no," Golnar Duchateau said.

After Wright related his story to her, Golnar Duchateau recalled that after they returned from vacation, Golotina had looked sheepish and withdrawn when she showed up for work. Golnar Duchateau noticed that her eyes darted immediately to a videotape lying on the windowsill.

Wright later told Golnar Duchateau that the Marine's identity might be traced through the videotape he left behind. He said a Marine's name was on the tape.[23]

Golnar Duchateau went to find the tape she had seen on the windowsill. It was gone. Her daughter said the nanny took it.

By now Wingate had been replaced as detachment commander by Master Gunnery Sergeant John G. Bradley, who won two Purple Hearts during the Vietnam War.[24]

Based on what Duchateau and Bracy told him, Mecke told Bradley he wanted Bracy out of the country on the next available plane. Bradley called Bracy into the secure "bubble" on the ninth floor of the embassy. Bracy saluted, and Bradley warned him of his rights.[25]

"You are suspected of violating Article Ninety-two of the Uniform Code of Military Justice: failing to obey a lawful general order," Bradley said.

Bracy readily admitted to seeing Golotina and not reporting it.

"I'm relieving you from post. I'm sending you back to MSG Battalion for disobeying a direct order," Bradley said.[26]

On orders from Mecke, Duchateau fired Golotina.

That night Corporal Robert J. Williams went to see Bracy in his room at the Marine House. Accounts differ on what was said. Williams later told the NIS that Bracy told him he had fallen in love with Golotina and had given the Soviets classified documents in exchange for thousands of dollars.[27] Like Bracy, Williams subsequently recanted, saying the NIS coerced him. Bracy also denies making the comments.

Yet others have said Williams told them essentially the same thing. His former girlfriend, Taina A. Laurivuori, told me in Moscow that she accompanied Bracy and Williams to the airport four days after Duchateau reported the incident in his apartment. A Finnish citizen, she was a nanny to Chase Dustin, an embassy employee.

Bracy looked sad, and Laurivuori asked Williams what was wrong with him. He said a Soviet girl had set him up.[28]

After Bracy confessed and was arrested, Williams called Laurivuori from Vienna, where he was then based. Williams asked if she remembered the day they took Bracy to the airport.

"Yes," she said.

"Don't tell anybody, but the day before we went to the airport, Arnold told me that he was doing that spy stuff," he said.[29]

"Don't tell me that bullshit," Williams said he told Bracy.

She said Williams called her again and told her not to tell anyone what he had said if she were interviewed.

I had already interviewed Williams, and I later asked him about this new information. He is a six-foot four-inch black Marine from the South Bronx. Initially, he thought the Marines didn't take blacks because he never saw a black Marine on a recruiting poster. When he saw his first black Marine on the street, he signed up.

Unlike Bracy, Williams felt the Marines were prejudiced against blacks. When he was at Camp Lejeune, several white Marines called him "nigger" and beat him up.

Williams told me that his former girlfriend had misunderstood him. He attributed this to her poor English. He said he told her that the NIS had told him Bracy had been spying.[30]

I felt her English was sufficient. She had said flatly that Williams had said Bracy told him he was into spying.

Williams suggested she might have made up the story because they did not part on the best of terms. Yet Williams continued to call her after he left Moscow. Moreover, his own love letters to her contradict his assertion.

"Right now I want to talk to you so bad!" he wrote to her on May 21, 1987. "I love you a lot," he said. In another letter, he wrote, "I've been thinking how we can meet. Maybe we can plan a serious trip. I don't care how much it costs."[31]

Besides Laurivuori, Lance Corporal Philip J. Sink, a Marine security guard stationed in Vienna, said Williams told him that Bracy had confessed to him. Sink asked Williams about the NIS investigation of Bracy on April 4, 1987, in Williams's room in the embassy in Vienna.

"Bracy came to me one night and was crying and telling me he was in over his head," Sink quoted Williams as saying. "He had done things he shouldn't have, and that he didn't know what to do." Williams said something about a $1,000 payment.[32]

That weekend, as Williams drove Sink and his girlfriend to the embassy, Williams muttered about "Bracy and greed."

"I immediately cut him off, because I did not want my

girlfriend to hear this and get involved. Williams picked up on it and dropped the subject," Sink said.

According to Sink, Williams later said to him, "Why don't you just forget about that stuff I said."[33]

I asked Bracy how everyone could be lying—Golotina, who said Bracy occasionally brought films to the apartment; Wright, who said he found him having sex with Golotina, a magazine stuffed in the door; Golnar Duchateau, who said a Marine's videotape had been left behind; Laurivuori, who said Williams told her that Bracy said he had engaged in spying; Duchateau, who said the bed was put together; and Sink, who said Williams told him that Bracy said he had gotten in over his head and had done things he shouldn't have done.

Bracy seemed uninterested. Perhaps, he suggested, the NIS had somehow interjected facts that colored what people had said. But I had verified each statement independently with the people involved.

"I don't lose no sleep over it," Bracy told me.

Looking at all the facts, the most likely scenario is that Bracy began having sex with Golotina in January 1986, a month before the embassy fired her, as Bracy told the NIS. According to his statement—which he later retracted—Lieutenant Colonel Stephen A. Bauer, an Air Force attaché, asked him to house-sit for him one weekend in January. He had intercourse with Golotina in Bauer's apartment that Saturday.[34] She then told him she wanted him to meet her "Uncle Sasha."

His report of a contact with her in the park would then be a ruse to allay suspicions. An embassy official may have seen them in the park together.

Ultimately, it was Bracy's lack of concern that was most disturbing to me. Could it have been because he knew he was innocent and did not care what was said about him? Or could it have been because he was guilty of something much more serious than lying about his relationship with Golotina? If indeed he had let the KGB into the CPU, as stated in his confession, whether or not he had sex with Golotina would be the least of his worries.

Based on more facts, I would later conclude that he was guilty of something much more serious than having sex with a Soviet.

On September 9, 1986, Bracy stood on an old Beijing carpet in front of Colonel C. Sean Del Grosso's desk in Marshall Hall and poured out his tale. As commander of the Marine Security Guard Battalion, it was Del Grosso's job to decide how to adjudicate the allegations against Bracy. He could either hold nonjudicial punishment or recommend to the base commander that he be court-martialed. He decided to hold nonjudicial punishment, or "office hours." It then became Del Grosso's job to decide if Bracy had violated orders, and if so, what punishment to mete out.

Del Grosso was an old-line Marine who talked like Colombo. He punctuated his sentences with jokes about proctologists. To weighty questions, he would reply, "That's above my grade."

With blotchy skin, a big nose, and an easygoing manner, Del Grosso had a way of jerking his head sharply up and down like a bull, signaling that he would not brook any compromise with his orders.

Of all the rules, the one that Del Grosso felt most strongly about was the one barring women from Marine's rooms. The thought of a mother seeing her son with a woman in his room in the Marine House made him apoplectic.

"There are no second chances," he would tell the Marines at security guard school. "I don't fine you and slap your hand. The golden rule here is women in the Marine House, you're coming home."[35]

In his twenty-five years in the Marines, Del Grosso had held "office hours" for hundreds of Marines. He thought he had seen it all and could judge whether a Marine was lying to him. Bracy failed the test. After hearing him out, Del Grosso decided Bracy was giving him a sea story.[36]

Del Grosso fined Bracy and demoted him from sergeant to corporal. He sent him to the Air Ground Combat Center at Twentynine Palms, California.[37]

Del Grosso told me he asked Marine headquarters to request an NIS investigation of Bracy. There is no record of such a request, and the NIS never got it.

Del Grosso had not seen Mecke's cables concerning Bracy. If he had, he might have taken stronger action. In particular, Mecke's cable of August 25, 1986, called for follow-up:

Bracy, who until the incident [involving contacts with Golotina] was generally regarded as one of the best and most popular Marines in the detachment, has told a story of his involvement with the former cook that bears a closer examination.[38]

We believe that there is more to the relationship either on the emotional side or intelligence side or both that because of feelings he has for the girl, embarrassment, or whatever, he is not divulging. Bracy should be further interviewed on the subject preferably in Washington in order to obtain an accurate picture of what actually transpired.

But the State Department had done nothing with the cables, and had not referred them to the NIS, the FBI, or the Marine Corps. The department was as concerned about Mecke's request that someone look into the circumstances surrounding Bracy's removal as it was about his request for new alarms for the CPU.

The State Department had a second chance to find out what happened at Moscow station. On September 4, 1986, the department's counterintelligence unit debriefed Bracy, a standard procedure for all Marines leaving the guard program.

This time, Bracy added a few new twists to his story. He said he agreed to Golotina's request to meet with her in the Duchateaus' apartment, a decision he attributed to his own "poor judgment."[39] He said he stayed with her an hour. During their talk, she said the KGB wanted her to introduce him to a man she was to identify as her uncle.

"At this point, Bracy followed her into the apartment bedroom while she went to get a highchair, and he told her that all of this had been reported to the RSO [regional security officer]," according to the memo on the debriefing.

Bracy had apparently forgotten that when he and Golotina emerged from the Duchateaus' bedroom, she came out holding a vacuum cleaner, not a highchair. Nor did he explain why she was getting a highchair when she was not supposed to be in the apartment in the first place.[40]

In contrast to what he told the State Department, Bracy later said at a press conference that Golotina did not know he was coming to the Duchateaus' apartment. He "just showed up there."[41]

Never mind the inconsistencies. As it had previously done with Mecke's cables, the counterintelligence unit filed the memo of the debriefing away.

James W. Lannon, who headed the unit, seemed mainly interested in lecturing security officers on how to handle security infractions without offending diplomats. Poor morale could lead to espionage, he would say. Beyond that, Lannon was coping with a staff of just five people. He had repeatedly requested more help.[42]

Looking back, Lamb, the assistant secretary of state for security, said the memos should have been turned over to the NIS or FBI immediately. He called his own staff's debriefing of Bracy "totally unsatisfactory, a sloppy investigative effort, and sloppy interrogation."[43]

For seven months, the memo of the debriefing and the cables from Mecke lay undisturbed in the State Department's vaults. Not until the NIS got a tip and finally interviewed Bracy did the State Department hand over the documents to the NIS.[44]

If the State Department had set out purposely to cover up what had happened, it could not have done a better job.

# CHAPTER 16

# Happy Birthday

Violetta seina let only a week go by after Lonetree left Moscow before writing to him in Vienna. After all, the KGB was as interested in what happened in the embassy there as it was in what happened in the embassy in Moscow.

"The whole week has passed since I saw you last," she wrote on March 17, 1986. "I couldn't bring myself to write you a letter. I tried several times but I could not. It appears to be very difficult to write on paper what I am thinking of."[1]

"You may be already in Vienna," she said. "You are full of new impressions. You see new places, new people. It must be interesting. I hope you are going to like it. And I am here. Alone."

Seina said she always thought of Lonetree.

"I can't get rid of the memories, and I don't want to," she pouted.

One could almost picture Yefimov dictating the letter to her as she prepared for her next "honey pot" or "honey trap"— intelligence lingo for a sexual entrapment.

Two weeks later, Lonetree called Seina at the Irish embassy, where she now worked.

"Darling! It was so good of you to call," she wrote to him later.[2] "After I talked to you I could do absolutely nothing. I was just sitting like a fool at my table (or like a stupid broad as you would call me) and could neither write nor read."

On April 12, she wrote that she had gone to bed but could not fall asleep.[3]

175

"You know, Clay, I'm just scared to death of losing you. I just don't know how I am going to live without you. Only a sense of hope that I will see you again keeps me going since you have been away. Please don't give me up. Okay?"

Then, in an ironic twist, she wrote:

"I love you, darling. I love you so much that you'll never forget me."

Lonetree alluded to Seina in a letter to his father and brother on May 4. In contrast to Seina's almost perfect English, his was full of grammatical errors, misspellings, and run-on sentences.

Lonetree called his duty in the Soviet Union "quite an intersting [sic] experience, the cultural life was insatiable, politically you began to see why they tick, as they do. While I was there I met so many interesting people. I do have intensions [sic] of returning should an opportunity come my way again.

"As of now," he said, "life here in the West is not to [sic] bad, but I guess I take it for granted and I'm sure it will always be here. One thing I'm certain of is that Americans are sure arrogant they don't relize [sic] that we [Indians] can be admired and respected, but we're to [sic] proud."

Then he mentioned that he had a new girlfriend, whom he "respects a lot."

". . . she's one year older than I and an interpreter (English/Russian)," he wrote.

He mentioned no other details about Seina.

Meanwhile, Seina was keeping the pressure on Lonetree. She reminded him that Yefimov would be seeing him soon.

"I want so much to be in Vienna, next to you," she wrote on May 10, "and share all your troubles so that you don't feel alone there. And I'm very glad that Uncle Sasha will come to Vienna. He likes you very much, and we spend a lot of time talking about you. He is eager to see you and give you my letter. I envy him because he will see you."[4]

By now, Lonetree's fantasies about somehow exposing Yefimov had vaporized  He was fearful that the KGB would do him in, and he decided he would see Yefimov after all.[5] Ever incompetent, he had memorized the dates of their next meetings, thrown away the slip of paper that listed them, then forgotten the dates.

Yefimov always gave Lonetree several alternate dates in case he could not make the first one. When Lonetree missed all the dates, Yefimov called him at the embassy. Without identifying himself, Yefimov began talking when Lonetree answered. Lonetree eventually recognized him and agreed to meet him at the Staatsoper, the Vienna opera house that was first built in the middle of the nineteenth century, then reconstructed after a fire.[6]

After switching duty with another Marine, Lonetree took a tram to the opera house. As the city where Beethoven and Mozart lived, and where Brahms, Schumann, and Schubert played, Vienna is defined by its music. No institution is more important to the Viennese than the opera house where Yefimov told Lonetree to meet him.

They met at the main entrance and walked along Vienna's spotless streets, past the Sacher, the hotel where the Sacher torte was created, and the Opern-Passage, a large subterranean tunnel that leads to a vast subway station. Yefimov said that Seina sent her regards. Since he had just gotten into town, Yefimov said, he didn't have much time. He gave Lonetree a slip of paper with another meeting date.

Thus began a slow dance that would draw Lonetree deeper into Yefimov's web. Lonetree would stall, trying to give up as little as possible, but each step drew him closer to the spider. Eventually, Lonetree would be eaten alive, but for now he thought he could outsmart the KGB officer.

Lonetree decided that at the next meeting, he would confront Yefimov about being in the KGB—a move as pointless as giving his high school teacher a notebook inscribed with Nazi epithets. After having lunch at the Wienerwald Restaurant, part of an Austrian chain, Lonetree and Yefimov sat by a pond. Lonetree peered into Yefimov's face and asked if he were in the KGB. Yefimov drew closer to Lonetree, and Lonetree wondered what he would do. Predictably, Yefimov denied he was in the KGB.

Their next meeting was near the Fisherhaus Restaurant in the Wienerwald, the Vienna Woods that begin on the outskirts of Vienna and extend to the Alps. Yefimov showed Lonetree a list of people assigned to the embassy. He asked what each of them did.

He also wanted to know the size of the Marine detachment and how many of the Marines were in counterintelligence.

Reaching into his pocket, he pulled out a newspaper clipping reporting the expulsion for spying of Michael C. Sellers.

"See what the CIA does?" Yefimov said.

This was the first time Lonetree had heard that Sellers had been expelled from Moscow. He blamed himself for having given him up.[7]

As he pondered what he had done, Lonetree decided he would turn the tables on Yefimov and entrap him. He would pay a local bar girl $100 to seduce him.[8] It was a silly idea, and like everything else Lonetree tried, it failed. After discussing the plan with the girl, Lonetree asked her to meet him at a café. She never showed up. As agreed with Yefimov, Lonetree went on to meet him that day at the twelfth-century Romanesque abbey in Klosterneuberg, an old market town along the Danube just outside of Vienna.

Lonetree brought with him photo ID cards he had stolen from post number one. He also gave Yefimov letters and photos of himself for Seina.

Yefimov looked at the ID cards as if he had found a gold mine.

"You are a true friend of the Soviet Union," he said.

The KGB officer gave Lonetree $1,000 in Austrian schillings. Lonetree declined the money, but Yefimov insisted. He said the money would cover the cost of taxis and trams. Lonetree hid the money under a blue sweater in his room at the Marine House. He spent it on dinners and beer for friends, a dress for Seina, and a silk tie for Yefimov.

Even though Yefimov was blackmailing him, Lonetree was so starved for affection that he thought anyone who talked with him for more than five minutes was a friend.


Back in Washington, pressure from Congress and the intelligence community was finally starting to have an impact on the issue of employing Soviets at the embassy. Like most moves affecting U.S.-Soviet relations, there were plots and subplots leading to the final denouement.

Incensed that the Soviets had shot down a Korean commercial airliner on September 1, 1983, Senator Walter D. Huddleston, a Democrat from Kentucky, began considering legislation that would shut down the Soviet consulate in San Francisco. Huddleston had long been concerned that the high elevation of the consulate enabled the Soviets to eavesdrop on a wide range of microwave communications in the U.S. The Soviet action gave him an excuse to press the issue.[9]

After consulting with the FBI, Huddleston realized the obvious: that the Soviets would only respond by shutting down the American consulate in Leningrad, impairing intelligence collection there. The FBI suggested an alternative. Since 1979, then–FBI director William H. Webster had been telling anyone who would listen that one of the most effective ways to prevent espionage in the U.S. was to reduce the number of Soviet diplomats in the country. Since roughly a third of them were KGB or GRU officers, it made sense to reduce their numbers rather than increase the number of FBI agents assigned to track them. The FBI suggested to Huddleston that he introduce legislation requiring that the number of Soviets assigned to the U.S. equal the number of Americans assigned to the U.S.S.R.

Difficult as it is to believe, the State Department had long ago allowed the number of Soviets in the U.S. to exceed the number of Americans in the Soviet Union. By the State Department's reasoning, the U.S. was ahead of the game because it employed a total of 240 Soviet nationals at the embassy in Moscow and the consulate in Leningrad. Since the Soviets had no Americans working for them in the U.S., the State Department figured its missions in the Soviet Union were larger than the Soviet missions in the U.S. Thus the State Department allowed the number of Soviets in the U.S. to exceed the number of Americans in the U.S.S.R. by 105.

The reality was that because of this policy, the Soviets had more spies in the U.S. than the Americans had spies in Russia. Moreover, the Soviets had another 240 spies working side by side with the Americans in their own embassy and consulate.

Later that year, Huddleston introduced the legislation the FBI had suggested as an expression of the will of Congress.

Predictably, the State Department opposed it. The State Department felt that if the number of Americans and Soviets in each country were equalized, the Americans would have to get rid of their Soviet employees. Ever concerned about their own creature comforts, the diplomats wanted to avoid that at all costs. Even if Congress was willing to foot the bill, the State Department preferred to retain the Soviet employees rather than have more Americans assigned to Moscow and Leningrad.[10]

"They gave us the excuse it was a hardship post, and it was difficult to get Americans to go there [to Moscow]," Huddleston said. "We were never able to understand why State was not as concerned as some of us were about the espionage aspects."

While the legislation did not pass in final form, it laid the groundwork. The next year, Senator Patrick J. Leahy, the Vermont Democrat, joined the effort. In 1985 the legislation passed in the form of a mandate that only the President could waive.

Emboldened by that success, Leahy and Senator William S. Cohen, a Maine Republican, proposed legislation in 1986 that would bring the number of Soviets assigned to the United Nations mission in New York more into line with the number of Americans assigned to the U.S. mission there. The measure still allowed more Soviets than Americans at the U.N. because they were on foreign soil.

Driven by these twin initiatives, the State Department began reassessing its position. Because it was seen as nonideologically inspired, the measure to reduce the number of Soviets in the U.N. gained broad support in Congress. Webster, who supported it, was not a reactionary anti-Soviet, and a mix of Democrats and Republicans were for it.

The reductions were to take place in October. At the end of August a new element entered the equation. After the FBI arrested Soviet U.N. employee Gennadi Zakharov for spying, the Soviets arrested Nicholas S. Daniloff, the *U.S. News & World Report* journalist.

With tensions between the two countries mounting daily, the Soviets said they would not comply with the ordered reductions in U.N. employees. That played into President Reagan's hands, and he then named the U.N. officials who had to leave—primarily key KGB and GRU officers.

The old American em-
bassy in Moscow.

The new American embassy, Moscow.

The American
consulate, Leningrad.

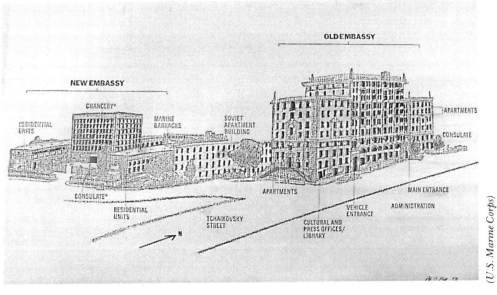

The old Moscow embassy and the new one filled with electronic bugs.

Marine post number three guarding access to the Communications Programs Unit, or CPU, as it appeared when Soviet firefighters entered the embassy in August 1977.

Sergeant Clayton J. Lonetree.

Corporal Arnold Bracy.

Secretary of State George P. Shultz in front of Uncle Sam's, a disco in the embassy courtyard. The photograph was taken during his visit to Moscow in 1985 following the death of Soviet leader Yuri V. Andropov. To the right are Vice President George Bush, Master Gunnery Sergeant Joey E. Wingate, and Ambassador Arthur A. Hartman.

Staff Sergeant Robert S. Stufflebeam (*foreground*) at the 1985 Marine Corps ball at Spaso House. The blonde to his right is Nina Sheriakovo, the Soviet cook. To her right is Galina N. (Galya) Golotina, the former embassy cook who was with Arnold Bracy in the Duchateaus's apartment.

Ambassador Hartman (*center*) with his wife, Donna, at the 1985 ball. Just over Hartman's right shoulder is Sergeant Lonetree. To Mrs. Hartman's immediate right are Master Gunnery Sergeant Wingate and his wife, Effie. In the rear row at the left is Corporal Bracy.

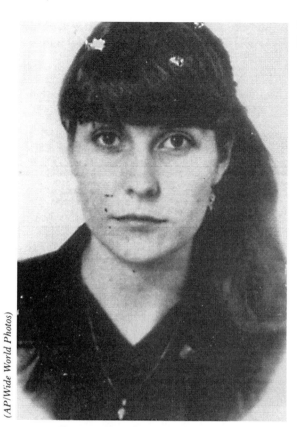

Violetta A. Seina, as she appeared in an embassy I.D. photo.

Ambassador Hartman at the 1985 ball.

Corporal Bracy dancing with an unidentified woman at the ball.

Staff Sergeant Stufflebeam at the ball.

"HALT! WHO GOES THERE? NATASHA? SVETLANA? VIOLETTA?..."

One of the hundreds of cartoons spawned by the Marine Corps scandal.

Lanny E. McCullah, who headed the Naval Investigative Service investigation of the Moscow security breaches.

William M. Kunstler (*right*) and Michael V. Stuhff (*second from the right*) praying with Clayton Lonetree's relatives and supporters during his court martial in 1987.

The author outside KGB headquarters, Dzerzhinsky Square, Moscow.

In October the U.S. began expelling U.N. and non-U.N. Soviets alike, and the Soviets responded in kind. As the expulsions reached their zenith, the Soviets withdrew all their remaining employees from the embassy in Moscow and the consulate in Leningrad.

Hartman and others in the State Department would later cite the withdrawal as proof that the Soviet workers were not so important to the KGB after all. But the Soviets knew that the days when they could roam the embassy were numbered. Because of the congressional pressure, the State Department had begun advertising for contractors who could supply American workers to the missions. Moreover, the embassy by now had confined the Soviets to the shacks in the courtyard, where they were far less effective at passing along information to the KGB.

When the fireworks subsided, the score was tied. Before the expulsions, the U.S. had 191 Americans in Moscow and 24 in Leningrad. The U.S.S.R. had 279 Soviets in Washington and 41 in San Francisco.

In addition, the Americans employed 240 Soviets at their missions in Moscow and Leningrad.

After the expulsions, the numbers were even—225 Americans in Moscow and 225 Soviets in Washington. Leningrad had 26 Americans, and San Francisco had 26 Soviets.[11]

The sudden withdrawal of Soviet workers placed a strain on the embassy, underscoring how much leverage the Soviets had had when they supplied the workers. In the background, there had always been the implied threat that the Soviets might retaliate for some action they didn't like by withdrawing their employees.

The result of the withdrawal was that with the exception of Hartman and Combs, everyone in the embassy from secretaries to CIA officers performed manual labor at least two days a month. Known as APD, or All-Purpose Duty, the work included shoveling snow, cleaning the public areas, and driving to the airport to pick up shipments. One day the APD squad unloaded 80,000 pounds of supplies.

Faced with a visible threat, the Americans put aside their differences and acted like the pioneers who founded the country. Even Benson and Verner, the two diplomats who complained about the new security rules, pitched in.[12]

But Hartman demonstrated his priorities when he made the first request for twenty-six Americans to replace the Soviets. Along with desperately needed plumbers and electricians, he requisitioned a driver for his Mercedes.[13]

In Vienna, Lonetree's relationship with the KGB was about to come to an abrupt end, but not before he would do significant damage to the CIA station there.

All along, Lonetree's interest in Seina had been more emotional than sexual. She gave him the love he had craved as a child, and that was more important to him than the four sexual encounters they had had. Now that he could no longer see her, the love relationship played nicely into the KGB's hands. It meant he was tied to her even though he might never see her again.

On October 27, 1986, Lonetree wrote to her to wish her a happy birthday.

"Your [sic] my priority nowe [sic] and I get sad at times when I think of you, but my love for you is genuine. But I smiole [sic] to [sic] and I know you love me. I'm certain of that. I feel the positive vibes in the air," he said.[14]

Lonetree had told Yefimov that if he missed a meeting, he should call him at the embassy and say he was Mr. Laurel from Finland. Yefimov had been impressed that Lonetree would think of this. When Lonetree missed a meeting in October, Yefimov did just that. They set up a meeting for 7:00 P.M. on November 15, 1986, at an obscure church in Vienna's sixteenth district.

Yefimov gave Lonetree pictures of Seina and conveyed her greetings.[15] He wanted to know everything about a particular political officer at the embassy and the ambassador's secretary. He seemed to be hinting that Lonetree should ask her out. He also wanted Lonetree to bring the embassy phone book next time.

Still making pitiful attempts to stall, Lonetree showed up at 7:00 P.M. on November 27 at another church. He said he forgot to bring the phone book. Yefimov was upset, and Lonetree used the occasion to ask Yefimov if he would blackmail him if he did not cooperate.

"I am your friend, and I want to continue our friendship," Yefimov said.

Lonetree could tell from the false note in his voice that he had better do as Yefimov said.[16]

In one of their earlier meetings, Lonetree had mentioned that he would like to visit the Soviet Union. He had not really meant it, but now Yefimov gave him $1,500 to cover the cost of the trip.[17] Lonetree spent most of it on gifts for Seina and Yefimov.

Lonetree showed up for the next meeting with an undated, abbreviated embassy phone book, along with the floor plans to the embassy.[18] He thought Yefimov would be more pleased with the plans than the phone book, but it was the other way around.

During this meeting and several others, Lonetree went down the list of employees and ticked off which ones were in the CIA. While he never knew for sure, he was a good guesser. Almost all of his identifications were correct.[19] He also told Yefimov which Marines had problems with drugs or alcohol, and which ones might be homosexuals.

As he had in Moscow, Lonetree marked up the floor plans to show the function of each office, its occupants, and their functions. He marked the locations of alarms and other security devices in secure areas and special doors guarding access to the CIA offices. He showed where the CPU was located and how it was alarmed. He told Yefimov how the Marines react to alarms, how they deal with walk-ins offering information, and how they enter secure areas without triggering alarms. In addition, he told Yefimov who the foreign nationals in the embassy were and which ones might be susceptible to KGB recruitment.[20]

Yefimov gave Lonetree $1,000, which he spent on dinners and beers for Marines. For the information Lonetree provided, the sum was low. As a rule, the KGB does not want to pay so well that agents will attract attention to themselves because they have excess money or have no need to come back for more.

At their next meeting, Yefimov said he wanted to turn Lonetree over to a friend, a KGB officer based in Vienna. Lonetree now realized this game would never end. While he had put in for leave so he could go to the Soviet Union in January, he dreaded the trip. Even though he would see Seina, he knew he would be in for heavy training sessions with the KGB. The fact that his alcoholism was growing worse did not help.

Lonetree was supposed to meet Yefimov on December 5 but instead wrote to Seina. In the letter he said he was tired.

"Just about every day for the last month if I'm not working, I'm out with friends including Sash, and I still have to meet people in the upcoming days," he complained to her.[21]

In Moscow, meanwhile, things had gone from bad to worse. Bradley, the new detachment commander, was not as tough and decisive as "Top" Wingate had been.[22] Before, the Marines had engaged in infractions on a retail basis. Now, it seemed, they had gone wholesale.

Nor were the infractions confined to Marines. While he was in Moscow, Mecke had to send home twenty-five Americans for rule violations ranging from black-marketeering to sleeping with Soviet women. While half of those Americans were contractors building the new embassy, the rest were Marines and several employees from other agencies represented at the mission.[23]

Stufflebeam had been replaced as assistant detachment commander by Staff Sergeant Vincent O. Downes. A gregarious, slightly built man from Yonkers, New York, Downes made up for Bradley's indecisiveness by being a firm leader. At the same time, he had not quite adjusted to his new role. Unlike Stufflebeam, he continued to go out with the Marines on liberty even though he was no longer a watchstander. It would lead to his downfall.[24]

Like the other Marines, Downes could not believe the state of security at the embassy. It was far looser than at his two previous posts, Tokyo and Budapest. He would never forget the feeling he got when he said he needed to enter the embassy's locked boiler room, only to be told a Soviet worker would escort him in.

If the embassy trusted the Soviets as much as the Marines, it seemed to Downes it was also a miniature Peyton Place. Five embassy wives, dubbed by the Marines "the Homewreckers," routinely picked up Marines at Uncle Sam's, the embassy disco, on Friday nights.[25]

Typically, one wife, whose husband might work for the State Department, would sit with a Marine and mention that another wife, whose husband might be a Seabee, was interested in him.

"If he wants her, she's up for grabs," was the not-so-subtle line.

As expected, the Marine would pass the information along, and the second Marine would take the woman to his room in the Marine House for a one-night stand. Then the same process would be repeated with another Marine and another wife.

In any other part of the world, the affairs might be considered the private business of the parties involved. But in a hostile environment like Moscow, they only invited KGB blackmail attempts. The fact that they took place so openly illustrated how out of control the embassy was.

One young State Department employee made it a practice to sleep with as many Marines and Seabees as she could. In September she took on three Marines at the same time in one of their rooms.[26] On her ID card on file at post number one, the Marines scribbled a variety of crude remarks: "I'm a slut machine"; "I took on three MSGs [Marine security guards]"; "We take on all comers"; and so forth.[27]

Downes meanwhile opened himself to entrapment by picking up a pretty hitchhiker and having sex with her with another Marine. One night they saw her thumbing while they were returning to the embassy from the Kosmos Hotel. Dark-haired and shapely, she was wearing blue jeans and a blouse. When Downes asked her for identification, she said she was German and had none. Given the fact that hitchhiking by women is unusual in the Soviet Union, it is likely the KGB planted her on the street corner. If not, the KGB most likely would have visited her after any encounter with an embassy employee.

After dropping two other Marines at the embassy, Downes and the second Marine took her to an apartment where the Marine was house-sitting. After downing a few drinks, the two Marines had vaginal and anal intercourse with her simultaneously, then took turns with her as the other watched. They referred to the former practice as "scrogging"; they called the later activity "tag team."[28]

Focusing on the important things, an NIS report on the incident would later note that the two Marines could feel each other's penises as they penetrated the girl.[29]

Now that the Soviet workers had been withdrawn, the Marines

for the first time held their annual ball without inviting Soviet women. One of the Marines got drunk and damaged one of the ambassador's metal statues, touching off a major investigation. Because the offending Marine had just had a death in his family, Mecke and Hartman decided to let him stay in Moscow.

A second party in December ended on a much more disastrous note. The party was held at one of the embassy's two dachas, a log house just inside the city limits. A young British student got drunk at the party, and several Marines brought her back to one of their rooms at the embassy. She passed out on the floor, and two Marines began having sex with her. As she came to, she screamed and severely scratched one of the Marines.[30]

Through interviews, Mecke established that the young woman had been sexually assaulted. While she did not press charges, Bradley and the new commander of Company A in Frankfurt ultimately sent the two Marines home, along with seven others who knew what was happening and did nothing.[31]

"Everybody broke a rule here or there," Downes told me. "Marines will get away with anything they can—they'll push it to the limit." He added, "There was a code of silence in the Marine House. 'You have fun, and I can have fun.' It was what we called the unwritten law. There were a lot of things the detachment commander didn't know about. He didn't know, and we didn't tell him."[32]

Now that Lonetree's drinking problem was getting worse, Gunnery Sergeant Darrell J. Enderlin, the detachment commander in Vienna, removed him as a squad leader and got him to join Alcoholics Anonymous. To Enderlin, Lonetree was a pathetic figure, lacking confidence in himself and incapable of taking charge of his life.[33]

Apprehensive about meeting the second KGB officer, Lonetree missed two meetings before he finally saw Yefimov at the church where they originally met in Vienna. They walked to the Heurigen Restaurant, where Yefimov introduced Lonetree to Yuri V. Lysov, a KGB officer whom he called "George."

Fifty-three years old with graying hair, Lysov looked to

Lonetree like former national security adviser Zbigniew Brzezinski. Lysov wore reading glasses and spoke better English than Yefimov. By the way Yefimov deferred to him, Lonetree could tell that Lysov was senior to him.

Lysov told Lonetree that he and Yefimov were friends, and he could trust him. Yefimov jumped in and confirmed that.

"If you need anything, just ask, including money. You should not be shy," he said.[34]

Now it was Lysov's turn to make demands on Lonetree. He wanted to know if Lonetree could enter the ambassador's office freely. He asked for a list of the cleaning personnel at the embassy. Finally, he wanted Lonetree to meet him at the Saint Laurenti Church at 7:00 P.M. on December 17, 1986, to make plans for his trip to the Soviet Union.

Lonetree never showed up.

Having failed to attend AA meetings, Lonetree was in an alcoholic fog much of the time. Confused and apprehensive, he approached the CIA station chief at a Christmas party given by then-ambassador Ronald Lauder on December 14, 1986. Edging him toward a crackling fire, Lonetree said he had been seeing some officials of the Soviet government in Vienna, and they wanted him to go to the Soviet Union. The station chief told Lonetree to meet him the next day at a McDonald's, where Lonetree began spilling the beans.

Still, he said he bore no ill will toward Seina. Thick-skulled to the end, he told the wide-eyed CIA officer, "If Sasha was really her uncle, then she was somewhat obligated to support him."[35]

Lonetree said he never fully appreciated what he had done until he began reading about Walker's spy activities. He speculated that his actions might have been motivated by hatred for the white man. But that was more of an attempt at self-aggrandizement than anything else. While Lonetree harbored resentments against almost everyone, he had never identified with his race.

His obtuseness even after the KGB and Seina had consumed him highlighted once again how inadequate the screening process was for selecting Marine security guards.

For the next ten days, the CIA continued to debrief Lonetree.

Since the CIA is not a law-enforcement agency, it had no interest in warning him of his rights, transcribing what he said, preserving evidence, or making sure he would talk in the future. The CIA only wanted to know how much damage Lonetree had done and whether he might be used as a double agent to get information.

The agency sent officers to watch Lonetree's next scheduled meeting with Yefimov, but because they were in covert capacities, the CIA did not want them to testify openly in court about what they saw.

These deficiencies reveal a weakness in how the U.S. government handles espionage by Americans overseas. Later, that weakness would come back to haunt the CIA.

# PART II

# CHAPTER 17

## "Tell Us a Lie"

BACK IN WASHINGTON, Lanny E. McCullah, the chief of the Naval Investigative Service's counterintelligence division, was about to go to an NIS Christmas party at the Officers' Club in the Navy Yard when he got a call that changed his plans. Over a secure phone, James W. Lannon, who headed the State Department's counterintelligence unit, told him that the CIA wanted to see them about a Marine who had said he was in contact with the Soviets in Vienna. From the way Lannon described it, it didn't sound like a big case.

"We have our Christmas party in an hour," McCullah said at 11:00 A.M. "Can it wait?"

Lannon checked with the CIA and told McCullah it could not.

With this inauspicious beginning on December 22, 1986, the NIS began an investigation of the security breaches at Moscow station. In the coming months, the NIS would establish a special task force of a hundred agents and support personnel to investigate the Marine security guards at U.S. missions in the Soviet Union and in other Soviet bloc countries. In the course of that investigation, the NIS would interview 487 Marines and 1,285 other people, open files on 136 Marine security guards, and administer polygraph tests to 260 people.[1] To carry out its investigation, the NIS would obtain an additional $1 million from the Navy. Not knowing that then, the man who would head that investigation was miffed that he would miss the NIS Christmas party.

Beyond a personable manner, there was nothing about

McCullah that would lead one to believe he would head one of the most important counterintelligence investigations in U.S. history. Named for Lanny Ross, an entertainer from the 1930s, McCullah was born in Garden Grove, California. After graduating with a bachelor's degree in police science and administration from San Jose State University, he joined the Menlo Park police force in 1961. In 1963 he joined the Office of Naval Intelligence, the predecessor of the NIS. He rose through the ranks, taking posts in the Philippines, Japan, and Annapolis, Maryland, before being named chief of the NIS regional office in New York. In 1984 he became chief of the counterintelligence directorate, known as Directorate Twenty-two, which investigates security breaches and espionage.[2]

Because of a spinal arthritic condition, McCullah has a stooped appearance. That, his shuffling gait, and the way he wears his dark hair over his ears had given him the sobriquet "The Prince of Darkness."

McCullah drove from NIS headquarters in Suitland, Maryland, to Lannon's office in Rosslyn, Virginia. Switching to Lannon's car, they drove along the George Washington Memorial Parkway, turning off at the exit to the CIA's gleaming white building. At the reception desk, they gave their Social Security numbers and passed through elaborate turnstiles operated by their visitor passes. An escort took them to the office of an agency officer who worked for Gardner R. (Gus) Hathaway, the chief of the CIA's counterintelligence staff.

The CIA officer told McCullah that the case was far more serious than what he had indicated on the phone—that Lonetree had, in fact, met with the KGB and disclosed sensitive information about the embassies in Moscow and in Vienna. He showed McCullah CIA cables describing how the case had started with Lonetree's approach to the CIA station chief in Vienna eight days earlier.[3]

"We'll take it," McCullah said.[4]

As espionage cases go, it should have been relatively easy. Lonetree had already confessed to taking $3,500 from the Soviets in return for classified information. He was still talking. By showing up at the next scheduled meetings with Lysov, the CIA would soon confirm that he had, in fact, been meeting with the

KGB. It remained for the NIS to warn Lonetree of his rights, take his confession, and tie up a few loose ends.

But that was too much to expect of the NIS, which was as good at investigating espionage as the State Department was at protecting security. In fairness to the NIS, the agency rarely had the opportunity to undertake espionage investigations by itself. Normally, the FBI investigates espionage. Only when the target of the investigation is a military man and no civilians are involved do the military investigative services have exclusive jurisdiction.[52] Since Lonetree was a Marine and therefore worked for the Department of the Navy, he came under NIS jurisdiction. Thus, the NIS did not have the experience required to handle espionage cases properly. Asking the NIS to investigate espionage was like asking a general practitioner to perform heart surgery.

In one form or another, the NIS had been around for more than a century. It did not become the NIS until 1966.[6] Besides conducting security clearance investigations of Navy personnel, its job is to investigate the equivalent of felonies in the civilian justice system. More minor crimes, such as thefts, are investigated within the Marines by the corps' own uniformed police, called the Criminal Investigative Division.

Although the NIS is part of the Navy, its director, J. Brian McKee, is a civilian who joined the NIS in 1962 after graduating from Cornell University. While many are former Navy or Marine officers, most of the 1,200 NIS agents are civilians.

In December 1986, when the Lonetree investigation began, McKee reported to Admiral Cathal L. (Irish) Flynn, who headed the Naval Security and Investigative Command. Flynn reported to the chief of naval operations and the Navy secretary.

What makes an espionage case so difficult to prove is that it leaves no footprints. In a bank robbery, there are witnesses who saw the robber and may have seen the getaway car, video cameras that record the scene in the bank, and possibly fingerprints left on the teller's window. The robber may also have accomplices with loose lips, and the money may be traceable.

As a rule, there is no physical evidence in an espionage case. The evidence of the crime is either an oral disclosure of secrets or documents that most likely left the country on the next Aeroflot plane. The accomplice is most likely a KGB or GRU officer who has diplomatic immunity and has usually left the country as well. Passing documents is as easy as eating ice cream. Even if there were a witness, it is unlikely anyone noticed that the documents were passed. Nor is there usually a paper trail to track as in fraud or other white collar crimes.

In some instances, such as the Walker case, the FBI may get lucky and receive a tip. It can then conduct surveillance until the suspect leaves documents for his Soviet handlers. If the crime already took place, there is virtually no way to get a conviction unless the suspect or an accomplice confesses.

For that reason, the FBI has refined its methods for getting confessions in espionage cases into something approaching a science. After developing as much evidence as possible, FBI agents sit down with psychologists and plan, over the course of several weeks, how they will approach the suspect. They decide what time of day would be the best time to confront the suspect, how they should dress, what words they should say, and how the chairs should be arranged in the room where they talk with the suspect. As a rule, lawyers from the Justice Department's internal security section also brief the agents on how much they can say without jeopardizing the validity of a confession in court.

Once the suspect agrees to talk, the FBI has on occasion spent ten days or more taking a confession.[7] The emphasis is on trying to get a full understanding of the crime so that any holes in the case can be plugged before the suspect decides to recant. Rather than using written confessions, FBI agents take notes or record the confession with hidden video recorders. Polygraph machines are used as an investigative tool rather than as a final arbiter of truth. The possibility that the suspect may have to take a polygraph test is often enough to prompt him to disclose additional details that he may have been hiding.

Before administering the test, FBI polygraphers spend days alone with the suspect learning about the crime. In framing questions for the polygraph exam, FBI polygraphers narrow the focus to particular events. Instead of asking if the suspect ever committed espionage, FBI polygraphers ask, "Did you take the KH-11 manual from the desk on December 25?" Because the polygraph is such an imprecise instrument, only a narrowly defined question can produce useful results.[8]

The most important requirement is that the agents come across as honest, sincere individuals trying to get at the truth. If the suspect gets any hint that the agents are trying to railroad him, he may either clam up or fail the polygraph test out of sheer nervousness.

The NIS approach tends to be quite different. It can be summed up as "Slam, bam, thank you, ma'am!"[9] While there are exceptions, NIS agents generally do not take nearly as much time to develop the facts as the FBI does. Instead, they expect the suspect to confess on the spot. If he does not, they use a variety of subtle and not-so-subtle techniques to try to get him to confess.

Instead of using polygraph machines as an investigative tool, they use it as a screening device, placing suspects on the box after only one or two interview sessions. Instead of framing questions narrowly, they tend to use broad questions like "Have you ever committed espionage?"

Unlike the FBI, the NIS relies almost totally on written confessions. The problem with that is that they tend to focus the investigator's attention on drafting the statement rather than developing a full understanding of the events. Because suspects ultimately control how they are written, such confessions can contain booby traps that defense lawyers later use to impeach the credibility of the entire confession.

The NIS has one advantage over the FBI. In theory, it cannot force a military man to be interviewed or take a polygraph test. In practice, most military men realize their careers will be over if they do not cooperate with the NIS. The NIS takes advantage of that fear to the hilt.

Not that the FBI doesn't make mistakes. A glaring example is the bureau's investigation of Karl F. Koecher, a Czechoslovak intelligence service officer who penetrated the CIA for the KGB. In obtaining his confession, New York FBI agents made promises they never intended to keep and threatened the personal safety of Koecher and his family. If Koecher had not been traded for Natan Sharansky, his case almost certainly would have been thrown out of court.[10]

But the FBI's track record speaks for itself. Since 1975 its investigations have produced indictments against fifty individuals in major espionage cases. Only one has resulted in an acquittal. While the NIS also gets convictions, they tend to be in minor security cases involving a sailor who gets drunk in a bar and threatens to tell the Russians everything.

Because many of the major spy cases have involved former Navy men, the NIS has assisted the FBI in important cases such as John Walker's. In addition, because Jonathan J. Pollard, the Israeli spy, worked for the NIS, he first came under suspicion by the NIS. But the NIS tends to exaggerate its involvement in these and other major spy cases, suggesting that it is better at public relations than catching spies. For example, the NIS has repeatedly claimed that it was primarily responsible for bringing Pollard to justice.[11] When Justice Department prosecutors who were in charge of the case heard that, they looked shocked.

"Anybody who was involved in that case would say the FBI was chiefly responsible for it," Joseph E. DiGenova, then the U.S. Attorney in Washington, said.[12]

The NIS claims to have been at least partly responsible for thirty-three "espionage or security-related convictions" since fiscal 1982. Only eight of the cases were investigated solely by the NIS. The rest were done with the help or supervision of the FBI. With the exception of Lonetree's, all of the cases investigated exclusively by the NIS involved thefts or other security breaches rather than espionage on behalf of a foreign country.

As its tendency to magnify its own importance suggests, the NIS has a massive inferiority complex—and with good reason. When FBI counterintelligence agents and Justice Department prosecutors rank the proficiency of the various military investigative agencies, the NIS is not at the top of the list.

Aside from the shoddy procedures, many NIS agents simply are not good investigators. There can be no better example of that than the way the NIS handled the Lonetree case.

After returning at 4:00 P.M. to his office on the third floor of NIS headquarters in Suitland, McCullah called in three counterintelligence agents and let them know what he had found out at Langley. Then he called the NIS regional director in London on a secure phone to tell him about the case. The next morning he sent what the NIS calls an "ALS (Open)"—an action lead sheet formally opening a case—by secure cable to the London office.

The cable referred to the case as "Bobsled," the code name assigned to it. It was sent "Specat," which means the communications officer on duty had to keep a record of receiving it and personally deliver it to the recipient. In addition, the cable carried the designation "Cabin Boy," a code the NIS uses on all its counterintelligence traffic to indicate which department is handling it.[13]

That same day, David Moyer, the head of the NIS London office, and two other agents received a briefing on the case from the NIS regional director for Europe. He assigned them to Vienna to take Lonetree's confession. Because of the Christmas crush, they did not arrive in Vienna until the following day.

The NIS agents met Lonetree at the Vienna Intercontinental Hotel in the late afternoon. Lonetree had orange juice and the agents had coffee in the coffee shop. They took him to the Strudlhof Hotel, a less expensive establishment near the U.S. embassy, and checked into a suite. As instructed by McCullah, the NIS agents gave Lonetree what is known as a "cleansing warning," letting him know that because the CIA did not warn him of his rights, anything he previously told the CIA could not be used against him in court. At 7:12 P.M., Lonetree signed a statement waiving his right to a lawyer.[14]

Over the next two and a half hours, Lonetree held forth about his escapades with Seina and Sasha. He was voluble and jocular, almost as if he were enjoying the sudden attention.

At one point, Lonetree told the open-mouthed agents that he knew Yefimov liked him because of the way he smiled at him. Lonetree was like a baby who had never left the crib. At the end of the interview, Lonetree gave the agents permission to search his room in the Marine House. That night he slept in one of the bedrooms in the suite. Although nothing was said, he was in the agents' custody from then on.[15]

The agents found a treasure trove of evidence in Lonetree's

room. Besides the black enamel box that Lonetree said Yefimov had given him, they found several drafts of letters to Seina, along with letters Lonetree had received from her, a pocket diary, and slips of paper with dates of meetings he had had with Yefimov.[16]

The next morning, the agents flew Lonetree to London, where they checked into the Holiday Inn near Heathrow Airport. It was Christmas Day, and the agents wanted to be with their families. They asked if Lonetree wanted to wait until the next day to be interviewed.

"No, I'd like to do it as soon as possible," he said.

As he told particularly damaging parts of his story, Lonetree would cry and look remorseful. At other times, he would smile to himself, as if mentally assessing how much he was implicating himself and whether he should tell more.

After two and a half days of interviews, the agents introduced Lonetree to Thomas E. Brannon, an NIS polygraph agent. Brannon talked with Lonetree for six hours on December 28.[17] The following day he began administering polygraph tests. After Lonetree signed a second statement based on what he told Brannon, he began registering deceptive on the polygraph machine. Brannon thought he was holding back some facts, which could show up as deception on all his answers.[18]

Brannon decided Lonetree must have taken classified documents from the embassy in Vienna, and he began pressing him on the point. Speculating on what Lonetree might have done, Brannon fired questions at Lonetree while Lonetree continued to deny that he took any documents. Brannon kept coming back to the same question with different twists. As Brannon increased the pressure, Lonetree finally said, "Do you want me to lie to you?"

"Yes," Brannon said.[19]

Choking up, Lonetree said he stole three documents from the embassy's CPU on the fourth floor.

"I bet they were top secret," Brannon said.[20]

Lonetree said they were. He said he also took 200 secret documents he was supposed to burn at the embassy.

Lonetree began hyperventilating and went into the bathroom to splash cold water on his face.[21] When he returned, he said he wanted a lawyer.

Brannon would later claim his statement to Lonetree had been taken out of context. He would then repeat that Lonetree asked him if he wanted him to lie, and Brannon said yes.[22]

Extracting the truth from someone who has everything to lose by telling the truth is difficult enough as it is without suggesting that he lie. Besides creating misinformation, it undermines the credibility of the interviewer. To get a suspect to confess, an investigator has to establish a degree of trust and convince the suspect that it is in his best interests to confess, either to help his country, clear his conscience, or obtain a less severe sentence. Telling a suspect to lie makes a mockery of the entire criminal justice system and impairs any faith the suspect may have had in the investigator. Without credibility, an investigator has nothing.

To this day, the NIS does not see it that way. Brannon's superiors who helped direct the NIS task force investigation of the security breaches in Moscow claimed that what Brannon did was perfectly proper. What was most remarkable about this was that they were not trying to cover for Brannon. They honestly believed that there was nothing wrong with telling a suspect to lie in order to keep him talking.[23] Indeed, one of those supervisors, with decades of experience in the NIS, said he had done the same thing on occasion. As he put it:

There are probably few investigators around who have never said something similar to that [tell me a lie]. In the confines of the interrogation room, a lot of things are said that if taken out of context really sound bad. What happened in that interrogation, and I personally have used the same words: You're sitting there after you've been there hour upon hour. The guy is just not saying much. Brannon has explained this to me. Lonetree was sitting there with his head hung down. They're trying to get the guy to talk. That's one of the things you do in an interrogation. You try to keep the guy talking. He's not saying anything. Brannon makes the comment, and I don't know if he used these words, but this is the way I would say it: "Goddammit Clayton, talk to me. Tell me anything. Tell me a lie. But tell me something." And that is the context in which that was said. And that to me is totally believable.[24]

The NIS reaction to Brannon's statement tells more about the NIS and its institutional values than anything learned from reading the agency's reports of its interviews with Marines.

Ultimately, it is impossible to know with precision what exactly took place during an interrogation. But when the supervisors of the investigation condone telling a suspect to lie and say they have done it themselves, it is clear that everything from that investigation must be looked at with a jaundiced eye.

Slow as he was, Lonetree realized there was no point in talking to someone who told him to lie. Within forty-eight hours, the NIS established that he had in fact lied to Brannon just as Brannon asked him to. The secret documents mentioned by Lonetree never existed. Nor was he standing watch when he said he took them.[25]

But the damage had been done. The NIS had taken a relatively simple case and almost lost it. By pressing Lonetree too hard and then losing his confidence, the NIS had lost the cooperation that is so vital in an espionage case. Before, Lonetree was willing to tell the investigators most of the details of what he did. He was even willing to help them find other Marines who might have been engaged in similar activities. Now he would say nothing.

As it turned out, Lonetree knew a lot more than he had told the investigators up to that point. But because of the NIS action, it was not until nearly a year later—after he had been sentenced—that he finally revealed in debriefings just how much he had given away. While he never implicated others, his knowledge of how the KGB went about recruiting Marines at the embassy would have been invaluable if the NIS could have learned about it in December 1986.

Yet this would be only the first of the NIS blunders.

# CHAPTER 18

# "Another Spy!"

THE MARINE CORPS announced Lonetree's arrest on January 2, 1987, with a five-paragraph press release. The release said he was suspected of espionage and was in pretrial confinement in the brig at Quantico. There were no further details. The press hardly took notice.[1]

On January 27 the Marine Corps specified the charges against Lonetree. The Marines charged him with giving information to Yefimov and Lysov and with falsely claiming he had given away top-secret documents from the Vienna embassy.[2] Since his prosecution ultimately would depend on the veracity of his confession, the Marine Corps eventually realized that charging him with lying in his confession was not a wise move. The Marines later dropped the perjury charges.

Under the Uniform Code of Military Justice, Lonetree was entitled to free military counsel. The Marine Corps assigned Major David H. Henderson, a respected military lawyer, to represent him. Lonetree could also hire his own civilian counsel. He chose William M. Kunstler, the noted defender of radical leaders, and Michael V. Stuhff, an obscure lawyer from Las Vegas, Nevada.[3]

Now that Lonetree's case had been publicized, the KGB wanted to know what had happened to him. In Moscow, Yefimov called Sean Byrnes, the political officer he had dealt with at the embassy, and suggested they have lunch on January 17, 1987.

201

Yefimov always saved the most important items for last. So it was this time. As they strolled toward the metro stop after lunch, Yefimov asked if Byrnes knew anything about the Lonetree case.

"Yes, I read about it in the *International Herald-Tribune*," Byrnes replied coyly.[4]

"Do you know the woman?" Yefimov asked.

"No, I don't," Byrnes said.

Then came the question the KGB was dying to know the answer to.

"Do you know if Sergeant Lonetree was discovered by U.S. authorities, or if he volunteered the information?" Yefimov asked.

"I don't know," Byrnes said.

"Well, you know, it's possible for people to fall in love, and this looks like a case of that happening in Moscow," Yefimov said. He then changed the subject.

A few weeks later Byrnes had Yefimov to his apartment for dinner. On instructions from Hartman, he asked Yefimov if he knew Lonetree and if he had handled him as his case officer. Yefimov did not seem surprised by the question. Looking Byrnes straight in the eye, he said, "I did not know Sergeant Lonetree, and never dealt with him. Please convey that to the ambassador and to Washington."[5]

On March 9, Yefimov called Byrnes to suggest a meeting. Byrnes said he had been instructed to cut off contact with him.

"I understand," Yefimov said.


Having lost Lonetree's cooperation through its own ineptitude, the Naval Investigative Service now had to turn to other Marines and embassy employees to determine more precisely what he had done. The fact that many of the employees had by now scattered all over the world made the work that much more difficult.

Like its interrogation of Lonetree, the NIS conducted these interviews on a rush basis with virtually no preparation. This led to more blunders. The NIS would later attribute its haste to the fact that under military rules, unless the defense requests delays, suspects must be tried within ninety days of their arrest. Yet the NIS did not have to arrest Lonetree immediately. In investigating espionage, the FBI frequently does not take suspects into custody, hoping that they will get in touch with their Soviet handlers or lead the bureau to secret caches of money. By keeping them under surveillance, the FBI ensures that they will not leave the country.[6]

Even after Lonetree was incarcerated, the NIS could have recommended to the Marine Corps that he be freed if the NIS still needed to gather more evidence. As it was, the NIS already had the evidence it needed against Lonetree anyway. Anything more would have been frosting on the cake. No one at the NIS looked at the larger picture or focused on what the investigation was trying to do. Asking the Marine Corps to free Lonetree would have required more foresight than the NIS was capable of mustering. Reminiscent of the code name for its investigation, the NIS ran its investigation of Lonetree and the other Marine security guards as if it were hurtling down an icy slope on a bobsled.

The other government agencies involved were in no hurry to help. The Christmas holidays and an inadequate computer program meant that the Marine Corps took three weeks to supply the NIS with a list of Marines who had been stationed in Moscow when Lonetree was there. After delaying several weeks, the State Department gave the NIS its so-called infractions list, showing which Marines had been removed from post. But the State Department did not get around to handing over the debriefing of Bracy or Mecke's cables about his case for almost three months.[7]

Meanwhile, the intelligence agencies so jealously guarded their own information that to this day the CIA has not told the NIS what Yurchenko said about the penetration of communications at the Moscow embassy.

By March 1987 the NIS had interviewed 200 Marines, CIA officers, diplomats, and military attachés who may have known anything about Lonetree. Still the NIS had not interviewed Bracy. Bracy was thought to be a 5.0 Marine—the perfect performance score. The NIS figured he would not have known Lonetree well. As a result, the NIS had placed him near the bottom of the list of people to be interviewed.

That changed on March 16, 1987, when David Moyer, the NIS

agent who had interviewed Lonetree in Vienna, was in Vienna to discuss Lonetree's case with the CIA station chief. Since the CIA had not kept a detailed record of its interrogation of Lonetree, there was no telling what Lonetree might have said that could have proven useful. Now, Moyer learned from the station chief that Lonetree had mentioned something about Bracy and Golotina.

As the station chief recalled it, Lonetree had said that Bracy told him in Moscow he was secretly seeing the Soviet cook, and she wanted to introduce him to her uncle. Lonetree warned Bracy to be careful.[8]

Three months had elapsed since the interrogation, and it was difficult to know if the station chief accurately recalled what Lonetree had said. When the NIS later debriefed Lonetree with the benefit of polygraph machines after his sentencing, he only recalled that he saw Bracy and Golotina holding hands and that he warned Bracy to be careful.[9]

Even this crumb was significant, since it further undermined Bracy's claim that he never had a romantic relationship with Golotina. If true, Lonetree's statement would mean Bracy was seeing Golotina well before what he claims to be their first encounter in the park in June 1986.

Recognizing that Lonetree's remark could mean the KGB had recruited yet another spy, Moyer cabled NIS headquarters in Suitland. He said the NIS should immediately interview Bracy, who was then at Twentynine Palms, California. Moyer suggested that NIS agents ask Bracy about "his knowledge of subj [an NIS abbreviation for subject, in this case Lonetree] and his personal relationship with . . . Golotina. In view of possible SIS recruitment of Sergeant Bracy, polygraph examination should be considered."[10] SIS is an abbreviation for the Soviet intelligence service, an umbrella term used by U.S. intelligence agencies for both the KGB and GRU.

One does not have to be a professional investigator to know that the last thing to do at this point was interview Bracy. It is basic to any investigation that all the facts are assembled before the target is confronted. If the NIS had gone about its job properly, it would have pulled every record on Bracy, including the record of his nonjudicial punishment at Quantico. It would have done what the FBI calls a background investigation, discreetly checking into Bracy's history and character. It would have interviewed Mecke and Duchateau of the State Department and Del Grosso of the Marine Corps. It would have reinterviewed the CIA station chief in Vienna to find out more precisely what Lonetree told him. Beyond that, it would have developed a thorough understanding of the embassy, its functions, layout, personnel, and alarm systems.

The NIS did none of this.

Driven by the ninety-day deadline the NIS had imposed on itself, Angelic White, a personable woman with blond hair who was in charge of the Lonetree case, frantically told the NIS resident agency—called a NISRA—in Twentynine Palms to interview Bracy immediately.[11]

White followed up with a rambling, confusing cable meant to tell them what they should ask Bracy. The cable said Bracy had been removed from Moscow for fraternizing and should be interviewed to determine if he was involved in espionage.

"It is possible that Bracy was unaware that he was being targeted by the KGB," the cable said. "It is not known whether subj was the first to be involved with a Soviet woman. Subj claims that he took the initiative in establishing his relationship with Seina. However, the possibility exists that Bracy encouraged the relationship or visa [sic] versa."[12]

The cable reveals that after three months the NIS had very little understanding of the Lonetree case, the embassy, or its workings. The cable warned that SIRO—a code word for the CIA—had identified Galya, Golotina's nickname, as a KGB officer. In fact, White had mixed up Galya the cook with another Galya employed by the embassy. Any Marine or security officer at the embassy could have told the NIS that the embassy employed at least two Soviets by the name of Galya. After 200 interviews, the NIS still did not know the difference between them.

Aside from the misinformation, White's cryptic cable gave virtually no data that would be helpful in interviewing Bracy. It was like telling a police officer that a neighbor may have committed murder, and expecting him to ask the neighbor if he did it.

White would later defend what she did by saying, "There wasn't any other information to get about him [Bracy]."[13]

In fairness to White, the NIS was not equipped to deal with the case. Having never undertaken an investigation of this magnitude, the NIS had no system for correlating and analyzing the stacks of reports that poured in every day. While a good manager, McCullah, who was in charge of the investigation, was not a detail man. He often quipped that he did not understand how a flashlight worked. The case agents did not have the organizational skills, the experience, or the attention span to sift through facts carefully and put them together into a coherent whole. To this day, NIS supervisors have only the haziest idea of the embassy's layout and the way its alarm system worked at the time.

"We did not have all the details we should have had," one of the NIS agents who later interviewed Bracy said. "I think they [NIS headquarters] weren't organized properly."[14]

Another agent who interviewed Bracy observed, "It's the system that screwed up."[15]

After receiving White's garbled cable, the NIS agents stationed at Twentynine Palms chatted with a former Marine security guard stationed at the base, located in the Mojave Desert forty miles northeast of Palm Springs. The NIS agents wanted to find out how the guard program worked. The former guard gave them background that the agents could have learned from reading any brochure on the program. Having never been to Moscow, he gave them an idealized version of how the program was supposed to work. Beyond the interview with the former guard and White's cable, the agents knew nothing about Bracy or the Lonetree case except what they had read in the papers.

After other agents fetched Bracy, NIS Special Agent R. Michael Embry began interviewing him at the NISRA on March 18, 1987. Just two days had elapsed since Moyer cabled NIS headquarters from Vienna. Bracy told Embry the State Department had already debriefed him about Golotina. Embry was surprised no one had told him about it.

With one difference, Bracy told Embry essentially the same story he gave Mecke in Moscow. This time he said he talked with

Golotina in the master bedroom of the Duchateaus' apartment. He did not explain why he selected the bedroom as the place where he would tell her to leave him alone.

Embry later told the other NIS agents on the case that he felt Bracy was lying when he said he had not had sex with Golotina. But he did not think Bracy had committed espionage.[16]

The next day, NIS polygraph agents James P. Pender and Patrick J. Hurt took Bracy to a Best Western motel near Twenty-nine Palms for lie-detector tests. At 8:39 A.M., they warned him of his rights.[17] When the operators told him he was registering deceptive reactions, Bracy began changing his story. Now he said he agreed to meet with Golotina at the Duchateaus' apartment. He said he took a taxi from the embassy at 7:00 or 8:00 A.M.[18]

According to his signed statement, "She was the only one in the apartment, and she told me the Duchateaus [had] gone somewhere on vacation. She moved closer to me and initiated the sexual contact, and we began making out. After a short period of time she suggested we go to the bedroom, where we had sex.

"After having sexual intercourse," Bracy said, "I asked her what was so important, and she told me that they had been putting pressure on her family so she would arrange for me to meet 'Uncle Sasha.' She implied that he really was not her uncle but that that was what she was supposed to tell me."

Bracy said he asked her what they were supposed to discuss.

"Anything you feel comfortable with," she said. For example, Golotina said, Bracy might talk about nuclear arms talks, the blacks' position in America, any complaints he had about the way things were run at the embassy, and the fact that America could be wrong, too.

She said her uncle would be interested in learning "who was leaving the embassy and who was going to replace them, and the names of the people working for the CIA."

Bracy told her he had reported her, and the embassy was "just waiting for the Russians to make a move." It was then that the ABC-TV sound man walked in, he said.

Bracy signed the second statement at 4:17 P.M. At one point, according to Embry, Bracy apologized to him for lying about not having sex with Golotina.

The following day, Bracy signed a third statement that would rock the intelligence community. According to that statement, Bracy ran into Lonetree one night in the kitchen of the Marine House in January 1986.

"He had been drinking and was very drunk," Bracy said in his statement. "I began talking with him, and during the course of the conversation, we were talking about the rules and regulations we had to follow, and he was bitching why he had extended in the first place to stay in Moscow.[19]

"He was obviously pretty worked up and mad at the system and how the Marine detachment was run," Bracy said. "He remarked that he was paying them back in his own way. I asked him what he meant, and he said, 'I've been letting people in the embassy.' I knew he was talking about Russians. I asked him how many times had he done it. He said he had done it many times. Then the conversation ended and he left the kitchen."

At the time, Bracy had thought Lonetree was babbling. He did not really believe him. The next day, Bracy asked Lonetree about it. Lonetree said he had been drinking and said he should not pay attention to what he had been saying.

About two weeks later, Bracy said he was on duty at post number one when he saw Lonetree escorting a Soviet man into the courtyard around midnight. As they walked by, Bracy asked Lonetree who the individual was.

"Nobody," Lonetree said.

Bracy said he next saw Lonetree escorting someone through the embassy around midnight in late January. Bracy asked who the man was, and Lonetree told him he was a Soviet driver whom he was taking to the Marine House for a few beers.

In February, Lonetree was standing post number two-A, the roving guard for the secure areas, while Bracy was standing post number three. Lonetree told Bracy he had been letting people into the secure spaces "for a while." He said he was doing it because he was in "big trouble" with the Russians.

"I felt sort of sorry for him, so I decided not to report what he had told me," Bracy said in his statement.

Bracy said that before Mecke established post number two-A, it was easy for the guard at post number three on the ninth floor to silence the alarms and let people into the CPU. He explained how a communicator had to reset them, and the Marine guard could claim they went off at 6:00 A.M. when they really had gone off at 2:00 A.M. Since the alarms were always giving false signals anyway, he said, it was common for the Marines to turn them off.

Once Mecke established the new roving post, Bracy·said in his statement, it was more difficult to let the Soviets in. That was why Lonetree asked for his help.

"He told me at that time that this had been going on all the time. I had been standing duty with him, and if I did not cooperate, I would be just as guilty as he was," Bracy said. Lonetree got the combinations to the CPU and other secure areas from the guard safe on the ninth floor, according to Bracy. He said Lonetree told him the Soviets were only looking at "office set-ups."

Beginning in February, Bracy said he agreed to turn off the alarms while Lonetree brought Soviets into the secure areas. He also warned him if the sergeant-of-the-guard was coming. He said he helped let the Soviets into the CPU on three occasions for an hour each time.

" . . . We were always able to convince the RSO and the duty communicator that it [an alarm] was accidental, and that no one was really in there," Bracy said.

Bracy said he continued to cooperate with Lonetree until he left for Vienna in March. He said Lonetree gave him a total of $1,000 for helping him.

Bracy told the NIS agents that he began having sex with Golotina in January 1986, while house-sitting at the apartment of the Air Force attaché. It was then that Golotina said she wanted to introduce him to her bogus uncle, and he agreed to see him.[20] Bracy also gave a new version of his meeting with Golotina in the park in June 1986. He said she asked him to meet her there after already having introduced him to her "uncle." The "uncle" told Bracy he wanted him to do "what Lonetree was doing."

After incriminating himself in espionage, Bracy continued to fail the lie-detector tests administered by Hurt and Pender. When he said he had engaged in espionage against the U.S., he passed. He also passed when he said he had never provided the Soviets with classified information.[21] But he failed when he said he had had no other secret meetings with the Russians besides those he had described, no personal meetings with Sasha, and no sexual activity with Golotina beyond what he had admitted to. Most significantly, he failed when he said he had never deliberately allowed a Russian unauthorized access to the embassy and its secure areas.

After the interrogation, NIS headquarters told the polygraphers at Twentynine Palms to "correct" their report to show that Bracy had failed all the questions.[22] When Bracy's lawyers got hold of both reports, they had a field day. Soon, there were stories in the press of a cover-up.

Ironically, the NIS this time had done things properly. By changing the report, the NIS was following Department of Defense guidelines based on years of experience in administering polygraph tests. Because the polygraph is such an imprecise instrument, the machine often registers correct responses only to one question in a series because the subject tends to focus on the one question that bothers him most. Rather than report a misleading result, the Defense Department rules say responses to all the questions in a series should be considered deceptive if the subject registers a deceptive response to one of them.

The FBI follows the same procedure.[23] On the other hand, the FBI would not ask if a subject had ever engaged in espionage because the word is subject to differing interpretations.

"What we try to do is find out what he did that may later be termed espionage. The less ambiguity, the better the results," a senior FBI polygraph examiner said. "The question [of whether the subject committed espionage] may also evoke an emotional reaction that we want to avoid."[24]

Bracy signed the final incriminating statement at 4:30 P.M. on Friday, March 10, 1987. At that point, according to Bracy, he overheard the agents talking with each other outside the room. One of them said, "We've got ourselves another spy!"[25]

One of the NIS agents later admitted that something like that was said. Instead of glee, the agent said, the comment was an expression of concern.[26] Nevertheless, registering any emotion in such circumstances is tantamount to suggesting that the subject recant. It tells the subject of an investigation that he has been had, shatters any trust he may have had in the investigators, and forces him to rethink what he has done. Predictably, as soon as he heard the comment, Bracy told the agents he wanted to retract his statement. They told him he could be charged with perjury for swearing falsely under oath. He said he would rather go to jail for perjury than espionage.

The next day the NIS brought Bracy in for a final interrogation at 9:27 A.M. He told them virtually nothing and refused to take another lie-detector test. At 10:49 A.M., Bracy said he wanted a lawyer. He never talked to the NIS again.

First the NIS lost Lonetree's cooperation by telling him to lie. Now the NIS had lost Bracy's cooperation by gloating. The NIS then compounded its blunders by arresting Bracy on the spot. After Bracy retracted his statement, the NIS had no evidence to hold him on. There was no corroboration for anything he had said. Without corroboration, the confession was worthless. But that did not deter the NIS. Based on what the NIS told the Marine Corps, the Marines placed Bracy in the brig at Twentynine Palms. Besides infringing on Bracy's rights, the NIS threw away the opportunity of watching Bracy to see if he would lead them to evidence that would corroborate what he had said.

The Marines, meanwhile, made matters worse by transferring Bracy to the same maximum-security section at the brig in Quantico where Lonetree was being held. The two were not supposed to talk with each other, but they did. Saying the NIS had pressured him into it, Bracy apologized to Lonetree for implicating him.[27] The two did crosswords by announcing what they had written in each box. From his cell, Lonetree would yell to Bracy, "What did you get for thirty-one down?" Bracy would yell back the answer.

If there were a conspiracy, it was a good way to ensure that it continue. NIS officials later admitted privately that arresting Bracy and placing him in the same cell block with Lonetree was a mistake, but they blamed it all on the Marine Corps.[28] While the Marines made the decision, they based it on NIS information, which lacked substance.

When I interviewed Bracy at the coffee shop outside the Quantico Marine base, he said that the NIS agents got him to implicate himself by telling him that the statements would only help in their investigation of Lonetree. He said they told him that his life as an American would be over if he did not sign them.

According to Bracy, the agents came up with the scenario that Lonetree and Bracy let the Soviets into the embassy. He said they asked him hypothetical questions, then wrote the answers as fact. For example, he said, the agents asked how the Soviets could have gotten into the secure spaces.

"I said post number three and number two-A would definitely have to be [involved] in it, because number three set the alarm and number two-A roams. So they wrote that down [as if it had happened]," Bracy said. "Then they asked about the CPU. I said he [Lonetree] couldn't have done it. They said, 'We know he did it because he did it in Vienna.' They said, 'He is a criminal, and even if it's not true, it will help us find the truth.'"

When he objected to what they had written, "They said if I didn't sign it, I'd never get another meal as an American citizen," Bracy said. "Or if I didn't admit to sex, I'd be administratively discharged."

Having talked with dozens of NIS agents and Marines who had been interviewed by NIS agents, I believe the agents made statements along those lines. The stories the Marines told of how the NIS interrogated them were too consistent and too detailed to have been fabricated or orchestrated.

When I asked the NIS agents about Bracy's claims, they emphatically denied making up the statement for him. But one of the agents said that in response to Bracy's question, he told him his security clearance would be lifted if he failed the polygraph questions.[29] Even the retouched version made it clear Bracy had been implicitly threatened.

Besides using questionable tactics, the agents had a tendency to get their facts confused. For example, they asked Bracy if he knew anything about Nicholas Daniloff and his arrest. Bracy said he only knew that the *U.S. News & World Report* journalist was on the access list at the embassy. Lacking any knowledge of the embassy, the agents thought that meant Daniloff was allowed into the secure spaces in the embassy. From that, they deduced that Daniloff may have been working for the CIA after all. They passed that along to their supervisors, who accepted it as fact. Yet Bracy was only talking about the kind of access any American journalist enjoyed at the embassy.[30]

The fact that the NIS used improper tactics and did not always get its facts straight was one thing. Bracy's guilt or innocence was another. Even if the NIS had tortured Bracy, his confession was not necessarily false. Like two sides of a tape recording, what happened in Moscow and the NIS version of it played on separate tracks.

From inquiring into Bracy's previous statements about the incident in the Duchateaus' apartment, I already knew that Bracy's claims of innocence were suspect. Based on my interviews with Bracy and with witnesses, there was no question in my mind that he was dissembling about his involvement with the Soviet cook.

The fact that Bracy had implicated himself in espionage made his claims of innocence that much more suspect. When pressed by the NIS, I could see why he might falsely implicate another Marine to get the agents off his back. Unless he were guilty, it was virtually impossible to comprehend why he would implicate himself.

In the end, the answer to the puzzle lay in his six-page final confession. Bracy's account of the way he let the Soviets into the CPU was unerringly accurate and telling. Most Marines did not realize that they could silence the alarms in the CPU and make up a story about when the alarms had gone off. Bracy was not only aware of that fact but had an impressive grasp of how the Marines could have let the KGB in. When Mecke and CIA officers read his statement, they felt it was authentic, too.[31]

On the other hand, there was a pervasive air of unreality to Bracy's description of Lonetree's involvement. The two were not close. Even if he were drunk, it was unlikely the reclusive Lonetree would admit to Bracy that he was letting the Soviets into the embassy. Over a period of many months, Lonetree had kept his affair with Seina to himself, even though it was a far less serious offense than letting the Soviets into the CPU. Moreover, the comments Bracy attributed to Lonetree sounded as phony as Bracy's story about why he went to the Duchateaus' apartment.

Ultimately, it became clear even to the NIS that Bracy had made up the story that Lonetree let the KGB into the embassy. While the Marines often switched schedules, each kept a detailed log of events that occurred during his shift. Bracy had claimed he helped Lonetree let the Soviets into the CPU in February 1986, while the two Marines were standing posts two-A and three at night. The logs showed Bracy and Lonetree stood posts two-A and three together at night only twice—once in October 1985 and once in November 1985.[32]

Beyond the logs, Lonetree ultimately passed lie-detector tests on his statement that he did not conspire with Bracy.

Bracy's confession was like a picture of a human face drawn by a schizophrenic. One side was real, the other—relating to Lonetree's actions—was not.

But what if Lonetree were taken out of the picture? What if Bracy let the Soviets in by himself? All of a sudden the face became whole.

According to this version of events, Bracy first began having sex with Golotina in January 1986, just as he said in his last statement. The affair began at the apartment of the Air Force attaché. At that time, according to the most likely scenario, Golotina introduced him to her "uncle." Afraid that he would be found out, Bracy began letting the Soviets into the CPU in February. The report of seeing Golotina in the park in June 1986 was then a ruse to throw off suspicion.

When the NIS confronted him, Bracy realized that the agents were after Lonetree, not him. Desperate to clear himself on the lie detector, he made up the story of Lonetree's involvement, thinking he would shift most of the blame to him. Unsophisticated as he was, he may not have realized that an aider and abettor or co-conspirator is just as culpable under the law as the perpetrator.

This scenario conforms with the Marine logs, which show Bracy frequently stood post number three on the ninth floor at night. It conforms with Lonetree's polygraph results, which show he did not conspire with Bracy. It also conforms with Bracy's polygraph tests. When he said he had never engaged in espionage and had never given away classified documents, he passed. When he said he had never let the Soviets into the secure spaces in the embassy, he failed.

In his untutored mind, Bracy could have thought that giving away classified documents constitutes espionage, while letting Soviets into the embassy is not. According to the FBI, the question about espionage was useless anyway because it was so general.

Most compelling is that this version of events conforms with Yefimov's debriefing of Lonetree. The KGB officer asked Lonetree to place bugs in the offices of the CIA station chief, the ambassador, and the regional security officer. He did not ask him to place bugs in the CPU, which should have been the KGB's first target—unless the KGB had already penetrated it.

By this scenario, the KGB was not trying to recruit Bracy to replace Lonetree. Rather, it was the other way around. By the time Yefimov began meeting with Lonetree in early February 1986, the KGB had already recruited Bracy, according to Bracy's statement.

The NIS never came to this conclusion. NIS headquarters was wedded to the idea that two or even three Marine security guards were needed to let the KGB into the embassy. Recognizing that Lonetree had not conspired with Bracy, the NIS spent countless hours trying to fit other Marine suspects into the conspiracy with him. In a classic sign of an amateurish investigation, the NIS drew up elaborate bar graphs to show which Marines spent the most time standing watch with Bracy.[33]

Since only one entry was needed to bug the CPU, the graphs were meaningless. Criminal cases are not statistical problems that can be solved with bar graphs. They are solved by hard investigative work—digging into the facts, sifting clues, interviewing, testing different hypotheses, understanding the environment where the crime took place, and coming to reasonable conclusions.

Inconceivable as it seems, a year into its investigation the NIS still had not prepared an analysis of Bracy's confession and where it had gone wrong.[34] With no target in its sights, the NIS lost interest.

Not until one visits the ninth floor of the embassy does one realize how easy it would be for the guard at post number three to let the KGB into the CPU. In this maze that passes for an embassy, KGB officers could hide in one of the offices on the ninth floor, slip into the CPU when no one was around, and leave before anyone noticed. According to technical experts, only a half hour to forty-five minutes would be needed to bug the CPU.

The guard at post number three knew where the other guards were at all times. The roving sergeant-of-the-guard checked in with him as he made his rounds to the new embassy site and the warehouse. The new roving guard, known as number two-A, also checked in with him as he entered each of the other secure floors. Roughly every hour he returned to the ninth floor to ask the guard to turn off the alarms on another floor so he could patrol the next one.

The KGB could enter the CPU while guard number two-A was on another floor. With the door to the CPU closed, the KGB could remain in the CPU even when number two-A returned to the ninth floor. The embassy had video cameras all around, but none that would show if anyone was in the CPU.

Most likely, the KGB would have chosen an American national holiday to enter the embassy. Then there would be less risk that a communicator might pay an unannounced visit to the CPU at night.

The NIS felt the KGB would not take such a risk. But the KGB took risks like that all the time. If caught, the KGB officers would pretend to be ordinary thieves. Ilya Dzhirkvelov, the KGB defector, had been prepared to say he was a burglar if caught breaking into the Turkish embassy. When FBI agents broke into embassies in Washington in the early 1960s, they were ready to make the same claim if necessary.[35] Then there was the possibility that the KGB would simply shoot its way out to avoid being caught.

Unlike the NIS, the FBI was familiar with the way the KGB operated and came to a totally different conclusion. Initially, the FBI assigned Michael Giglia, a gregarious counterintelligence agent from headquarters, to act as liaison with the NIS. Prodded by Senator Ernest F. Hollings, the South Carolina Democrat, the FBI in May 1987 began its own investigation of civilians assigned to the embassy.[36] Giglia then became its headquarters supervisor while continuing to act as liaison with the NIS.

The investigation was conducted by the CI-6 counterintelligence squad in the Washington field office, one of two squads that arrested John Walker. Normally, CI-6 is one of two thirty-member squads that track GRU intelligence officers in Washington. Because of the importance of the case, the FBI temporarily assigned the squad to conduct the investigation. Under the direction of the squad, sought to determine if any CIA, NSA, or State Department personnel had committed espionage.[37] During the investigation, the FBI interviewed 15 percent of the 1,200 people assigned since 1980 to the embassy in Moscow and the consulate in Leningrad.

In November 1987 the FBI sent five agents, including Giglia and James L. Kolouch, one of two agents who arrested John Walker, to Moscow and Leningrad to examine the embassy and consulate and take photographs. After two weeks, the agents concluded that only the guard standing post number three was needed to let the KGB into the CPU at the Moscow embassy. In fact, the FBI decided that security was so lax that the KGB could have gotten into the CPU by simply distracting the attention of the Marine at post number three, possibly with a girl.

The FBI had done its homework. The NIS had not.


In my last interview with Bracy, I told him I did not believe his story about his relationship with Golotina. I enumerated the additional details Golnar Duchateau had given about Wright's entry into the Duchateau's apartment: the sexual noises he heard; the bedroom door slamming; the vacuum cleaner going on; and Bracy coming out of the bedroom buttoning his clothing, looking embarrassed, and saying he had been inspecting the apartment.

Bracy chose to focus on the question of whether he was buttoning his clothes. He said he was wearing a baseball uniform which had no buttons.

"I had on a sweatshirt under a softball shirt," he said. "Either you're dressed or not. How can you hear noises if a door slams? I don't know. Like I say, I don't lose no sleep about it."[38]

I mentioned Golotina's statement that Bracy came over occasionally to show her videotapes. Bracy again suggested that she might be saying that for "political" reasons. But when I explained that the Soviets had every reason to minimize what had happened, he agreed.

Bracy said he would not have gone to the apartment regularly because he did not know when Golnar Duchateau worked.

"I never understood why I'd be going over there more than that time," he said tentatively.

Could he have been having sex with Golotina while Golnar Duchateau was working and her daughter was going to nursery school?

"I thought she was a housewife," he said, contradicting what he had said earlier about her work hours.

"You don't seem to be able to keep your own story straight," I told him.

Bracy said it was hard to remember what happened two years ago. "They asked did you do this and did you do that," he said, referring to the NIS agents. "I told them what happened: nothing happened. If they don't want to believe me, they don't have to."

I told him that my first problem with his story was that he told me he had been talking with Golotina in the living room when the Wrights came in. Then I learned from others he was in the bedroom with her.

Like a kaleidoscope, it seemed Bracy changed his story every time I asked a question. Now he said he talked with the Wrights in the living room after they found him and Golotina together in the bedroom. As for the question of what Golotina was holding as she came out of the bedroom, Bracy said it was a highchair, not a vacuum cleaner as Wright had said.

Why would she be holding a highchair if she wasn't supposed to be in the apartment? Displaying his facility at deflecting difficult questions, Bracy said, "That didn't come out until later, that she wasn't supposed to be there."

I told him flatly I did not believe him—that there were too

many irreconcilable conflicts in his story and that his story changed all the time.

"Everyone is entitled to his opinion," he said. "You write what you want to write. You've got to make your book interesting, I can understand that. But as for me saying I had sex with this woman when I didn't, that's not going to happen. Because of what Mrs. Duchateau said she heard from the Wrights? These people [the Wrights] won't say what they heard because they still want to work there [in the Soviet Union]? Come on."

Bracy had conveniently overlooked the fact that Wright had given the same version of events directly in his interview with ABC-TV.

His story was unlikely on the face of it. Why would anyone go to someone's apartment to say he would not see the person?

"Like I said," Bracy said, "I didn't know what it was about until I got there." Earlier, he had told me he knew why Golotina wanted to see him: the KGB was pressuring her to compromise him.

"Are you saying to me she and I were running around for months?" Bracy asked.

Yes, I said, and I mentioned his story—later retracted—that he had started having sex with Golotina in January 1986, at the apartment of the embassy's Air Force attaché. Adroitly sidestepping the issue, Bracy asked why the NIS did not include that incident in the statement he signed. Instead, he said, the NIS included it in a report on his interview. One of the agents had told me he simply forgot to include it in the statement.

Now I brought up Bracy's admission that he helped Lonetree let the KGB into the CPU and the other secure areas of the embassy. I told him I felt his admission was true except that Lonetree was not involved with him.

Bracy said that based on what he had been told, the CPU had been shipped back to Washington and no bugs were found. He then mentioned that the NIS did not know what questions to ask and had incorrectly assumed that he and Lonetree were close— another irrelevancy.

"Come on," he said. "I'm really tired of the whole thing. I think you're the only person kicking this thing still and keeping it alive."

I mentioned that two people had verified that Williams told them Bracy had admitted he was into spying. He asked why they had not come forward earlier. "You don't protect someone for espionage," he said. "It never happened with Lonetree or anybody else. I always thought it wouldn't work because of the way the security system worked."

I told him I hadn't expected to come to this conclusion. Ultimately, there is no credible way to explain why he would admit to espionage unless he had been tortured or were guilty.

"I didn't let anybody in the building," he said. "You're going to believe what you're going to believe, and as long as you have your facts straight, you don't have anything to worry about. If I did anything, I'd be in the brig like Lonetree. I'm out of the brig, so it didn't happen."

I thought about the NIS's frantic rush to interview Bracy. I also thought about the NIS case agent's claim that there was nothing more to find out about Bracy before interviewing him. If the NIS had learned how the embassy worked and had interviewed Duchateau before talking with Bracy, the agents might have been able to home in on Bracy's story enough so that they later could have corroborated his confession. If the agents had not been so gleeful at the conclusion of his confession, Bracy might have kept talking.

Now Bracy had a simple explanation for it all: he was not in the brig; therefore, it didn't happen.

# CHAPTER 19

# Russian Posters

BRACY'S CONFESSION ignited a firestorm in Washington. Now it seemed there was no question the KGB had gotten into the jewels at Moscow station. There was only one problem: Bracy had recanted. Nor was there any corroboration for his story. But that did not deter the NIS, despite his retraction, from trumpeting Bracy's confession all over town. Soon the press began running the same incomplete version of events.

The Marines announced Bracy's arrest with a short press release on March 24, 1987. The release said Bracy was suspected of espionage but gave no further details.[1] The story ran only five inches on page A-11 of the *Washington Post*.

Two days later the Marines followed that with a more detailed press release announcing that additional charges had been filed against Lonetree. According to the new charges, Lonetree let the Soviets into the CPU and other sensitive areas of the embassy while Bracy acted as lookout. The new charges were based solely on Bracy's confession. Nowhere did the press release mention that he had retracted that confession.

Suddenly the Marine security guard scandal was front-page news.

"Severe Security Breach Alleged; Two Guards Accused of Letting Soviets See Secret Areas of Embassy," said the lead story in the *Washington Post* of March 28, 1987. Then Defense Secretary Caspar W. Weinberger said the U.S. had, the same day, suffered a "very great loss."[2] From there, the scandal escalated.

On March 30, 1987, the Marine Corps announced that it was replacing all twenty-eight guards then at the Moscow embassy. A few weeks later, the Marines replaced all the guards in Leningrad. Just as the Marines had placed Bracy in the same cell block with Lonetree, the Marines returned all the Moscow guards to the same detail at Quantico, where they were told to pick up cigarette butts and empty garbage cans.

If any of the other Marines had been involved in espionage, it was a perfect way to make sure they got their cover stories straight. But it was more convenient for the Marine Corps to have all the former Moscow Marines together, just as it was more convenient to send inexperienced Marine security guards to Moscow. Meanwhile, Marine headquarters ordered the returning Marines not to talk to the press "until further notice."[3]

Expanding on his previous comment, Weinberger said Soviet espionage operations within the embassy had been "massive." He compared them to "Iran's actions in seizing our embassy in Teheran."[4]

Saying he was "deeply concerned over the breach of security in our Moscow embassy," President Reagan took the opportunity to focus attention on the new embassy, which he said might have to be torn down if it could not be protected from Soviet eavesdropping.[5]

With George Shultz scheduled to visit Moscow in April to discuss an arms agreement, Georgi Arbatov, director of Moscow's Institute for U.S. and Canadian Studies and a chief Soviet spokesman, said the U.S. was trying to create imaginary problems before the meeting. Even though Lonetree had been arrested four months earlier, he complained, details were only now coming out.

"It is absolutely obvious that there are rather influential people—groups, maybe institutions—that are against any normalization of relations between the United States and the Soviet Union," he charged.[6]

Meanwhile, Representative Daniel A. Mica, a Florida Democrat, and Representative Olympia J. Snowe, a Maine Republican, flew to Moscow and held a press conference to call attention to the security problems at the embassy. This infuriated State Department officials.[7]

The NIS formed what became known as the Bobsled task force, widening the probe to other Soviet-bloc countries. McCullah, who had headed Directorate Twenty-two, became director of the task force. The task force took separate offices on the fifth floor of an office building on deserted Buzzard's Point, where the FBI's Washington field office also has its quarters. As his deputy, McCullah chose Goethe W. (Bud) Aldridge, a seasoned, white-haired NIS agent. Eventually, the task force consisted of more than 100 agents and support personnel.

For the Marines, the blow that hurt most was the cover of *Time* on April 20, 1987. It showed a Marine with a black eye.

Now that the NIS thought it was onto one of the biggest espionage cases in history, the agency became almost hysterical. On March 27, 1987, Angelic White, the agent in charge of the Lonetree case, issued a shrill cable to agents working on the case:

President Regan [*sic*] has been briefed on this case, expressed concern, and requested frequent updates. As such, this investigation takes priority over any matter now being handled by NIS and must be responded to accordingly.[8]

Misidentifying Golotina as a KGB officer, White recounted Bracy's confession.

"It is assumed all safes, communications channels, and spaces have been compromised since their [Bracy's and Lonetree's] espionage activities began," White said. The cable also said Bracy's statements are "valuable in corroborating charges against subj [Lonetree]."

Nowhere did the cable mention that Bracy had retracted his statement and that Bracy therefore had corroborated nothing. Nor did it mention that Lonetree's statement had already been corroborated. Instead, buried in the middle of the second page, was a fainthearted disclaimer that Bracy is "now claiming he was coerced into making his statements."

To this day, the NIS, in its internal communications, refers interchangeably to statements that have been retracted and those that have not as if they had equal weight. Even an internal NIS chronology of the Lonetree case makes no distinction between facts that have been verified and retracted claims.

In this Alice-in-Wonderland atmosphere, no one in the NIS had a clear idea of what was fact and what was rumor, suspicion, or falsehood.

Having bungled the Lonetree and Bracy investigations through their own impatience, NIS officials had an obligation to warn the agents of the previous mistakes and advise them to prepare for interviews more carefully in the future. Instead, White's cable patted the agents on the back for a job well done and turned up the heat even more.

"Investigative strides in this case are being made due to the excellent work being conducted by NIS agents worldwide," the cable said. Ever mindful that the NIS's image suffered by comparison with the FBI's, Agent White boasted that the NIS was in charge of the case. "The prosecution of this case is still within the exclusive jurisdiction of NIS and the USMC: Dept. of Justice is not involved," the cable said.

As if the country were at war, the cable warned:

Under normal circumstances, a suspect is not arrested until the bulk of the casework has been accomplished. However, in this case apprehensions were made upon termination of interrogations. With the case work and the 90-day trial deadline ahead, the final days before subj's trial are approaching and the urgency for corroboration is more critical than ever. Simultaneously, the clock is now ticking on time allotted until subj's [Bracy's] trial. Both could receive capital punishment for offenses committed after March 1986.

The cable instructed agents to conduct new interviews with people already interrogated and imposed even more severe time constraints than before:

All leads are to be completed and transmitted within 72 hours of receipt of lead. . . . 0022 [the counterintelligence directorate] should be notified immediately if an interview turns into an interrogation. Contact should be made while the interview is in progress, not, repeat, not after.

To get subjects to confess, successful FBI agents often spend weeks taking them out to lunch and dinner, making small talk, and getting the suspects to relax and trust the agents. By demanding that investigators call in while the interviews were going on, the NIS created so much pressure that agents were bound to use coercive tactics. NIS headquarters seemed to think that interviewing espionage suspects was like covering a fire for a wire service.

The cable concluded with a list of twenty rambling questions that the agents should ask during the interviews, including whether the subject knows "Slut Face." In its headlong rush, the NIS thought that Hartman or some other State Department employee had referred to Seina as "Slut Face." From that, the NIS jumped to the conclusion that she was commonly known by that nickname. In fact, Hartman had not referred to her that way. Given his diplomatic bearing, it was unlikely that the word "slut" even existed in Hartman's vocabulary. Instead, his characterization of Seina was that she was "inappropriate."[9] No one, least of all Hartman, had ever heard of her referred to as "Slut Face." Most likely, an NIS agent made it up. Nevertheless, White's cable attached great significance to the name.

"Do not mention that Violetta is 'Slut Face,'" the cable warned sternly. "Give the interviewee a chance to state who they think 'Slut Face' is."

"Good luck," the cable said.


The NIS agents who interviewed Bracy thought he had said something about Stufflebeam being involved with Soviet women. Nowhere in Bracy's statement or in the agents' reports does Stufflebeam's name appear, and the agents later had somewhat differing versions of what Bracy supposedly said.[10]

Five days after Bracy terminated the NIS interviews, NIS agents told Stufflebeam they wanted to interview him at Camp Pendleton in California, where he was now a Marine infantry platoon sergeant. Like the other Marines assigned to Moscow, Stufflebeam was shocked at the spy allegations he had been reading about. As the former assistant detachment commander, he thought the NIS agents would want to ask him about the other Marines and the security procedures at the embassy.

Like most of the Marines, he thought of NIS agents as

authority figures. Like his commanders, they were to be respected and obeyed. Without first consulting a lawyer, he readily agreed to talk with them.

Embry began interviewing Stufflebeam on March 26, 1987. It quickly became clear that Embry was more interested in him than in getting help with the investigation. Embry asked him if he had fraternized with Soviet women. He said he had not.

That night, Embry asked for Stufflebeam's permission to search his room and his Jeep. Again, Stufflebeam consented. The NIS agents found two newspapers published by the Communist Party—papers Stufflebeam had purchased out of curiosity. Then they found even more ominous material—Victor Suvorov's *Inside Soviet Military Intelligence,* Karl Marx's *Das Kapital,* and *Socialism for Beginners.* They seized the publications as evidence—of what it is not clear. If the agents had been well-informed on counterintelligence matters, they would have had similar publications in their own homes.

The next day NIS polygraphers Pender and Hurt joined Embry. Why did Stufflebeam have the publications? they wanted to know. It seemed to Stufflebeam it was beyond the agents' comprehension that a Marine could be interested in reading anything other than comic books.

"I said I'm interested in political science and other ideologies," Stufflebeam told me. "They said, 'Well, not me. They tell me what I have to fight for, and that's all I need to know.'"

The agents also wanted to know about a check they had found. It was made out to Bracy from Stufflebeam. Stufflebeam explained that he had supplied the embassy with Marines who cleaned the secure floors in their off-hours. The check was payment for Bracy's work. The agents weren't so sure.

Before the agents strapped Stufflebeam to the polygraph machine, he admitted he had gone to off-limits bars and had had sex with prostitutes who were possible Soviets.[11] Normally high-strung, Stufflebeam felt the agents were being accusatory. He began failing all the questions—including whether the KGB recruited him in Africa before he was sent to Moscow.[12] As the questioning became more confrontational, the agents accused Stufflebeam of being an "ideological Communist."

Polygraph machines are only as good as their operators, which is one reason their results are inadmissible in court. If subjects sense that the operators are not objectively trying to get at the truth, or have already arrived at conclusions, they become apprehensive.[13] On a polygraph machine, apprehension translates to deception. Instead of using the polygraph as an investigative tool to help in eliciting information, the agents were relying on the machine as if it actually could detect lies.

"If a guy has a lot of respect for law enforcement and they jerk him around, he could become apprehensive and fail the test," said a senior FBI polygraph examiner. "You can't rely on it [the polygraph] totally. You have to have additional facts."[14]

Based on the polygraph results and little else, the agents decided Stufflebeam was a spy. Later, NIS headquarters, which tended to be even more suspicious than the agents in the field, embellished what the agents found and decided that Stufflebeam was the ringleader of a nest of spies.[15] The NIS bolstered that conclusion with a series of unfounded assumptions.

First, NIS headquarters insisted that two or even three Marine security guards were needed to let the KGB into the CPU. Second, the NIS figured someone had to arrange the guard schedules so that the Marines involved in the conspiracy were standing the sensitive posts at the same time. Third, the NIS did not think Bracy and Lonetree were smart enough to pull such a conspiracy off by themselves. Someone had to mastermind it. As assistant detachment commander, Stufflebeam made up the guard schedule, so logically he was the mastermind.

It was that simple—and that tragic.

The assumptions were as far off base as the NIS's conclusion that Daniloff was working for the CIA. People not familiar with the Moscow embassy always pictured it as more secure than it was. The fact is, one guard—no matter how dumb—could have let the KGB in. There was no need to rearrange guard schedules; they were constantly changing. At one point or another, each Marine in the detachment stood guard with every other Marine.

In its race for glory, the NIS overlooked two facts. One was that Stufflebeam, along with Wingate, recommended Lonetree's removal from the Marine security guard program in September

1986, well before Lonetree began seeing Seina. If Company A
had taken his advice, Lonetree would not have been in Moscow
when he began committing espionage. Stufflebeam would have
been a mastermind without his key spy. The second fact was that
Stufflebeam scheduled Lonetree and Bracy to work together at
the sensitive posts only twice. Both occasions were well before
Lonetree and Bracy began dealing with any Soviets. If Stufflebeam were the mastermind, he was not very good at it.

Never mind that each fact, taken separately, was enough to
puncture the NIS's conspiracy theories. Its agents were determined to become the Sam Spades of the espionage trade. So
wedded was the NIS to its Stufflebeam-as-master-spy theory that
it perceived the fact that he was hard on Lonetree as further
evidence of a plot. In the view of the NIS, Stufflebeam was trying
to throw off suspicion by seeming to be hard on him. Or perhaps
he was being hard on him to drive him to become a spy.[16]


Now that the agents at Camp Pendleton were sure Stufflebeam
was guilty, they decided that the Soviet Stufflebeam mentioned as
his language tutor was his KGB handler. She was blond and
good-looking—enough to make anyone suspicious. Moreover,
Stufflebeam had recommended her as a language teacher to
Lonetree—reason enough to conclude that she was their go-
between.

When Stufflebeam told them he planned to apply someday to
the FBI or CIA, they knew they had hit pay dirt. Later, NIS
headquarters found he had applied for a Soviet-bloc assignment.
Headquarters also learned he had wanted to go to language
school and become a Marine translator. Because the Marines
needed Stufflebeam's specialty, which was the infantry, he had
been turned down. Stufflebeam had thought that going to a
Soviet-bloc country would give him added foreign language
experience that would help him get into the program.[17] To NIS
headquarters officials, however, it was further evidence that he
was a Soviet mole.

The NIS's conspiracy theories would have been laughable if
they were not so damaging. Their approach gave new meaning to

the phrase "Keystone Kops." Nor was their approach to Stufflebeam an aberration. Throughout the investigation of the
Marine security guards, the NIS latched onto Russian posters on
the Marines' walls, books on intelligence, a desire to get into
intelligence work, or a Soviet-bloc family background as evidence
of something sinister. Yet the reason the Marine security guards
had gotten into so much trouble in Moscow was that they had not
read enough books about the KGB and intelligence.

If one were to look at the world through NIS eyes, Murat
Natirboff, then the CIA station chief in Moscow, was suspect
because his parents were born in the Soviet Union. Donald
Stukey, the chief of the Soviet section of the FBI's intelligence
division, was suspect because he decorated his office at FBI
headquarters with Russian flags. CIA officers and FBI counterintelligence agents were suspect because of their interest in intelligence work.

The NIS's misdirected focus was a natural outgrowth of the
agency's lack of competence. It is so much easier to seize Russian
posters and intelligence books as evidence than to do the hard
investigative and cerebral work necessary to bring about a successful espionage conviction.

Recognizing that he was getting nowhere, Stufflebeam became
increasingly exasperated during the four days of interrogation.
At one point, one of the NIS agents slapped him on the knee.

"Don't you ever touch me again," Stufflebeam said coldly.[18]

One of the agents told me the other agent slapped him "to
emphasize what he was saying."[19] The other agent said he patted
Stufflebeam on the knee in friendly fashion, saying, "Hey!
Relax!"[20]

At the end of the interviews, other NIS agents took Stufflebeam in custody. They were sure he had done something, even
if it was not clear what it was. After the NIS told the Marine Corps
about his admissions, the Marines charged him with fraternizing
with Soviets and going to off-limits bars. Yet, since they didn't
carry around their birth certificates, no one knows to this day if
the women Stufflebeam had sex with were Soviets.

For this, the Marines flew Stufflebeam across the country in
shackles and handcuffs to the maximum-security section of the

brig at Quantico, where Bracy and Lonetree were incarcerated. NIS headquarters remains convinced Stufflebeam was a master spy who directed the entire operation.

"Stufflebeam asked for bloc assignments," a senior NIS official told me. "He had trouble on the polygraph on whether he was recruited in 1985," he said. "Stufflebeam had a [Soviet] language instructor who was seeing him for lessons. Stufflebeam rode Lonetree's ass. Shortly after that, he met Violetta. Is he a good NCO or did he spot him and assess him as being susceptible to recruitment?"

Then the final nail in Stufflebeam's coffin:

"Lonetree was told if he got in trouble they [the Soviets] would know. How would they know unless they had someone inside. Was he [Stufflebeam] a sleeper?" the NIS official asked rhetorically.[21]

Stufflebeam had become caught up in a web of nonsense. He never got over the sense of hurt, anger, frustration, and sorrow he felt because the NIS had accused him unfairly. I interviewed him more than a dozen times over many months. Unlike Bracy, he was totally believable—a Marine who looked me straight in the eye, answered fully every question I had, and was willing to show me any record I wanted to see.

Each time he talked about what had happened to him, Stufflebeam choked up. From the best Marine in the Moscow detachment with a good future ahead of him, he had become a pariah. As the NIS quietly let the word slip that he was dirty, the Marine Corps slammed every door in his face, even barring him after he had been freed from setting foot in the Marine security guard school at Marshall Hall.

Having recommended Lonetree's removal before he began spying, Stufflebeam should have been considered one of the heroes of Moscow station. Instead, he was considered a traitor. But the NIS was not interested in hearing anything that might detract from its paranoid theories. When I asked one of the agents who had interviewed Stufflebeam if he knew that Stufflebeam had recommended Lonetree's removal, he said he did not. He then changed the subject.[22]

One of the NIS agents said the Marine Corps jumped the gun

by insisting on jailing Stufflebeam and Bracy before enough evidence had been gathered. While admitting that "there were a lot of flaws in our investigation," the agent said, "I think we allowed the Marine Corps to interfere too much in the actual investigation. We should have had the intestinal fortitude to resist that pressure."[23]

But that was another smoke screen. It was the NIS that conveyed the information on the cases to the Marine Corps. It was also the NIS that arrested the Marines. If the NIS had made it clear there was no reason to place the two suspects in the brig and that filing charges against them would interfere with the cases, the Marine Corps would have backed off.

On March 31, 1987, the Marine Corps issued a press release saying Stufflebeam had been "identified as a possible suspect in the ongoing NIS investigation of Marine security guards in Moscow."[24] Even though the spy case against him was never brought, much less proven, his name thus became inextricably intertwined in newspapers around the world with the Moscow espionage scandal.

# CHAPTER 20

# "A Witch-Hunt"

Now THAT the Naval Investigative Service's Bobsled task force had turned up the pressure, NIS agents began badgering Marine security guards all over the world. The agents would round them up, herd them into a bare room, hook them up to lie-detector machines, and ask with varying degrees of aggressiveness what happened at Moscow station.

To get them to talk, many of the agents told the Marines they were not interested in pursuing minor infractions like fraternizing or black-marketeering. The Marines would then admit to these violations. Then the agents would use the admissions as levers to pry information from them about Bracy and Lonetree. Later, the Marine Corps took the admissions of minor infractions and brought charges against the Marines.

The approach was all wrong. The way to find out about espionage was not to threaten them but to solicit their cooperation or, after the facts were known, offer the lesser figures immunity from prosecution. Thanks to the Marine Corps's policy of keeping the Moscow Marines together, word of the NIS's tactics quickly spread, and many refused to talk. While it was true that the Marines protected their own, the methods used by the NIS only led to misinformation and retractions.

Instead of developing espionage cases, the NIS was left with endless cases of fraternizing and black-marketeering that were by now beside the point. Those few interrogations that brought out allegations of espionage tended to collapse as soon as the Marines left the interrogation rooms.

Staff Sergeant Vincent O. Downes's experience was typical. Downes had replaced Stufflebeam as assistant detachment commander in Moscow. Like most of the Marines stationed in Moscow, he had something to hide. He had picked up the female hitchhiker who said she was German but was most likely a Soviet. He and another Marine had had sex with her. Downes also took a girl to his room at the Marine House on New Year's Eve in 1985.

NIS agents interviewed Downes at the Navy Yard in Washington. When Downes told them he knew nothing about Bracy's espionage, they told him his military career would be over if he did not come clean.

"They told me that my life would never be the same because they would open a file on me called the 'Person of Particular Interest' file," Downes said.[1] "They told me that someone would always be looking into my life—if not the NIS, then the FBI."

One agent pointed to an article in a newspaper about Bracy. Throwing the paper in his face, the agent said, "You're responsible for this. You don't want to talk about it, and people are being killed."[2]

After days of tiring interrogations punctuated by polygraph tests that he repeatedly failed, Downes said Bracy had told him that he met with Golotina and a KGB colonel in an apartment and had given the KGB officer floor plans to the embassy.[3] He also said Bracy told him he let the Soviets into the embassy.[4]

The day after signing the last statement, Downes saw a military lawyer and retracted his statements.

Like Stufflebeam, I found Downes to be very believable. But in several interviews with him, I noticed that he sometimes became confused about where and when he had learned information about Bracy. As assistant detachment commander at the time, he had prepared the reports on Bracy's removal from post. He therefore knew a lot about the case. He seemed to have trouble keeping straight what he learned from typing the reports and what Bracy may have told him earlier. That confusion would have been enough to account for some of the statements he made and later retracted about Bracy. Beyond that, as he told me, he succumbed to pressure, threats, and his own weariness.[5]

"After being totally confused and these guys lying to us, with no support from the Marine Corps, I became mentally fatigued and signed the statements," he said.[6]

Corporal Robert J. Williams told a similar tale about his interrogation by NIS agents in Vienna. He was the Marine who talked with Bracy in his room just before Bracy was removed from the Moscow post. He also rode with Bracy to the airport.

According to Williams, the NIS agents told him that Bracy had implicated him. They then used that to try to get him to implicate Bracy. He said the agents told him he was withholding evidence and therefore was just as guilty as Lonetree and Bracy.

"One day I told them, 'I'm tired, and I want to go home,' " he told me. "They said, 'Well, you walk out that door right now, and you are going to get relieved off the program.' "[7]

At another point one of the agents shook her finger in his face. He told the agent that if she ever put her hands in his face again, "That would be the last person to put her hands in my face."[8]

Williams said the agents told him the statement they wanted him to sign was " 'just for investigative purposes. You don't have to testify,' " he said.[9] "I finally agreed to it [the statement] because I just didn't want to be bothered anymore and I was tired," he told me.[10] The statement said Bracy told him that the KGB had given him $35,000 for spying. Williams said the NIS supplied the figure.

When Williams saw that the agents were sending the statement to an NIS office in Brasilia, where other Marines were about to be interviewed, he realized the information would be used after all. He then said he would not stand behind it.

"They thought I couldn't read that message," he said. "I read message traffic all the time."

Like Downes, Williams saw a military lawyer and retracted his statement. But in his case, several people say he made the same statements to them. He told his former girlfriend, "Don't tell anybody, but the day before we went to the airport, Arnold told me that he was doing that spy stuff."[11] He made similar statements to Lance Corporal Philip J. Sink, mentioning a payment of $1,000.[12]

The larger issue is not whether Williams was lying but the fact that the NIS created enough smoke to render all the statements from Marines suspect. The interrogations did nothing to advance the espionage cases or help determine what had really happened in Moscow, and they infringed on the Marines' rights as well. Having the NIS conduct espionage investigations was like asking department store security guards to solve murder cases.

Not every Marine fell for the NIS's tactics. Sergeant John A. Martinson, a Moscow Marine, consulted a military lawyer before he would agree to take a polygraph test.[13] Martinson told the lawyer, Major Richard (Rick) Walton, that he was afraid the Marine Corps would think he was unpatriotic if he did not agree to take the test. The lawyer showed him a pile of files on his desk. He pulled out one and said, "I'll show you what will happen if you're loyal and patriotic to the Marine Corps." He then displayed a list of charges against the Marine.

"I have eight clients who could get anything from 'office hours' to a court-martial," Walton told him. "But there's one Marine who's going to walk out of here. He requested to talk to us." Martinson never took the test but was charged anyway with a minor infraction. Ultimately, the Marines did not press the charges.

When NIS agents interviewed Sergeant Todd Roen, another Moscow Marine, they tried to get him to talk about Bracy by making up stories about him, Roen said. They called Bracy "'a closet racist who hated white people,'" according to Roen. They said Bracy "'went out with white girls to get at white guys.' I knew it was a bunch of crap. They were trying to get me to say things. All it did was upset me and make me feel like not talking to them," Roen said.[14]

Before he took a polygraph test, Roen consulted with his father, who advised him to see a lawyer first. When he refused in Panama to take a polygraph test, Roen became "public enemy number one," he said. "I was their third man. They said they don't know why I would want to speak to a lawyer unless I was trying to hide something."

Because he would not take the test, the Marines returned Roen to Quantico along with some eighty other Moscow and Leningrad Marine security guards. There, the guards picked up trash from the lawn and bitched about the Marine Corps. Some of the Marines threatened others who had made statements against them, and one Marine had to be moved to a hotel for his own protection.[15]

During Roen's first two weeks at Quantico, the Marine security guard battalion refused to let Roen consult with his Marine lawyer, Major Walton.[16] The Marine Corps eventually charged Roen with minor infractions and reduced his pay and rank.

"These were not criminals," said Walton. "These were good guys who were superpatriotic Marines. They wanted to help their country. Instead, the Marine Corps turned against them."[17]

On April 8, 1987, the Marines announced that the NIS had arrested Sergeant John J. Weirick. Weirick had been removed from the Leningrad consulate for seeing a Soviet woman in 1982.[18] He also later admitted to black-marketeering in Leningrad. Apparently, the State Department and the Marine Corps thought fraternizing with a Soviet woman qualified him for a better assignment: they sent him to Rome to guard the embassy there.

Weirick was a big talker who remarked to someone in a bar that he had made a lot of money in Leningrad. This got back to the NIS, which began interrogating him.

Weirick described to me the usual NIS pressure tactics. He said he finally made up a story that he had had sex under a bridge with a Soviet woman. He told the NIS the KGB took photographs of the scene and that he later let the Soviets into the first and second floors of the consulate, which were not secure.

"At ten [at night], I said, 'You want a story? I'll tell you a stupid-ass story.' So I told them a story. And they believed it," he said.[19]

Because the military then had a two-year statute of limitations for espionage, the NIS referred his case to the Justice Department.[20] Weirick has not publicly retracted his statements.

If the NIS extracted any truth from these interrogations, it was a miracle. After spending an extra $1 million in Navy funds, the NIS knew little more about Bracy and Lonetree than when it started. Nor had its interrogations produced any new whiff of espionage, with one possible exception. That exception focused on Sergeant Albert D. Diekmann, who had been stationed in Bucharest.[21]

The NIS found out about Diekmann when a former Marine security guard in Bucharest admitted he had fraternized with Romanian women. Adding that others had done the same thing, the former guard named Diekmann. After checking with the State Department, the NIS found he had been removed from his post for fraternizing on August 20, 1985.[22] The State Department said it had no other information on him.

After he failed NIS lie-detector tests in the spring of 1987, Diekmann confessed that he had had a Romanian girlfriend who introduced him to her "uncle," possibly a Romanian intelligence officer. On several occasions, Diekmann became drunk with the "uncle." He said he may have given the man information from a document classified top secret, according to his statements.

Before Diekmann was transferred to Quito, the "uncle" set up meetings with him at his new post. Another man showed up at the meetings, but Diekmann told him he would not cooperate any further. The Romanian girlfriend then showed up with a baby at the embassy in Bucharest and claimed the baby was his. The Marine Corps sent him back to Quantico, where he was cleared of fraternizing.

Just as it had debriefed Bracy, the State Department debriefed Diekmann in 1985, and Diekmann admitted that he had had an affair with the Romanian girl and may have given away classified information to her "uncle." As in the Bracy case, the State Department sat on the information. Not until Diekmann told the NIS that the State Department had debriefed him did State finally turn over to the NIS the summary of the debriefing.

Because of the two-year statute of limitations then imposed by the Uniform Code of Military Justice, the NIS referred his case to the Justice Department for possible prosecution. After considering the case, Justice declined to prosecute because of lack of any corroboration for his admissions.

Now based at Twentynine Palms, California, Diekmann said

the one mistake he made was having an affair with a Romanian national. He said both the State Department and the NIS asked if he could have disclosed top-secret information to the girl's uncle, and when he said anything was possible, the agencies wrote that it had happened.

"I am not a traitor," he said. "I didn't betray anybody." He said the NIS turned his life upside down.

"I've been through too much, I've been harassed too much. . . . I've been treated wrong," he said. "You got to be there to understand the way it was. You get lonesome, get horny, and things happen. If they sent married Marines over there, there wouldn't be no goddamned problem."[23]

Almost as soon as the NIS learned about Lonetree's confession in Vienna, General P. X. Kelley, the Marine Corps commandant, issued orders to leave "no stone unturned, regardless of the consequences," to get to the bottom of the spy allegations.[24]

In part because the commandant is not supposed to influence legal decisions in the military, Kelley did not become actively involved in the Marine security guard cases. What he knew about them came almost entirely from the NIS. Like President Reagan, he seemed to have Teflon hands, managing to avoid any criticism by making forthright statements about the scandal.

"One of the reasons I was not reluctant at all to take the heat for this thing was the fact that this was good for the U.S.," he told me. "In this case, we could recognize what the KGB was, what they were doing, and take corrective action."

But the Marine Corps's legal apparatus, called the Judge Advocate Division, had a vested interest in retaining control over the cases. Even though the military has jurisdiction in military cases, the Justice Department may step in and preempt the Judge Advocate Division, particularly if civilian cases arise from the military investigation. Recognizing that Justice and the FBI could sweep all the cases away from the Marines, Colonel Michael E. Rich, the deputy director of the Judge Advocate Division, wrote a memo warning that if that were to happen, it would be a "politically unpalatable result."[25]

As Rich saw it, "If the FBI assumes investigative jurisdiction, we lose any ability to influence the scope and thrust of their investigation."

Rich proposed a joint task force consisting of the military and the Justice Department to "allow us this influence." Beyond controlling the cases, he said, including Justice would mean the military would get more help from the CIA. As it was, he wrote, "We still are not receiving the full cooperation of the CIA."

Kelley approved Rich's idea, as did James Webb, the new Navy secretary, and Caspar Weinberger, the secretary of defense. But the Justice Department wanted nothing to do with it.

Since shortly after the case had broken, John L. Martin, the chief of Justice's internal security section, and his staff had been reviewing the reports of the NIS investigations. Martin was distressed. By their nature, espionage cases are complex, usually involve large numbers of people, and require investigations of activities occurring outside the U.S. To Martin, it appeared the NIS investigation was being conducted more as an administrative or security inquiry into fraternization and sexual activities than as an espionage investigation aimed at prosecutions. There is a way to supervise and manage fast-breaking spy cases. The NIS did not know what it was. Nor, it seemed, did the NIS have the kind of leadership and investigative experience to learn how to do it.

Martin knew that very few investigators had the knowledge and experience necessary to make an espionage case that would withstand the scrutiny of a criminal trial. Yet the NIS had not consulted anyone with any experience in espionage investigations or prosecutions.

Since 1980, Martin had been the government's chief prosecutor of spies. During that time, the Justice Department had brought espionage indictments against thirty-eight defendants. Only one case had resulted in an acquittal. Moreover, there had been no charges in the press or in courts of cover-ups or sloppiness. Martin knew how difficult it was to rehabilitate cases that had not been properly investigated from the start. Martin had no intention of prosecuting a case like that.

The idea of a joint task force with the military held even less appeal for him. Reading between the lines, he saw in Colonel

Rich's memo an effort by the Department of the Navy to reap the glory for solving the cases while spreading the blame if they went awry. Moreover, Justice officials had instructed him not to become involved.

Despite the orders, Martin and John J. Dion, his chief assistant for espionage prosecutions, quietly helped the Marine prosecutors. Among other things, they recommended that the Marine Corps drop the charges that Lonetree made up his third confession, the one following the NIS's suggestion that he lie. They also put the prosecutors in touch with experts like John Barron, the author of *KGB Today*, and KGB defector Stanislav Levchenko, to give them insight into how the KGB works. At the same time, Martin would not take responsibility for the cases. The FBI's intelligence division, known as Division Five, also decided it would not become involved in any joint investigations with the NIS.

Martin's judgment that the cases were flimsy was soon borne out. On April 19, 1987, Williams retracted his statements against Bracy. The Marine Corps promptly charged him with making false statements.[26] On May 10, 1987, Bracy formally retracted his statements, saying they were coerced by the NIS. Five days later, the Marine Corps dropped those charges against Lonetree that were based on Bracy's confession. Finally, on June 12, the Marine Corps dropped espionage charges against Bracy. It was the lead story in *The New York Times*.

In recommending dismissal of the charges, Bracy's prosecutor, Major Charles A. Ryan, admitted there was no corroboration for his confession but said he still believed Bracy was guilty. Unless there was "significant coercion," he wrote in a memo, "there is no conceivable reason why any Marine would ever confess to a crime such as espionage unless he had actually engaged in this conduct against his country," he said. "There has not been the slightest evidence of coercion surrounding the taking of Corporal Bracy's confession. . . . The inescapable conclusion I am forced to draw is that Corporal Bracy was involved in espionage against the United States."[27]

With the help of Lieutenant Colonel Michael L. Powell, his aggressive military lawyer, Bracy began a series of public relations moves designed to highlight his innocence. On June 12, 1987, he held a press conference at the Quantico Marine base and charmed the press. Said one of his military lawyers, Captain Brendan B. Lynch, "Just to paraphrase Raymond Donovan [the former Labor secretary] last week when he was talking to the district attorney in New York, where does Corporal Bracy go—and I'd address this question to the NIS—where does Corporal Bracy go to get his good name, his good reputation in the Marine Corps, back?"[28]

A reporter asked if Bracy had confessed.

"No, sir," Bracy said.

"Well, what was it?" the reporter asked.

"It was a scenario, sir. It was a story that was cooked up."

"Who actually committed the crimes that you were charged with?" another reporter asked.

"Well, what I was charged with never happened, ma'am."

"How have your fellow Marines been dealing with you? Do they regard you with suspicion?" another asked.

"Well, I've been in the brig, sir," Bracy said to laughter. "Everybody wants to hear the sex scandal."

"No sex scandal at all, huh?" a reporter asked.

"No, ma'am. Not on my part, anyway," Bracy said to more laughter.


Red-faced, the NIS began a counteroffensive to convince congressional and administration officials that it knew what it was doing after all. The effort largely consisted of private briefings given to congressional committees and executive branch officials. The NIS selectively leaked details of ongoing investigations, criticized other agencies, and came across as good guys. The NIS was much better at public relations than criminal investigations, and the effort largely worked.

For example, on June 16, 1987, McKee, the NIS director, and McCullah, the head of the Bobsled task force, briefed the staffs of the Senate Select Committee on Intelligence and the House Committee on Intelligence.[29] McKee told the staff members the investigation was difficult because the crime had occurred in Soviet territory, and the NIS had to work "backwards" from a confession. Therefore, the NIS had not had time to develop the necessary background that would have helped to corroborate Lonetree's confession. This was something like a new millionaire complaining that he never learned how to work for a living because he had inherited all his money.

McKee criticized the Marine Corps for confining Lonetree immediately and the State Department for failing to notify the NIS in a timely fashion about its material on Bracy and Diekmann.

In this and other briefings, the NIS brought along impressive-looking statistics on the number of people interviewed and polygraphed. The briefing material said four Marine security guards had confessed, neglecting to point out that some of them had recanted. Ultimately, three of the four—Bracy, Weirick, and Diekmann—recanted.

The staff members of the intelligence committees expressed satisfaction with the briefing and suggested the NIS should do more to counter its bad image in the press. With the exception of Senator Hollings, no one in Congress took a serious interest in finding out what had happened. Violating the rights of Marines was not a politically sexy issue. Their parents had little clout back home, and when they wrote to members of Congress to complain, their staffs accepted the NIS and Marine Corps explanations.

As morale at Bobsled task force headquarters plummeted, a photograph of a homeless man warming himself over a grate appeared on a wall. Under it, someone had written "NIS Agent Basking in the Glow of Bobsled Investigation." NIS officials wove a protective cocoon around the agency by constantly sending messages of praise to the 170 NIS offices around the world.

"Our critics expect perfection, ignoring the realities of the imperfect world in which we are required to operate," Aldridge, the deputy director of the Bobsled task force, told NIS agents.[30] "We have been attacked by uninformed government officials, and all too often by the press. We will never still the critics, the sayers of doom, or the uninitiated. But we must, with resolve, stay our course and continue to strive for unqualified excellence."

Meanwhile, Rear Admiral John E. Gordon, a lawyer who had been deputy assistant secretary of defense for legislative affairs, became the new commander of the Naval Investigative and Security Service, which includes the NIS. Navy Secretary Webb told him to take a "hard look at everything" under his command and report in ninety days. Basing his conclusion on the NIS's own investigation of itself, Gordon pronounced the agency in fine shape.

The same pattern repeated itself all around town. The lack of cooperation and the outright warring that gave rise to the security breaches at the embassy now manifested themselves in internecine battles over who was at fault. Each of the agencies defended its own actions and pointed a finger in every other direction.

The problem, according to General Kelley, the Marine Corps commandant, was not that the Marines were sending single, innocent, inexperienced young men to do battle with highly professional KGB operatives. Rather, it was the deterioration in the "moral fiber" of Americans since the antiwar riots of the 1960s and the Watergate scandal of the 1970s.[31] At the heart of it all was the fact that half of all American mothers now work: "Children are not getting the upbringing we had," he pronounced.

In a memo, Colonel C. Sean Del Grosso, head of the Marine Security Guard Battalion, complained to Major General Carl E. Mundy, Jr., the Marine Corps director of operations, that the State Department was not getting its share of the blame.

"Public fixation, to include Marine alumni, is squarely on the Marine Corps and not the leadership responsibilities of State," Del Grosso told Mundy.[32] Nor did the public realize that the security program at the embassies was administered by the same people responsible for the new embassy construction "debacle." Del Grosso said State and the Marine Corps had never worked well together. He wrote that, as a rule, "cooperation is continually feigned (similar to the Navy–Marine Corps team) and none is intended; DOS [Department of State] does not see this enterprise as a joint venture, not even a junior partnership, and will always try to dominate the relationship; DOS views MSGs as hired hands and the lowest rung on the pecking order inherent to the country team.

"Since security and diplomacy, like oil and water, don't mix, the undersigned has carefully observed the DOS approach to security matters," he continued. "Their quintessential strategy has not been designed to identify problems and move quickly to fix them. Their overriding leitmotiv, rather, has been to deflect, buy time, and wait out the pressure. It is difficult to hurl a congressional lightning bolt at Jell-O.

"If this crisis can be viewed as a war, the Marine Corps is losing," he said. "We are ripping ourselves apart." But Del Grosso warned that the worst thing would be to disengage, signaling "to the Soviets the USMC has been wounded and is institutionally retrograding from the battlefield," he said.

When the NIS proposed expanding its probe into Soviet bloc embassies, Mundy observed, "It is time to tell NSIC [the command that includes the NIS] to kiss off. We have before commented—we will continue to comment—that this is a hare-brained witch-hunt without measurable purpose or hope of successful benefit to this nation."[33]

On another level, the agencies realized they needed to continue to deal with the people they were criticizing and issued public avowals of support.

"I want to say publicly that your Marine Corps is very appreciative of the tremendous effort and loyal support and plain hard work the NIS has done on our behalf," Lieutenant General Alfred Gray, who replaced Kelley, told a general officers meeting at the Pentagon.[34]

Brigadier General David M. Brahms, the judge advocate general of the Marine Corps, told his staff in a memo that they should refrain from participating in a new sport called "NIS bashing."

"As all things—this too shall pass—and sooner rather than later, if you join me in setting the record straight whenever the base canard, 'NIS screwed up the Moscow/Leningrad cases,' is offered," he said. "This is in order not only because friends ought to stand by friends in times of trouble, but also as a matter of self-interest," he wrote.[35]

The NIS frantically solicited other statements of support from FBI and CIA officials, who told congressional committees in closed hearings that they knew of no flaws in the NIS investigation. Justice Department and FBI officials said privately that they had no choice but to support the NIS if they wanted to continue to do business with it. At the same time, the FBI did not itself examine the cases and therefore had little firsthand knowledge of them.

The General Accounting Office, meanwhile, issued an interim report saying it had "failed to uncover any notable problems in the quality of the investigation conducted by the NIS." It based this on talks with NIS officials and reviews of NIS case files. According to its report, the GAO had not talked with a single Marine interviewed by the NIS. It was then not surprising that the final report virtually exonerated the NIS of any culpability.[36] That report, dated July 28, 1988, said the NIS had conducted a "thorough and professional investigation, and evidence was found to indicate that the NIS was aware of the constitutional rights of the MSG's and took steps to protect them."

Finally, the State Department, while publicly taking much of the responsibility for what had happened, leaked stories minimizing the security breaches.

No one, it seemed, was interested in finding out what happened or why, much less in doing something about it.

# CHAPTER 21

# Indian Feathers

WILLIAM M. KUNSTLER'S RÉSUMÉ reads like a history of the civil rights and antiwar movements. Over the years, he has represented Dr. Martin Luther King, Jr., and Stokely Carmichael; Adam Clayton Powell and Daniel Berrigan; Abbie Hoffman and Bobbie Seale. He also represented a defendant in the Wounded Knee uprising, the last major Indian resistance to white settlement in America. Because of Kunstler's involvement in that case, Spencer Lonetree chose him to represent his son.

If Kunstler was the right man to defend political activists, he was the wrong man to defend a Marine charged with espionage. Lonetree was not seeking to overturn a discriminatory law or redirect U.S. foreign policy. Quite simply, he was horny and had fallen for the oldest trick in the KGB's book. The fact that he was an Indian had as much relevance to his crime as the race of a car thief. There was nothing appealing about his case or about him. Moreover, Lonetree had confessed, and his confession had been corroborated.

Under these circumstances, probably the best thing a lawyer could have done for Lonetree was strike a deal with the government. Lonetree had much to offer. The CIA wanted to know the details of what he had done and what the KGB was interested in. In return for a guilty plea, Lonetree could have gotten a lighter sentence. But to Kunstler, the Lonetree case was larger than life—another in a long procession of government abuses.

Despite his own impressive credentials from Yale University

and Columbia University School of Law, Kunstler saw himself as a foe of privilege. To him, the law was a tool used by the "haves" against the "have-nots." He favored a radical redistribution of the nation's wealth, although he was hazy on how that should be accomplished. Despite the Bronze Star he won as a major in the U.S. Army, Kunstler was not sure espionage was such a bad thing. Perhaps if both sides knew each other's secrets, we would not have wars, he told me in his Greenwich Village town house. In any case, he saw no reason to prosecute spies like John Walker when the makers of the Dalkon Shield were not prosecuted.[1]

Early on, Major David H. Henderson, Lonetree's military lawyer, wanted to negotiate a plea agreement for his client. Henderson was a slow-talking country boy from Oakland City, Oklahoma, who had lost two fingers while making a rolltop desk. A member of the Order of the Coif, which consists of the top 10 percent of law school graduates, he knew the law and he knew the military. To him, the best course was to plead Lonetree guilty. But Kunstler and Michael V. Stuhff, who had been chosen by Lonetree's mother to represent him, were determined to go to trial.

Like Kunstler, Stuhff saw the government as a predator. With Lake Headley, a chain-smoking, hard-bitten private investigator, Stuhff had won acquittals for several Indians charged with assault or murder. Stuhff was nothing if not tenacious. To defend Lonetree, he drew on a $10,000 line of credit from a local bank and even borrowed from his parents.

"It was because Sally [Lonetree's mother] asked me," Stuhff said in his Las Vegas office decorated with Indian carpets. "The kid wasn't going to get a defense otherwise."[2]

In retrospect, it was a wonder the three lawyers put together any defense at all, so different were their approaches.


There are some who say military justice is a contradiction in terms. That is probably unfair. Lawyers who have practiced in both systems say many aspects of the military system give clients more rights than the civilian system. The fact that sentences for the same offenses vary wildly within the civilian courts demonstrates that what counts most is the outlook of the individual rendering the verdict.

In the military, justice is administered by the office of the judge advocate. Like a full-service bank, it provides the judges, the prosecutors, and the defense lawyers who serve clients free of charge. The Marine Corps has 450 judge advocates, split about evenly between those who handle civil litigation and those assigned to military justice.[3]

The most important figure in the system is the commanding general of the base where the accused is stationed. Known as the convening authority, he decides whether charges shall be brought, whether they will be adjudicated in nonjudicial proceedings or in a court-martial, and whether the sentence ultimately imposed will be sustained. He also decides which type of court-martial to convene. A general court-martial can impose any punishment, including death. A special court-martial can confine the accused for up to six months and reduce his pay and rank. A summary court-martial deals only with minor offenses akin to misdemeanors in the civilian system.

In Lonetree's case, the process began when Lieutenant General Frank E. Petersen, Jr., then commander of the Quantico Marine base, convened an Article 32 investigation, or hearing. Named for the provision in the Uniform Code of Military Justice that prescribes its use, the Article 32 investigation serves the purposes of a preliminary hearing and a grand jury in the civilian system. It differs from its civilian counterparts in that it is usually open to the public. In addition, the defense may call and cross-examine the government's witnesses and discover its evidence. During cross-examination, the defense can uncover weaknesses in the government's case and lock witnesses into their stories, then look for ways to rebut their versions. In the civilian system, such probing must wait until a trial.

The investigating officer who presided over Lonetree's Article 32 hearing found there was probable cause to prosecute him. Petersen then convened a general court-martial, which is the trial, and chose the jurors, or members of the court. While at least five must serve, Petersen chose eight jurors. Unlike the civilian system, which requires twelve jurors and a unanimous verdict, only a two-thirds majority is needed to convict in the military system.

Lonetree's trial began at 9:28 A.M. on July 22, 1987, in LeJeune Hall at the Quantico Marine base. Named for General John A. LeJeune, a revered former Marine commandant, the red-brick building houses Petersen's offices as well as the courtrooms.

Kunstler and Lonetree's relatives immediately established a circus atmosphere. His mother, grandmother, and an aunt carried eagle feathers and Indian spiritual symbols. Outside the court, Indians demonstrated against the proceedings.

Kunstler, meanwhile, took advantage of breaks in the proceedings to hold press conferences and issue what he called "white papers"—newspaper op-ed pieces railing against the tyranny of the military system.

"As his civilian defense team, we feel utterly compelled to publicize the savagery that is being practiced upon him in a Mephistophelian effort to ensure that he is convicted," one such "white paper" said.[4]

In his opening statement, Major David L. Beck, the chief prosecutor, referred to attempts to divert attention from the central issue, which was Lonetree's crime. "Whatever the motive this accused had . . . whatever the defense might try to establish concerning what other Marines or other organizations could or should have done about security, I would ask you on behalf of the government, gentlemen, to ignore any smoke screens which the defense may try to fill up this courtroom with, or divert your attention from what the evidence will show is the obvious fact of this accused's guilt."[5]

In his opening statement, Stuhff tried to win sympathy for his client. He referred to his family's tradition of military service, the fact that his father had pushed him beyond his capabilities, his tendency to be swayed by authority figures, and the abysmal state of security at the embassy.

"Lonetree did make a very serious mistake," he conceded. "He thought he could match wits with the KGB in a one-on-one situation. He thought he could match Sasha on his own terms."

It was not an argument that would sit well with any American, let alone a Marine.

Recognizing that Lonetree had a tendency to blurt things out and would not come across well, Kunstler and Stuhff elected not to have him take the stand.[6] As it turned out, they also called no witnesses. They had wanted to call Philip B. Agee, a former CIA case officer who published a book listing names of several hundred CIA officers, agents, and organizations. The idea was to show that names of CIA officers were publicized all the time.[7] The judge in the case, Navy captain Philip F. Roberts, ruled that such testimony would be irrelevant. On the other hand, Roberts allowed as evidence Lonetree's notebook with his Nazi scribblings. Written when he was fifteen, it had as much relevance to the case as Agee's list of CIA officers.

The prosecutors called a string of witnesses, including John Barron, who testified about Soviet recruitment methods.

From the beginning, Kunstler and Stuhff pinned their hopes on mounting a successful appeal. The military has an elaborate review system that includes both civilian and military courts. If cases present constitutional issues, the U.S. Supreme Court may ultimately review them.[8]

Kunstler and Stuhff argued that the CIA had not warned Lonetree that what he said could be used against him. They objected as well to the testimony of an anonymous CIA officer who saw Lysov show up for the planned meetings with Lonetree in Vienna on December 27 and 30, 1986. Because the officer was in a covert capacity, the CIA did not want to reveal his identity or his background. Finally, the lawyers planned to appeal Roberts's ruling that they could not introduce testimony that would show the NIS pressured Lonetree and other Marines to make up stories.

While the objections highlighted serious problems in the way the government handled the case, most of them were not insurmountable from a legal point of view. Since the CIA is not a law-enforcement organization, it is not specifically required by law to warn suspects of their rights. Nor were any of Lonetree's statements to the CIA used in court. As for the NIS's tactics, Lonetree's lawyers could not show that they influenced the confessions at issue in his case. The only objection that had a chance was the use of an anonymous CIA witness. The CIA clung so fanatically to the principle of not revealing its officers' identities that it initially refused to let the man testify even anonymously.

The agency would have rather let a traitor go free than transfer one of its employees out of a covert capacity. Should an appeals court throw out Lonetree's conviction, the CIA would have to decide whether to reveal the witness's identity in a second trial.

The only other defense the lawyers raised was a halfhearted attempt to show that Lonetree was playing the role of double agent, pretending to spy for the Soviets but actually working for the U.S. government. Cross-examining Sean Byrnes, the embassy political officer, the lawyers tried to show that Byrnes must have known about Lonetree if he was meeting with Yefimov monthly.

The strategy didn't work.

After three hours of deliberations on August 21, 1987, the jurors found Lonetree guilty. In a separate proceeding three days later, they sentenced him to thirty years at hard labor. They also reduced his pay and rank and fined him $5,000. Finally, they ordered him discharged dishonorably from the Marine Corps when he completes his prison term.


With the trial over, disagreements among the unlikely mix of lawyers came to the surface. The catalyst was Lawrence D. Cohen, a former mayor of St. Paul who was Spencer Lonetree's lawyer. After watching their tactics and discussing the case with Henderson, he became troubled by Kunstler's and Stuhff's approach. While Cohen had no experience with the military system, he knew it was not smart to attack the judges and the legal system.

In effect, "Kunstler was attacking the virility of the Marine Corps. Bad strategy," Cohen said later.[9] "I see state courts screw up all the time, and I don't attack the court, the state of Minnesota, and all its police officers."

Cohen decided that Kunstler and Stuhff had not objectively evaluated the facts. If they had, they would have pleaded Lonetree guilty in return for a reduced sentence. Beyond that, Cohen felt the defense should have emphasized Lonetree's lack of intent—the fact that he did not set out to give away secrets and eventually turned himself in.

When, after the trial, Kunstler and Stuhff began pushing to have Lonetree appear with them on "60 Minutes," Cohen decided that enough was enough. To Kunstler, publicity about a case could overturn verdicts. To Cohen, it meant alienating those who rendered the verdicts. A straight-talking man who peppers his conversation with Yiddish phrases while puffing on Marlboro Light 100's, Cohen advised Lonetree against appearing.

Together with Henderson, Cohen recommended that Lonetree cooperate with the NIS by agreeing to be debriefed about his activities. In return, the Marine Corps would reduce his sentence by five years. By now, it was the only realistic way to help Lonetree, but Kunstler and Stuhff felt the reduction was not enough.

While Henderson and Cohen were objecting to the plan to put Lonetree on TV, Kunstler and Stuhff were objecting to their decision to let Lonetree cooperate with the NIS. Cohen thought Kunstler was more interested in attracting publicity than in helping his client.[10] Kunstler and Stuhff, meanwhile, thought the military was responsible for keeping Lonetree off TV and charged as much in an interview with *The New York Times*. The story quoted the lawyers as calling the offer of a reduction of five years from Lonetree's sentence "absurd."[11]

In a letter of complaint to General Petersen, Kunstler said there is "presently a plan afoot, engineered by the military, to prevent Sergeant Lonetree from appearing on the CBS network program '60 Minutes' in order to subvert the widespread dissemination of his side of the case.

"Sergeant Lonetree received an unfair and barbaric court-martial, followed by a Draconian sentence," Kunstler continued. "He has become the scapegoat for the Marines, NIS, the State Department, and the CIA. I felt that you, of all people, would not tolerate all of the above, so I am bringing it to your attention in the forlorn hope that you will take the necessary action to prevent any further erosion of Sergeant Lonetree's Fifth and Sixth Amendment rights."[12]

The phrase "you, of all people" was a not-so-thinly-disguised reference to the fact that General Petersen is black. To suggest that a three-star general would be swayed by such a crude reference to his race was laughable. Petersen had become one of the highest-ranking officers in the Marine Corps by being a good Marine, not a black man.

A week after Kunstler wrote his letter, Lonetree fired Kunstler and Stuhff. In a letter that Cohen drafted, Lonetree wrote to both of them, "My decision to terminate you is solely my own, as was the decision to not be interviewed by '60 Minutes.'" He added, "Both of you are instructed to not discuss any matters about my case with anyone."[13] Nonetheless, Stuhff announced his intention to write a book about the case. This touched off further discord among the lawyers.

Saying Lonetree had totally cooperated with government investigators since his sentencing, General Petersen in May 1988 reduced Lonetree's sentence to twenty-five years and lifted his $5,000 fine. He will become eligible for parole after serving a third of his sentence. Compared with espionage sentences in the civilian courts, it was a light sentence. Thomas P. Cavanagh, who offered to sell the plans for the Stealth bomber to the Soviets, was sentenced to two life prison terms, even though the FBI caught him before he gave away any secrets. On the other hand, Lonetree did not set out deliberately to sell secrets for cash, as Cavanagh had.[14]

Cohen is convinced that the sentence would have been even lower if Lonetree had cooperated from the beginning.

Even as he sat in the brig at Quantico because of the trap Violetta Seina had laid for him, Lonetree pined away for her. Insisting that he still loved her, he asked Cohen and his father to find her and tell her he was okay.

Having gone through a trial and 200 hours of debriefings by the NIS, Lonetree still did not seem to know what had happened to him. When Cohen told him he thought she had conned him, Lonetree said, "People who feel that way are entitled to their beliefs. But I believe she loves me."[15]

# CHAPTER 22

# A New Power Line

By the end of 1987 the State Department had begun leaking stories that no evidence of a penetration of the embassy in Moscow had been found.[1] The stories overlooked the fact that the KGB had penetrated the embassy by introducing bugged typewriters into secure areas and by obtaining a wealth of secret information about the embassy and its employees from Clayton Lonetree. Instead, the stories focused on the claims that Marines had let the KGB into the embassy.

Based on the information made available to the State Department and the press, the stories fairly summarized the situation. After all, the only publicly known allegation that the KGB entered the embassy had come from Arnold Bracy. Not only had he recanted, but so had two other Marines who had corroborated his story.

What the State Department and the press did not know is that evidence of a penetration *had* been found, but the CIA and NSA had covered it up.

In March 1987 the State Department shut down all secure communications with Moscow and Leningrad. Diplomats and CIA officers either flew to the U.S. or sent messages in diplomatic pouches. Meanwhile, NSA sent technicians to Moscow and Leningrad to go over every inch of their CPUs, looking for bugs. They found nothing.

Several months later, the State Department shipped the entire

CPU and all the communications equipment from both missions—120 crates from Moscow alone—to a secure building in Virginia. After the FBI took custody of the material, some twenty NSA technicians began examining each part using X-ray, spectroscopic, and infrared analysis.

In August 1987 the NSA made a chilling discovery. The power line to the CPU in Moscow had been replaced. The discovery meant the KGB could have diverted signals from cipher machines within the CPU to the outside. Next the NSA found that eight-by-fourteen-inch circuit boards, along with chips the size of quarters, had been replaced in the printers. The new components appeared to be diverting uncoded signals from the "red side" of the communications circuits to the power line, bypassing electronic filters that were supposed to trap any signals inside. In September 1987, NSA found similarly sinister devices in the CPU from Leningrad.

The KGB had turned the CPU into a gigantic listening device, just as it had turned the new embassy into a massive antenna. As in the bugs in the typewriters, the listening devices were so well concealed that it was almost impossible to find them, even if American technicians knew they were there.

Because the Soviets could compare the uncoded "red side" signals with the encoded "black side," they most likely could replicate the cipher keys—the unique data that was needed to decipher the messages—used by other American embassies throughout the world. That raised the possibility that the KGB had been listening in not only on communications from Moscow and Leningrad but also from Vienna, Helsinki, and London. Since equipment in the CPU had been replaced in 1984, the penetration of the jewels to Moscow station could have gone back that far.

Only a dozen people, including President Reagan, were told of the findings. But the truth began to leak out, and as it did, the CIA and NSA began issuing cover stories within the intelligence community. According to these versions, orchestrated by the CIA, the devices found in the CPU were "anomalies" that were still being studied and might turn out to be "benign." The CIA used the same language when it found bugs in the new embassy. Both agencies claimed some of the replacements might have been done legitimately by technicians repairing circuit boards. With a few exceptions, the agencies produced neither records nor individuals to show that the changes had been made legitimately. On the contrary, those in charge of the CPU said records had been kept of every authorized repair. To ensure secrecy, they were not told of the findings either.

Admittedly, determining how the Soviets had bugged the CPU was no easy task. If spread out, the various plans to each circuit board filled entire rooms. Moreover, a plastic spray used on the circuit boards to identify them as originals before they were installed was found to be unreliable. After examining samples of the plastic substance that seemed to vary from the original, the FBI laboratory concluded that the differences could have occurred because the spray can had not been shaken before the plastic was applied to the circuit boards. Just as the bugs found in the typewriters did not transmit unless triggered by the Soviets, the bugs in the CPU normally did not emit signals. In the case of the bugs in the new embassy, the CIA and the NSA to this day do not understand fully how the devices work. Yet suggesting that dozens of foreign objects found in the CPU could have gotten there legitimately was like saying a man with a knife in his back might have fallen on it.

The fact that any differences had been detected, or that the NSA was still studying those differences, was never disclosed to the State Department much less the press. Nor did the CIA and the NSA ever flatly tell the other intelligence agencies that no bugs had been found. Instead, the CIA and the NSA said that a dozen "anomalies" remained "unexplained" and would have to be studied for another year. Very few in the intelligence community knew that Vitaly Yurchenko had also reported that the KGB could read embassy communications.

In deciding to keep the findings secret, the CIA and NSA could always claim that there were legitimate national security reasons for doing so. Just as it initially put a clamp on its findings of bugs in the new embassy, the CIA could claim it was studying CPUs in other embassies to see if they were similarly bugged. The CIA could also claim it was considering introducing disinformation on the lines to fool the Soviets. In any case, the CIA always made it a practice to reveal nothing even if the Soviets knew all about it anyway.

To those few individuals with knowledge of the findings, the more important reason for the secrecy was embarrassment.

"There's a cover-up to hide embarrassment, to cover ass," said one intelligence official.

According to these sources, the result of the communications penetration was the decapitation of the CIA's operations in the Soviet Union. Beyond roll-ups of nearly a dozen CIA officers, at least twenty-five Soviets have been executed in the Soviet Union since 1984 on suspicion of collaborating with the CIA. At least ten of those executed were, in fact, Soviets working for the CIA. The rest were innocent.

While Edward Lee Howard, the CIA officer who defected to the Soviets, was responsible for several of the executions, he knew CIA agents only by their code names. Intelligence sources with knowledge of NSA's findings believe the majority of the damage to CIA operations was caused by a penetration of Moscow station communications.

In its report of its investigation of the security breaches, the FBI suggested how that could have happened. Because NSA said it would take another year to complete its report, the FBI had to rely primarily on the people it interviewed as part of its Power Curve investigation. The final report, completed in June 1988, ran to some 2,000 pages. Classified "sensitive compartmented information"—a level beyond "top secret"—the report was so sensitive that each copy randomly contained different wording. If a copy leaked out, it could be traced to the individual who had signed for it.

The FBI report enumerated dozens of instances of CIA, State Department, NSA, and military personnel engaging in prohibited activities, from black-marketeering to sleeping with Soviet women. It catalogued the security weaknesses at the embassy, the determined efforts of the KGB to penetrate it, and NSA's findings of unexplained "anomalies" within the CPU. While the report drew no conclusions, anyone reading it would conclude that the KGB probably entered the CPU and planted bugs. The report said a final determination would have to await NSA's findings—findings the CIA wanted kept secret.

While individuals could be disciplined by their agencies as a result of the FBI probe, no other action will be taken. Because the Naval Investigative Service so bungled the case, the Justice Department concluded that no successful prosecutions of either Marines or civilians could be mounted.

The same ineptitude that led to the security breaches in the first place now conspired to protect the perpetrators. Bracy, who probably was not the first Marine to let the KGB into the embassy, got off scot-free. As the scandal faded from the newspapers and the General Accounting Office said the NIS had done a good job overall, the cover-up became complete.

The CIA had no comment.


To get the Soviet side to the story, I decided I would try to interview the KGB while I was in Moscow in January 1988. And how does one interview the KGB? I knew of no better way than to knock on its door.

With my wife, Pamela Kessler, I took the subway to Dzerzhinsky Square, which is dominated by a statue of Felix Dzerzhinsky, the Soviet revolutionary leader and founder of the Soviet security police. KGB headquarters are at 2 Dzerzhinsky Square, but it was difficult to tell which streets corresponded with which numbers. Pointing to the most massive building in the square, I asked a taxi driver if that was KGB headquarters. He looked sheepishly at me and averted his eyes. When I asked again, he nodded ever so slightly—just enough to confirm that it was the place I was looking for without letting onlookers know he had done so.

We crossed the street to the gray, marble-trimmed building. On the front was a bas-relief of Yuri Andropov, who headed the KGB until he succeeded Leonid Brezhnev as chairman of the Communist Party in 1982. Clearly, this was the place. Yet there was nothing to indicate it was the headquarters of the combination CIA, FBI, NSA, and state police of the most security-conscious country in the world. Since it was a Saturday, no one was entering or leaving the building. The only sign of authority was a militiaman directing traffic in the square.

I knocked on the tall oak door. Nothing happened. I tried it, and it opened. Inside was an elegant scene—lush red carpeting, marble floors, a winding staircase, and massive crystal chandeliers. Instantly, three very tense, very surprised-looking uniformed KGB officers appeared. On their hats they wore the distinctive green bands that identified them as KGB officers. In my sparse Russian, I tried to explain that I wanted to deliver a letter. Addressed to Colonel Gennadi Ageev, deputy chairman of the Committee for State Security, or KGB, it asked for an interview. As I fumbled for it, the guards motioned for me to leave. With my wife, I quickly scurried out, only to be confronted at the front door by the traffic cop.

Having been summoned by radio, the militiaman wanted to know who I was. I told him I was a journalist and that I was seeking an interview with Ageev. He asked for my press credentials. I said I had none, since I wrote books. Instead, I showed him my passport. As he examined the photograph and compared it with my face, a second, sterner-looking officer appeared. He seemed to be a supervisor. He asked where I was staying. As he wrote down my room number and "National Hotel," another KGB officer appeared. Wearing a suit and an overcoat, he was bigger than the others and seemed much more polished. Even though he didn't appear to be able to speak English, it was clear he wanted us to go with him. I didn't know if I was to be arrested or was already under arrest. I had no choice but to follow him. We crossed the street and went around the corner to what appeared to be a KGB substation. Down a flight of stairs, we went into a small entryway where another uniformed KGB officer pointed to a wooden inner-office mailbox. I dropped the letter in the box. Marveling at how well coordinated the entire operation had been, I left.

That Monday, I called to request an interview with Gennadi I. Gerasimov, the chief spokesman for the Soviet Foreign Ministry. Gerasimov's one-liners enlivened television coverage of Mikhail Gorbachev's visit to Washington in December 1987 and President Reagan's visit to Moscow in June 1988. The next day, I met with Gerasimov in his mahogany-paneled office on the second floor of the Soviet Press Center. Gerasimov, who wore a red vest, was in a jocular frame of mind. Offering me coffee, he asked how the embassy scandal had started. Was it some kind of personal vendetta? I told him defectors had disclosed a penetration well before Lonetree confessed in Vienna.

"What do you mean, 'penetration'?" he asked. "Marines penetrated into our girls. This is real penetration. This was the real penetration. We didn't make a big fuss over it," he said.

"Penetration in the sense the KGB was allowed to run around and put bugs in the CPU," I said.

"In my view it's a real case of spy mania and personal vengeance," Gerasimov said. "It has nothing to do with our intelligence. That's my position."

Gerasimov said the Soviets have no problems at their embassies because they do not use Marines who are hungry for sex. "This is the problem. They have to have sex," he said.[2] He suggested the solution would be to teach the Marines to have sex by themselves. "Then our seducers would be unemployed," he said, a big smile on his face.

Because of the scandal, some traditional American phrases will have to be changed, he said. "You used to have 'a Red under every bed,' which is now obsolete," he said. "You must change it to 'a Red in every bed' to update the saying."

I mentioned the bugs that had been found in the embassy's typewriters, demonstrating that the KGB had previously penetrated the embassy.

"These are games some people play. In my view, the results approach zero," Gerasimov said. So far, he said, the Americans have yet to produce a single bug found in the new embassy, despite Soviet requests to do so. "It's just another example of spy mania," he said.

"I understand the Soviets intercepted and read all the secret communications into and out of the embassy," I said.

"And do you think it makes exciting reading?" he asked with aplomb. "It's very dull."

I asked about the roll-ups of CIA operatives and the twenty-five Soviets who had been executed. Looking shocked, he said he knew of no such number and said it was "highly improbable" anyone had been executed.

"Suppose Violetta had an affair," he said. "Why do you think it was a spy case? Maybe it was just a case of two consenting adults."

Noting that the Naval Investigative Service had pressured Marines, he said, "Shame on you; shame on your interrogators. What kind of a country is this? Is it a free country or some kind of a Stalinist regime over there?"

Gerasimov said he would look into the possibility of arranging an interview with Seina. "If she is not sleeping around somewhere then I can maybe find her. But if she is sleeping around in the Middle East somewhere, no."

Gerasimov gave me a lift back to my hotel in his chauffeured car. We chatted about his impressions of New York: "It's a hell of a town," he said. The next day I called him. His tone seemed colder. He said he could not locate Seina. I said I would like to interview the KGB instead.

"And how would one do that?" he asked. "Knock on their front door, perhaps?"

While I never got a response to my request for an interview, I did hear indirectly from the KGB. I was staying on the sixth floor of the National Hotel, but when I returned there the following day, I got off the elevator on the third floor to meet my wife in a tearoom. As I stepped out, a chunky-looking young Soviet woman asked if I was from the U.S. When I said I was, she said agitatedly, "You got off at the wrong floor—this isn't your floor."

After checking, I told her I had gotten off at the right floor. Clearly, she knew who I was. She then said she was a student who needed to buy some items in the souvenir shop downstairs for a class. Since the shop only takes "hard currency," she needed American dollars.

"I need five dollars. I will give you rubles," she said.

Recognizing it as an attempt to entrap me in a black-market transaction, I told her I could not help her. As she got back on the elevator, she turned to me and said, "You are right. There are many police informants in this hotel."

After spending months writing about entrapment of Marines by the KGB, I had become a target myself.

Today the embassy in Moscow is under the control of Jack F. Matlock, Jr. A short, balding man with a North Carolina accent, Matlock speaks Russian fluently and served three previous tours in Moscow in various capacities. Before becoming ambassador in 1987, he was special assistant to the President for national security affairs.

I interviewed Matlock in his office on the ninth floor of the embassy, just a few feet from the CPU. It became clear immediately that his attitude toward security is quite different from that of many of his predecessors. Matlock said he sees nothing wrong with helping to find bugs. He questions whether Marines should guard the embassy and is perfectly happy to be free of Soviet workers there.

"I certainly do not see finding bugs as inconsistent with my duties as a diplomat to take reasonable precautions to have private conversations," Matlock said. "One of the most fundamental rights under international law is the right to have confidential conversations with your government. I . . . think it's totally consistent with my duties as a diplomat."[3]

While George Shultz, a former Marine, is committed to continued use of Marine security guards, Matlock said a better guard force might be found.

"I think in the long run that as security becomes more highly technical in an environment where the threat is mainly a technical threat, and where you don't have terrorists, that there are advantages to [considering using] more mature guards who might come with their families," he said.

Matlock said he has long had reservations about using Soviet workers at the embassy because the Soviets could always withdraw them, in effect holding the embassy hostage.

"The argument was made by some that we needed them to operate in Soviet society," Matlock said. "Frankly, that's an argument made more by people who are not specialists in the area."

Together with the new regional security officer, John Drotos, Matlock has established new rules prohibiting employees or their spouses from having contact with Soviets unless their jobs require it. He has banned all cars from entering the embassy courtyard unless they are owned by the embassy. And he has done away with the exemption that allowed diplomats to leave classified documents out as long as someone was on the floor.

Unlike his immediate predecessor, Matlock has not exempted himself from cleaning chores. So far, 90 Americans have replaced 206 Soviet nationals. They do the work better and faster. Typically, they earn $7.50 an hour and receive free housing for such jobs as cleaning tables in the cafeteria.[4] Until more Americans can be brought in, the diplomats still perform some of the chores. Noting that he usually drives his own car, Matlock said, "Americans, of all people, given the right context, will do any job. We are self-sufficient people."

Beyond these changes, Marines no longer have access to the CPU, which is manned by communicators twenty-four hours a day and scanned by video cameras. Since the new embassy may never be occupied, the State Department is planning on spending $30 million to renovate the old one and improve security there. Secure communications were resumed in the spring of 1988. Meanwhile, embassy employees have moved into the residences that are part of the new embassy.

Yet many of the problems identified by Fred Mecke when he was regional security officer remain. When I visited the embassy, the gate blocking entrance to the courtyard was stuck in the "up" position. For years, the Marine security guards had complained about the gate. More than two years earlier, Mecke had ordered a new one. It had yet to arrive. While black-marketeering is prohibited, the embassy continues to permit the same practice under the guise of a "flea market."[5] Because the "flea market" is held on embassy grounds, the Soviets cannot prosecute the participants. Raya, a Soviet previously in charge of personnel at the American embassy, has reappeared wearing a new mask: that of a copying machine repair person. When the embassy employed her, she was thought to be a KGB officer because she was so inquisitive, and the other Soviet employees seemed to follow her orders. While the machines she services are not in secure areas, bugging devices placed in the machine could provide the KGB with a wealth of useful information about the American employees.

In Leningrad there were similar examples of negligence. A

single Marine on the third floor still controls access to the entire consulate, which has no metal detector. The U.S. military employs more than 2 million people, yet cannot spare an extra guard to protect one of the most sensitive American outposts in the world. Despite all the publicity, congressional criticism, and expense of shutting down communications, the security of the consulate still depends on the integrity of one young man on the KGB's own turf. While some alarms have been replaced, others in the CPU still do not register the time when they go off, permitting Marines to circumvent them.[6] When I got there, Soviet workers had just refinished the floors to the Marine House. While they were watched by an American, they undoubtedly installed bugs in the consulate, just as Soviet construction workers installed bugs in the old embassy in Moscow in 1953.

Like the State Department, the Marine Corps has made minor changes. Training in KGB entrapment methods at Marine security guard school has been extended from two hours to three. Tour lengths have been reduced, and extensions of tours in Communist countries are now prohibited. Marines can no longer request a post in Soviet-bloc countries.

The changes are like giving a tune-up to a car that needs a new engine. The State Department still insists on sending inexperienced, immature young Marines to guard the embassy. Like a crazed bull repeatedly knocking its head against a brick wall, the Marine Corps still sends new guard school graduates to Moscow, still insists that they remain single, and still prohibits them from having girls in their rooms.

The KGB itself could not have devised a better way to ensure that the guards remain vulnerable to compromise. As Ilya Dzhirkvelov, the KGB defector, told me, he much preferred single young men as recruitment targets when the KGB assigned him to penetrate embassies in Moscow.

"They have no experience. They need sex," he said. "If you are married, there is no need to see Russian girls. Young guys sometimes can lose their minds over a girl."[7]

As the Marine Corps's attitude suggests, little has changed in the larger scheme of things since Lonetree confessed to the CIA station chief in Vienna. The State Department's Soviet experts continue to insist that employing Soviets was a good policy. If the Soviet government allowed them to return, they would welcome them back. The diplomats, for the most part, still consider security a dirty word and look down their noses at security officers. Matlock's strictures have set off a round of grumbling at the embassy, particularly among spouses who want to continue to see Soviets and do not understand why they cannot. The fact that the Hartmans were more engaging hosts than the Matlocks counts for more in many diplomats' minds than whether the embassy is secure. As soon as Matlock leaves and the publicity dies down, the diplomats can be expected to begin cutting corners again.

The Marine Corps still thinks that Marines are incorruptible and that Marine security guards are doing a good job, despite a 10 percent removal rate for everything from drug use to criminal assault. In the aftermath of the scandal, the Marine Corps has sought to downplay what happened, pointing out that only one Marine was convicted.

Despite its counterintelligence responsibilities overseas, the CIA continues to display little interest in protecting embassies from KGB penetration. While William Webster, as CIA director, has tried to upgrade the importance of the counterintelligence staff, the personnel for the most part remain largely untrained in the subject. The agency insists on keeping secret information that the Soviets already know, creating the kind of unreal atmosphere that contributed to the bugging of the new embassy.

The Naval Investigative Service still believes it is acceptable to tell a suspect to lie and still thinks it knows how to investigate major espionage cases.

Rather than identifying the problems and correcting them, the U.S. government agencies responsible for the security of the embassy have engaged in fierce battles among themselves. After the scandal erupted, at least a half dozen committees or individuals weighed in with recommendations. James R. Schlesinger, the former CIA director and defense secretary, reported on the new embassy, while Melvin R. Laird, another former defense secretary, and Ambassador William Brown studied the problems at the old embassy. In addition, the President's Foreign Intelligence Advisory Board looked into the scandal.

While none of the recommendations went far enough, each of the reports made useful suggestions. Nevertheless, the agencies for the most part ignored the findings. Responding to the Brown report's criticism of Marine security guards, Colonel Del Grosso, the commander of the Marine Security Guard Battalion, haughtily wrote to his superiors, "The speculation . . . that [Marine security guard] conduct was a function of limited recreation and sexual opportunity is a continuing misperception on the part of this committee and is adjudged as a non sequitur."[8] Pointing the finger at other agencies, the internal memo noted that the report detailed "numerous incidents of alleged sexual misbehavior" at "all levels" of the State Department and other civilian agencies.

Sounding like the diplomats who preferred Soviet workers over Americans, Del Grosso told me sending married Marines to Moscow would be a mistake. ". . . What we do is put in more people who can be targeted [by the KGB]," he said. "After further study, people pulled in their horns. It took six months for some of the hysteria to die down."[9]

By his reasoning, the Marines in Moscow should be replaced by Soviets, since the KGB can target Marines.

Rather than finding out how to improve, the NIS similarly devoted its resources to writing rebuttals. Rear Admiral Gordon, who heads the command that includes the NIS, wrote to his Navy superiors that senior NIS managers reviewed the NIS investigation of the Moscow Marines and found only minor administrative errors. "Notwithstanding the adverse media coverage, NIS policy directs supervisory review of all investigations to ensure quality control," he wrote. The review found "no evidence of agent misconduct [or] improper behavior."[10]

In explaining away the minor errors, the NIS says hindsight is better than foresight. Yet it requires neither to know that an espionage suspect like Bracy should not be interviewed until something is known about him.

With the exception of low-ranking Marines, no one in the U.S. government has been demoted or fired as a result of the scandal. The Marine officer who turned down a recommendation to remove Lonetree from Moscow before the KGB recruited him is still a Marine officer. The ambassador who insisted he wanted the Soviets to know 80 percent of what he was saying was allowed to retire gracefully after being given a large bonus. The State Department officer who sat on Mecke's cables requesting an investigation of Bracy still works for the State Department. The CIA officers whose insensitivity to Yurchenko's needs contributed to his redefection still work for the CIA. The CIA official whose committee devised the strategy that led to the bugging of the new embassy suffered no consequences. The NIS agent who expressed glee at Bracy's confession is still working Marine cases.

At the same time, the lives and reputations of the Marines, who were the least powerful members of the embassy community, have been ruined over infractions like going to an off-limits bar or taking girls to their rooms.

To the readers of this book, the solutions to the scandal will be self-evident. The Marines should be replaced with mature, married professionals similar to the Executive Protective Service officers who guard foreign embassies in Washington.[11] The regional security officer at each embassy should report directly to Washington. FBI agents should be assigned to each embassy to supplement the efforts of CIA counterintelligence officers. The NIS should not be allowed to investigate major espionage cases without the involvement of the FBI and the supervision of the Justice Department.

These are not radical proposals. Yet far less ambitious changes have already been shot down. The State Department has rejected a proposal to have the regional security officer report to the deputy chief of mission instead of the administrative counselor, who is twice removed from the ambassador. Another proposal to have the assistant secretary of state for security report directly to the secretary of state has also met with resistance and has been shelved.[12]

At the heart of the problem is the government's basic lack of accountability. From paying $9,606 for Allen wrenches to neglecting to fortify the Marine barracks in Beirut, the federal government repeatedly makes unthinkable mistakes. While private companies may also engage in unethical conduct and cover-ups, they will go out of business if they don't get the job done. In government, there are no such constraints.

In theory, the people will elect a new President if the previous one failed to lead. Yet in practice, Americans have come to accept government ineptitude just as Soviets accept food lines caused by bureaucratic bungling. The idea that federal bureaucrats are entitled to their jobs and their pensions despite the most monumental screw-ups has become embedded in the American psyche. A man who steals $100 gets a jail term. Yet those officials who allowed the Soviets to build their embassy on the second-highest site in Washington, whose policies led to American defeat in the Vietnam War, who presided over the redefection of Yurchenko, and who mishandled CIA officer Edward Lee Howard have suffered not even public approbation.

Behind it all is a bureaucratic mind-set that takes the short rather than the long view, that avoids taking action wherever possible, and that puts selfish interests above the national interest—a tendency magnified by the secrecy that pervades the intelligence community. While there is nothing new about this, under President Reagan the problem grew geometrically. His repeated refusal to remove from office those who engaged in gross ethical violations officially sanctioned the proposition that federal officials are untouchable.

A cartoon by Bill Schoor in the *Kansas City Star* illustrates how out of control the government has become. Two Reagan administration officials enter the White House dining room and wait for the maître d' to seat them. As the two officials peer into the divided room, the maître d' asks, "Indicted or unindicted?"

It was the ultimate irony that Reagan, who came to office with a conservative mandate to strengthen the nation's defenses, wound up presiding over the worst intelligence debacle since the CIA's abortive 1961 invasion of Cuba at the Bay of Pigs.

Unfortunately, there are no short-term solutions. Until a U.S. President holds bureaucrats accountable for their actions, monumental bungling by the U.S. government will continue. The embassy in Moscow will remain vulnerable to KGB penetration. And the government will continue to be incapable of bringing those responsible to justice.

# Epilogue

Clayton Lonetree is serving a twenty-five-year prison term at the U.S. Disciplinary Barracks at Fort Leavenworth, Kansas. He is the only participant in the Marine scandal to have confessed without recanting, and he is the only one to have been convicted.[1]

The Marine Corps discharged Arnold Bracy honorably in April 1987. He married another Marine and is now guarding a computer firm in northern Virginia while attending a two-year college.[2]

A court-martial found Robert S. Stufflebeam guilty of dereliction of duty by going to an off-limits bar. The Marine Corps demoted him one rank to sergeant. He received an honorable discharge in January 1988. Stufflebeam began protecting executives in Washington, D.C. Because of his court-martial and the publicity surrounding it, police departments rejected his applications, and some clients refused to let him protect them. Eventually, a wealthy Lebanese hired him to protect his son.

"I'm very bitter," he told me.[3] "The Marine Corps is just as much to blame for this as the Naval Investigative Service. Nothing will happen to the NIS officers because they're officers. We were thrown to the wolves. That's the bottom line. Our careers have been ruined, and we'll carry this around with us for the rest of our lives."

In an illustration of the inconsistency of the Marine Corps's response to the scandal, the judge presiding over Stufflebeam's court-martial read Duane Parks his rights when he admitted he lied to the NIS about the number of Soviet women he had taken out. Later, Parks admitted to the NIS that he also had engaged in black-marketeering and had taken LSD while a Marine. In contrast to Stufflebeam, who was court-martialed for going to an off-limits bar, the Marine Corps brought no charges against Parks. He was discharged honorably and is working as a carpenter.[4]

Because he retracted his statement about Bracy, an administrative discharge board found Robert J. Williams guilty of false swearing. Williams received a general discharge under honorable conditions, a rung below an honorable discharge.[5]

After returning to Quantico from Moscow, Vincent O. Downes received office hours for undermining the overall discipline and good order of the Marine detachment by going to the Kosmos Hotel with watchstanders. Charges that he asked a Marine to change a logbook entry to show he had arrived within the curfew, that he lay on his back during a New Year's Eve party while blowing on a noisemaker, and that he took a girl to his room were dismissed. Because he retracted his statements about Bracy, the Marine Corps charged him with false swearing. Like Williams, he received a general discharge under honorable conditions, which he is appealing. He is working as a security guard in northern Virginia.[6]

Joey E. Wingate retired from the Marine Corps in January 1988 and began working as a private security guard. After the scandal erupted, the Marine Corps withdrew him from Athens and assigned him to Quantico. As the detachment commander in charge of the Marines when the scandal broke in Moscow, Wingate feels he has been unfairly blamed. Wingate points out that he and Stufflebeam requested Lonetree's removal before he became involved with the KGB, but they were overruled.

"I feel the Marine Corps let me down," he said. "They let a lot of the Marines down. This saying they look out for their own is a bunch of baloney. They don't. They don't want to be tainted. They don't want to have anything to do with you. When you have a Marine who's in trouble, especially after twenty-nine years, you'd think someone would say, 'Look, this guy's got a [good] record.' And I do. It's written down."

"Where were the CIA people?" he asked. "Who's responsible for the damned Marine Corps? How come [Kelley] wasn't relieved?

General P. X. Kelley retired on schedule in June 1987. He is senior vice president of Star Mountain Inc., which helps Third World countries maintain military supplies.[7] A shrewd politician, he has remained impervious to the scandal.

Richard Klingenmaier is in charge of worldwide communications for the State Department's bureau of diplomatic security. He denies security was lax at the embassy and believes Americans employed there now are potentially more of a threat than the Soviets they replaced.

Robert Lamb, who continues as assistant secretary of state for security, has found that congressional interest in improving security at American embassies has already waned.

"A year after the publicity, congressional interest has moved to other things," he said. "The funding for the programs that we need for security improvements is becoming a problem for us again. We're not talking big money, but it doesn't look like there's any interest in paying for these programs."[8]

Incredibly, money already budgeted by Congress for improving security has not been appropriated, in part because State Department officials who associate good security with McCarthyism have not asked for it. Meanwhile, President Reagan decided in October 1988 that the entire new embassy in Moscow should be torn down, but he left the question of funding the work and the construction of a new embassy to the next administration.

After resigning as ambassador, Arthur Hartman received a $9,000 bonus from the State Department.[9] He is a consultant on European affairs for a Washington firm and is working on a report on Soviet internal changes for the Johns Hopkins University School of International Affairs.[10]

A presidential commission headed by former defense secretary Melvin R. Laird concluded that Hartman should be held responsible for the misconduct of Marine security guards in Moscow. Hartman indignantly disputes this, saying that what happened at the embassy was overblown and that the Marines failed to police themselves.[11]

"I think a lot of people made a lot of foolish statements . . . which they should be correcting, but I'm sure they won't," he said. "Washington is a rather ungrateful place."

Lanny E. McCullah, who headed the NIS investigation, began

looking for another job in part because of frustration with the outcome of the investigation and the criticism he received.

"There are times when I thrilled to the chase and other times when I wished my parents had had me a year earlier so I could have retired and walked away," McCullah said.[12]

When he did not find a suitable job in the private sector, the NIS promoted him to deputy director.

Even though he improved security at the embassy, Frederick Mecke was asked to leave Moscow ten months earlier than planned. At first, he felt the scandal had tainted his reputation. He is still unsure what the ultimate effects on his career will be.[13] He is stationed in Washington working on security issues related to the Soviet Union.

"I am disappointed with the way the U.S. government has handled this problem," he said. "The Soviets have gained from this by getting information from a recruited agent. But what is of even more concern is the U.S. government's inability, largely because of petty rivalries and overexercised egos, to deal with the problem without savaging innocent people and paralyzing institutions crucial to our worldwide interests."

"It almost isn't worth looking for who is to blame," said Lincoln D. Faurer, the former head of NSA. "There were so many who could have thwarted the whole [penetration] scheme. . . . It's not just the ambassador or that person. They all screwed up."[14]

Faurer added, "I'm pessimistic that that will change."

# Notes

## 2 The Great Seal, pp. 19–30

1. George F. Kennan, *Memoirs: 1925–1950*, Atlantic Monthly Press, 1967, page 59.
2. Ibid., page 63.
3. Charles E. Bohlen, *Witness to History: 1929–1969*, W. W. Norton & Co., 1973, page 15.
4. Ibid., page 20.
5. Ibid., page 21.
6. Will Brownell and Richard N. Billings, *So Close to Greatness: A Biography of William C. Bullitt*, Macmillan Publishing Co., 1987, page 157.
7. In a letter of April 7, 1988, to the author, Kennan commented, "When the U.S. embassy was established in 1934, we were not at war with the U.S.S.R.; there was no significant military rivalry between the two countries; and despite the ideological differences, the U.S.S.R. did not figure in the eyes of official Washington as primarily a hostile power."

The work of the embassy that required strict confidentiality formed only a small part of its official activity, he said. "As for the remainder, there was no reason the Soviet authorities should not have knowledge of it, and there were even reasons why it was better that they should have it. Problems of security therefore formed only a small part of the mission's concern."

8. FBI memo from Special Agent Beck to Director Hoover dated November 13, 1940. Hoover sent the memo to President Roosevelt on December 13, 1940.
9. Hayden B. Peake, *Foreign Intelligence Literary Scene*, National Intelligence Study Center, March/April 1986, page 1. The fact that the documents had been received by British officials was enough to give the British jurisdiction over Kent.
10. Kennan, op. cit., page 155.
11. Ibid., page 157.
12. Interview on February 1, 1988, with Elizabeth Stannard.
13. Rhodri Jeffreys-Jones, *American Espionage: From Secret Service to CIA*, Free Press, 1977, page 128.
14. Interview on November 5, 1987, with Roger Provencher.
15. Bohlen, op. cit., page 345.
16. *Microwave Radiation at the U.S. Embassy in Moscow and Its Biological Implications: An Assessment*, U.S. Department of Commerce, March 1981.
17. Interview on December 9, 1987, with Toon. Asked about it on February 22, 1988, Rusk said he did not recall the incident.

18. Interview on December 9, 1987, with Toon. The cartoon, by Etta Hulme, appeared on June 1, 1979.

19. Interview on November 28, 1987, with Carl Provencher, who was ten years old when he and other children of diplomats at the embassy discovered the tunnel.

20. Interview on November 5, 1987, with Roger Provencher.

21. Interview on February 1, 1988, with Kohler.

22. Interview on November 5, 1987, with Provencher.

23. Interview on December 9, 1987, with Toon.

24. Interview with Richard W. Shear in the author's 1988 book, *Spy vs. Spy: Stalking Soviet Spies in America*, Charles Scribner's Sons, page 113.

25. General Accounting Office, "U.S. Embassy Moscow: Why Construction Took Longer and Cost More Than Anticipated," October 1987, page 12.

26. Ibid., page 14.

## 3 The Station, pp. 31–40

1. The Soviets identified Natirboff as the CIA station chief when they presented new charges against Nicholas Daniloff, the *U.S. News & World Report* correspondent. See *New York Times*, September 14, 1986, page 1. According to embassy officials, Natirboff's identity was widely known within the embassy and among the Soviets.

2. John J. Dziak, in *Chekisty: A History of the KGB*, Lexington Books, 1988, has called the Soviet Union the "counterintelligence state."

3. Stanislav Levchenko, *On the Wrong Side: My Life in the KGB*, Pergamon-Brassey's, 1988, pages 86 and 121.

4. Interview on December 4, 1987, with Levchenko.

5. Interview on October 29, 1987, with a former CIA official.

6. Interview on March 29, 1988, with Hartman.

7. State Department report dated February 14, 1986.

8. Interview on October 29, 1987, with a former CIA official.

9. Interview on December 14, 1987, with a State Department official.

10. Interview on November 30, 1987, with a former CIA official.

11. Interview on March 23, 1988, with a former CIA official.

12. FBI report of June 15, 1960, to J. Edgar Hoover from the New York field office. The report includes the results of interviews with James B. Donovan and Thomas M. Debevoise II, two of Abel's defense lawyers. Donovan has since died; Debevoise said he did not recall talking to the FBI.

13. Peer de Silva, *Sub Rosa: The CIA and the Uses of Intelligence*, Times Books, 1978, page 68. The information was corroborated by an interview on November 6, 1987, with a former CIA official.

14. Interview on November 6, 1987, with a former CIA official.

15. See the author's 1988 book, *Spy vs. Spy: Stalking Soviet Spies in America*, Charles Scribner's Sons, page 179.

16. Interview on November 17, 1987, with a former CIA official.

17. Interview on November 30, 1987, with a former CIA official.

18. John Barron, *KGB Today: The Hidden Hand*, Reader's Digest Press, 1983, page 363.

19. Oleg Penkovsky, *The Penkovsky Papers*, Doubleday & Co., 1965.

20. Peter Wright, *Spy Catcher*, Viking Penguin Inc., 1987, page 208.

21. Interview on November 12, 1987, with Korczak.

22. Interview on February 16, 1988, with an intelligence officer.

23. Interview on February 18, 1988, with a former CIA official.

## 4 The Opposition, pp. 41–51

1. The figure of 1.2 million KGB employees comes from FBI sources. Comparing the KGB staff with the staffs of American law-enforcement and intelligence agencies is a virtually impossible task. KGB employment is usually compared with the NSA's 120,000 employees (including those who work for the military), the CIA's 20,000 employees, and the FBI's 23,000 employees, totaling 163,000 employees. But the KGB also performs many functions carried out in the U.S. by dozens of other law-enforcement and intelligence agencies, including the state police; local sheriffs; the Marshals Service; the Drug Enforcement Administration; the Bureau of Alcohol, Tobacco, and Firearms; the Customs Service; the Immigration and Naturalization Service; military criminal investigative agencies; the State Department; the Postal Inspections Service; the Securities and Exchange Commission; the Secret Service; the Internal Revenue Service; and the Executive Protective Service. In addition, the KGB carries out some functions performed in the U.S. by private guard services and the Federal Protective Service, as well as intelligence functions performed in the U.S. by the Defense Intelligence Agency and Army, Navy, and Air Force intelligence. Besides the KGB, the equivalent Soviet agencies would also include the GRU, or Soviet Military Intelligence, which has 18,000 employees.

2. Ilya Dzhirkvelov, *Secret Servant*, Collins, London, 1987, page 171, supplemented by an interview with Dzhirkvelov on May 25, 1988. Harper & Row published the U.S. edition of the book in 1988.

3. Interviews on November 5, 1987, and April 12, 1988, with Provencher.

4. Dzhirkvelov, op. cit., page 171.

5. Ibid., page 212.

6. Interview on December 4, 1987, with Levchenko.

7. Interview on May 25, 1988, with Dzhirkvelov.

8. Interview on November 5, 1987, with Provencher.

9. The description of Scarbeck's espionage comes from his unpublished memoir, made available by his lawyer, Samuel C. Klein. It is corroborated by the newspaper accounts and legal documents concerning his case, plus interviews with then ambassador to Poland Jacob D. Beam and Klein, along with the prosecutor, FBI agent, and State Department security officers involved in his case.

10. Interview on March 27, 1988, with Klein.

11. Interview on January 4, 1988, with Knauf.

12. Interview on January 4, 1988, with Dikeos.

13. Interview on February 21, 1988, with Vincent.

## 5 Guard School, pp. 52–66

1. Clayton Lonetree's testimony about his father from page 1960 of Lonetree's court-martial. The fact that Clayton felt this way about his father was confirmed by Cohen, counsel for both Spencer and Clayton Lonetree, in an interview on November 2, 1987.

2. Interview on November 12, 1987, with Tsotie; also stated by Spencer Lonetree's lawyer, Cohen, in an interview on November 2, 1987.

3. Lonetree's testimony on page 1958 of his court-martial proceeding.

4. Interview on February 23, 1988, with Snyder, Clayton's first girlfriend. Snyder was first interviewed by Pete Earley of the *Washington Post*. Also an interview with Spencer Lonetree on November 3, 1987.

5. Page 1958 of Lonetree's testimony during his court-martial proceeding.

6. Interview on November 3, 1987, with Broich.

7. Page 1611 of Dahl's testimony at Lonetree's court-martial. The notebook was introduced as Exhibit 51.

8. Page 1613 of Dahl's testimony at Lonetree's court-martial.

9. Interview with Spencer Lonetree on November 3, 1987.

10. Interview on November 2, 1987, with Cohen, counsel for Clayton and Spencer Lonetree.

11. Testimony by Clayton Lonetree from page 1960 of Lonetree's court-martial. Also an interview on February 23, 1988, with Snyder.

12. Interview on November 3, 1987, with Spencer Lonetree.

13. Interview on February 23, 1988, with Snyder.

14. Snyder's letter of March 10, 1988, to the author.

15. Page 1960 of Lonetree's court-martial. Other biographical data comes from a Marine Corps release on Lonetree of January 2, 1987.

16. Lonetree's percentile score on the AFQT aptitude test was 33, according to the test results listed on his application to the armed forces.

17. Daniel Da Cruz, *Boot: The Inside Story of How a Few Good Men Became Today's Marines,* St. Martin's, 1987, page 37.

18. Letter of March 10, 1988, from Snyder to the author.

19. Reference Section, History and Museums Division, Marine Corps headquarters, *The Origins of the Marine Security Guard Battalion,* October 1986.

20. Interview on December 19, 1987, with Wingate.

21. Marine Corps headquarters, *Marines* magazine, June 1985, page 13.

22. Interview on December 28, 1987, with a State Department security officer, supplemented by interviews with representatives of the French, British, and Canadian embassies in Moscow. The May 16, 1988, *Washington Post* on page A-1 listed the cost of a Stealth bomber as $450 million.

23. Lonetree's application to Marine Security Guard School of May 17, 1984.

24. Interview on March 28, 1988, with Timothy Droogsma, press secretary to Boschwitz.

25. Commandant of the Marine Corps, *Marines* magazine, June 1985, page 15.

26. Interview on February 3, 1988, with Del Grosso.

27. Interview on March 1, 1988, with Del Grosso. Since the controversy erupted over the guard program, the total time spent on entrapment has been extended by an hour.

28. The course on answering critics of the U.S. has since been dropped from the guard school curriculum.

29. Lonetree's professional evaluation form.

30. Memorandum dated May 18, 1984, from Mabry.

31. Department of State, *Marine Security Guard Program Disciplinary Infractions, 1980–1987.* Another thirty-three Marines were removed for medical reasons.

32. Memo of June 25, 1987, from Cohn to NIS case agents and NIS task force director.

33. Letter dated June 23, 1987, from Mundy to Lamb.

34. Interview on February 24, 1988, with NIS officials.

## 6   Snapping In, pp. 67–78

1. Interview on December 9, 1987, with Toon.

2. Interview on January 5, 1988, with a State Department official.

3. Interview on December 28, 1987, with a State Department security officer.

4. Interview on December 19, 1987, with Wingate.

5. U.S. Marine Corps, *Narrative Description of Guard Posts.*

6. Interview on December 11, 1987, with Roen.

7. Interviews on December 13, 1987, with Cooke and on December 7, 1987, with Downes.

8. Interview on December 13, 1987, with Cooke.

9. Interview on November 14, 1987, with Stufflebeam.

10. Interview on December 13, 1987, with Cooke.

11. Interview on December 19, 1987, with Wingate.
12. Interview on December 11, 1987, with Roen.
13. Interview on December 19, 1987, with Wingate.
14. Kris had no comment.
15. Interview on December 19, 1987, with Wingate. Kris declined to comment.

## 7  Swiss Cheese, pp. 79–90

1. Interview on January 5, 1988, with a State Department official assigned to the embassy at the time.
2. Ibid.
3. Interview on December 11, 1987, with Roen.
4. Interview on December 13, 1987, with Cooke.
5. Interview on March 29, 1988, with Hartman.
6. Ibid.
7. Interview on December 28, 1987, with Hartman.
8. Interview on December 19, 1987, with Wingate.
9. U.S. Marine Corps biographical information, April 1, 1987.
10. Interview on November 14, 1987, with Stufflebeam.
11. Ibid.
12. Ibid. In an interview on December 28, 1987, a State Department security officer confirmed that this was the policy at the embassy.
13. Interview on December 19, 1987, with Wingate.
14. Ibid.
15. Interview on December 11, 1987, with Roen. Wingate, in an interview on December 19, 1987, confirmed that the Kosmos disco and Bier-Stube were not off-limits even though they served drinks and took foreign currency.
16. Interview on November 14, 1987, with Stufflebeam.
17. Ibid.

## 8  Finding Bugs, pp. 91–104

1. The figure of twenty-six comes from Thomas Switzer, a State Department public affairs officer. The figure of thirty-four is from Dana Weant, the regional security officer in Moscow.
2. Interview on December 23, 1987, with a former official of the Leningrad consulate.
3. Interview on October 29, 1987, with Pope.
4. Ibid.
5. Interview on April 16, 1988, with Squire.
6. Interview on January 30, 1988, with Goddard.
7. Interview on October 29, 1987, with Pope.
8. Interview on November 26, 1987, with Weirick.
9. Interview on January 7, 1988, with a State Department security officer.
10. Interview on April 22, 1988, with a State Department official.
11. Interview on January 7, 1988, with Faurer.
12. Interview on December 16, 1987, with a State Department official.
13. *Washington Post,* March 11, 1983, page A-1.
14. Associated Press, April 19, 1987. Sellers, on March 20, 1988, declined comment.
15. Reuters news agency, October 22, 1986.
16. The Associated Press, April 19, 1977.
17. Interview on December 16, 1987, with a State Department official.
18. It is impossible to know with certainty whether a clever move by the opposition is attributable to inside information or good guesswork.

19. Interview on December 28, 1987, with Hartman.

20. Senate Select Committee on Intelligence, *Report on Security at the U.S. Missions in Moscow and Other Areas of High Risk*, September 9, 1987, page 3.

21. For a full discussion of the building techniques used by the Soviets at Mount Alto, see the author's 1988 book, *Spy vs. Spy: Stalking Soviet Spies in America*, Charles Scribner's Sons, page 116.

22. Interview on February 16, 1988, with an intelligence officer.

23. Interview on December 16, 1987, with a State Department official.

24. Interview on April 13, 1988, with Warnecke.

25. Interview on March 15, 1988, with Lamb.

26. Interview on April 18, 1988, with Martin.

## 9    The Hairdresser, pp. 105–11

1. Interview on January 27, 1988, with a State Department official.

2. Interview on November 28, 1987, with Carl Provencher.

3. Interview on February 22, 1988, with a State Department security officer. The information picked up by Valentina had to do with a character weakness. Hartman, in an interview on March 29, 1988, said he had fired her because he was fed up with being questioned while he was having his hair cut.

4. Interview on April 11, 1988, with Stufflebeam.

5. Letter of January 28, 1988, from E. Charlene Kurth. Hartman said he had no recollection of his involvement.

6. Interview on January 27, 1988, with a State Department security officer, and on January 12, 1988, with a State Department official.

7. Interview on March 18, 1988, with Hlatky.

8. Letter of January 28, 1988, from E. Charlene Kurth, confirmed by testimony by Hlatky on page 258 of Lonetree's Article 32 hearing; an interview on December 1, 1987, and on April 11, 1988, with Stufflebeam; an interview on February 2, 1988, with Shirley Benson; and an interview on December 28, 1987, with a State Department security officer.

9. Interview on January 25, 1988, with E. Charlene Kurth.

10. Interview on December 1, 1987, with Stufflebeam. Charlene Kurth's letter of January 28, 1988, said her husband reprimanded Stufflebeam for his "rudeness and lack of reasonable judgment." Admiral Kurth, in an interview on March 6, 1988, said he had read his wife's letter and agreed with it.

11. Interview on January 7, 1988, with Faurer.

12. Letter dated October 23, 1985, from the commanding officer, Marine Security Guard Battalion, to the State Department.

13. U.S. Marine Corps, *Moscow Marine Detachment Individual Score Sheet*, inspection dates September 25–29, 1985.

14. Kris felt the only automatic causes for removal should be use of drugs, matters affecting integrity such as a cover-up, and fraternization.

15. Interview on November 14, 1987, with Stufflebeam.

16. Interview on December 19, 1987, with Wingate.

17. Interview on February 20, 1988, with Hlatky.

18. Interview on December 19, 1987, with Wingate.

## 10    The Swallow, pp. 112–20

1. The information on Seina's background comes from the personnel card the embassy had on her.

2. Interview on March 29, 1988, with Hartman.

3. Seina's subsequent letters to Lonetree were written in nearly perfect English,

suggesting she either purposely made errors when addressing Hartman's letters or that the KGB wrote her letters to Lonetree for her.

4. Interview on March 29, 1988, with Donna Hartman.

5. Interview on December 28, 1987, with Hartman.

6. Lonetree's statement of December 26, 1986. The statement was introduced as evidence at Lonetree's subsequent court-martial and has not been retracted by him.

7. Interview on December 4, 1987, with Levchenko.

8. NIS cable of March 17, 1987.

9. Embassy card on Seina. Seina has since moved. A letter to her old address asking for comment got no response.

10. Interview on January 12, 1988, with a State Department administrative officer.

11. Mataitis's testimony on page 277 of Stufflebeam's court-martial, confirmed by an interview with him on April 14, 1988.

12. Interview on November 14, 1987, with Stufflebeam, and statement by Stufflebeam for his later court-martial on March 29, 1987.

13. Interview on November 22, 1987, with Stufflebeam.

14. Interview on December 5, 1987, with Parks.

15. Interview on December 11, 1987, with Roen, and on April 11, 1988, with Stufflebeam.

16. Interview on April 30, 1988, with Parks.

17. Interview on December 5, 1987, with Parks together with an NIS cable reporting the results of an interrogation of Parks at Camp Lejeune on April 1, 1987.

18. Interview on April 12, 1988, with Stufflebeam.

19. Interview on December 5, 1987, with Parks.

20. Ibid.

21. Ibid.

22. Interview on April 30, 1988, with Parks, and on May 1, 1988, with a Marine officer.

23. Lonetree's statement to the NIS on December 26, 1986, which has not been retracted by him.

24. Testimony by Byrnes beginning on page 1732 of Lonetree's court-martial proceedings.

25. Testimony by Byrnes from page 1746 of Lonetree's court-martial proceedings.

## 11 A Defector's Information, pp. 121–32

1. Interviews with three intelligence sources confirm that Yurchenko revealed KGB penetration of the embassy's communications.

2. John Barron, *KGB Today,* Reader's Digest Press, 1983, page 379.

3. Interview on July 28, 1987, with Costa.

4. Alexandra Costa, *Stepping Down from the Star: A Soviet Defector's Story,* G. P. Putnam's Sons, 1986.

5. Interview on September 10, 1987, with Levchenko.

6. Interview on August 11, 1987, with Lisa Jameson.

7. Interview on July 30, 1987, with Jameson.

8. Interview on October 12, 1987, with Wyatt.

9. Interview on July 22, 1987, with Geimer.

10. Interview on February 16, 1988, with a government official who was privy to the briefing of Reagan.

11. Interview on February 10, 1988, with a high-level intelligence officer.

## 12 A Slide Show, pp. 133–41

1. Interview on December 21, 1987, with Lamb.

2. Interview on December 28, 1987, with Hartman.

3. Interview on January 6, 1988, with Lamb.

4. Ibid.

5. Interview on December 28, 1988, with Hartman.

6. Interview on December 21, 1987, with Lamb.

7. NSA and CIA budget figures are estimates by reliable intelligence sources.

8. Interview on January 7, 1988, with Faurer.

9. The twelve spies arrested or charged in 1985 were John A. Walker, Michael L. Walker, Arthur J. Walker, Jerry A. Whitworth, Sharon M. Scranage, Michael A. Soussoudis, Jonathan J. Pollard, Anne Henderson-Pollard, Larry Wu-Tai Chin, Ronald W. Pelton, Randy M. Jeffries, and Edward Lee Howard. With the exception of Howard, who is considered a fugitive, all were convicted.

10. Interview on December 14, 1987, with a State Department official.

11. Hartman sent his cable to Shultz "NODIS," meaning it was to be read only by the secretary with no distribution to others in the State Department or intelligence agencies.

## 13    A Promotion, pp. 142–50

1. Lonetree's statement of December 26, 1986, which has not been retracted.

2. Internal NIS chronology of the Lonetree case based on Lonetree's admissions.

3. Associated Press, April 19, 1987. Sellers, on March 20, 1988, declined comment.

4. The declassified version of Lonetree's statement of December 29, 1986, shows he admitted that Yefimov asked him to place bugs in the ambassador's office. He has not retracted that statement. An unclassified internal NIS chronology shows Yefimov also asked him if Natirboff were station chief and requested that Lonetree place bugs in Natirboff's and Mecke's offices. An interview on March 8, 1988, with an NIS official confirmed that Lonetree revealed that Natirboff was station chief.

5. Stanislav Levchenko, *On the Wrong Side: My Life in the KGB*, Pergamon-Brassey's, 1988, page 88.

6. Most of the details of what Lonetree gave Yefimov have not been publicized before. The charges against Lonetree relating to Moscow were that he gathered names and photographs of covert agents, met with Yefimov and gave him photographs, and gathered information on floor plans and office assignments. As summarized on page A-8 of the August 23, 1987, *Washington Post*, the charges relating to Moscow included revealing several identities of several CIA operatives and giving the Soviets plans of some of the floors in the embassy.

The new details come from 200 hours of secret debriefings of Lonetree by the Naval Investigative Service, with the participation of the CIA and other intelligence agencies, after he was sentenced. Lonetree passed polygraph tests on each statement.

7. Lonetree's statement of December 29, 1986, which he has not retracted.

8. Ibid.

9. Michael Daly, "I Spy," *New York* magazine, April 6, 1987, confirmed by an interview with Bhoge. The contract read, "I, Leakh Bhoge, agree to work for the U.S.S.R. for seven to ten years, and after that, if I am willing, then the contract can be renewed or extended."

10. Lonetree's statement of December 26, 1986, which has not been retracted.

11. Byrnes's testimony on page 1742 of Lonetree's court-martial proceedings.

12. Interview on December 19, 1987, with Wingate.

13. Interviews on December 1, 1987, with Stufflebeam; on December 19, 1987, with Wingate; on December 7, 1987, with Martinson; on December 28, 1987, with a State Department security officer.

14. Interview on December 28, 1987, with a State Department security officer.

15. Interview on December 13, 1987, with Cooke, confirmed in an interview December 28, 1987, with a State Department security officer. Shirley Benson, in an interview on February 29, 1988, confirmed that she complained that her son's bag had been searched. "I felt people who lived in the building shouldn't have their bags searched," she said.

16. Interview on February 2, 1988, with Shirley Benson.
17. Interview on December 18, 1987, with Raymond Benson.
18. Interview on February 2, 1988, with Shirley Benson.
19. Interview on December 19, 1987, with Wingate. Benson, in an interview on February 29, 1988, said he recalled speaking with Wingate about a problem involving Doder but never asked for an exception for him. In a letter of March 25, 1988, Doder, now Beijing bureau chief of *U.S. News & World Report,* confirmed he complained to Benson when the Marine guard could not read his Soviet press card.
20. Interview on December 19, 1987, with Wingate, confirmed by a State Department security officer in an interview on December 28, 1987, and by Stufflebeam in an interview on March 1, 1988. Verner said he had already discussed his complaints about security with the appropriate officials and had no comment.
21. Interview on November 29, 1987, with Bracy.
22. Interview on March 18, 1988, with Hlatky.

## 14  Finding a Replacement, pp. 151–58

1. Interview on November 29, 1987, with Bracy, and on April 2, 1988, with Theodore Bracy.
2. Interview on March 14, 1988, with Frieda Bracy.
3. Interview on April 2, 1988, with Theodore Bracy.
4. Interview on November 29, 1987, with Bracy.
5. Biographical data from a March 29, 1987, release from the Marine Corps.
6. Interview on November 29, 1987, with Bracy.
7. NIS listing of "Espionage/Significant Security Related Convictions," October 1982–August 1987.
8. Interview on February 15, 1988, with a former NIS official, corroborated by interviews with FBI officials.
9. Interview on November 29, 1987, with Bracy.
10. Interview on May 25, 1988, with Dzhirkvelov.
11. Interview on March 8, 1988, with an intelligence officer.
12. Interview on March 15, 1988, with a State Department security officer.
13. Interview on November 29, 1987, with Bracy.
·14. Ibid.
15. Interview on November 20, 1987, with Williams. Bracy said he walked out before the girls got undressed.
16. Interview on December 11, 1987, with Roen.
17. Interview on March 1, 1988, with Stufflebeam.
18. Interview on March 12, 1988, with Downes.
19. Mecke's cable of June 30, 1986, to the State Department.
20. Interview on December 28, 1987, with a State Department security officer.
21. Ibid.

## 15  The Duchateaus' Bedroom, pp. 159–74

1. Mecke's cable of August 21, 1986, to the State Department; an interview on December 10, 1987, with Duchateau; and an interview on April 24, 1988, with Golnar Duchateau.
2. Interview on February 3, 1988, with Del Grosso, and on March 8, 1988, with Powell.
3. Interview on December 28, 1987, with a State Department security officer.
4. Ibid.
5. Ibid.
6. Interview on April 24, 1988, with a State Department official.

7. Mecke's cable of August 21, 1986, to the State Department.

8. Bracy's statement of March 20, 1987, to the NIS and NIS "results of interview" with Bracy on the same date. Bracy has retracted both statements.

9. See *The New York Times*, July 20, 1987, page A-8. The story said contradictions and discrepancies in Bracy's case cast doubt on whether he committed espionage.

10. Interview on November 29, 1987, with Bracy.

11. Interview on December 18, 1987, with Duchateau.

12. Interview on November 29, 1987, with Bracy.

13. Interview on April 23, 1988, with Golnar Duchateau.

14. Interview on January 5, 1988, with Wright.

15. Transcript of the interview of Stephen Wright as it appeared on ABC-TV on April 2, 1987, provided by the Sherman Grinberg Film Library Inc., New York City.

16. Interview on March 4, 1988, with Westwood, and on December 18, 1987, and April 23, 1988, with Duchateau.

17. Interview on December 23, 1987, with Bracy.

18. Interview on January 25, 1988, with Bracy.

19. Interview on January 15, 1988, with Golotina.

20. Interview on January 25, 1988, with Bracy.

21. Interview on April 23, 1988, with Golnar Duchateau.

22. Interview on April 24, 1988, with Golnar Duchateau.

23. Since Wright previously said the tape was in the VCR, Golotina might have moved it once they were caught in the apartment.

24. Interview on April 24, 1988, with Bradley.

25. Ibid.; interview on December 7, 1986, with Downes.

26. Interview on December 7, 1986, with Downes.

27. Williams's statement to the NIS of April 2, 1987, retracted by him in a statement to the NIS on April 19, 1987.

28. Laurivuori's statements of July 26, 1986, and May 13, 1987, to the NIS, confirmed in an interview in Moscow on January 21, 1988. She said in the interview, "Williams told me Bracy had been spying. He told Williams. The statement [to the NIS] was true."

29. Laurivuori's statement of July 26, 1986, and May 13, 1987, to the NIS, confirmed in an interview on January 21, 1988.

30. Interview on February 2, 1988, with Williams.

31. Letters to Laurivuori from Williams were entered as exhibits 82 and 83 in Article 32 proceedings against Williams.

32. Sink's statement to the NIS of July 31, 1987, confirmed in testimony by him on page 512 of Williams's Article 32 hearing. Sink was given a draft of the book manuscript referring to him and did not suggest any corrections.

33. Sink's statement to the NIS of July 31, 1987, verified by his testimony under oath on page 527 of Williams's Article 32 investigation.

34. NIS's "Results of Interview with Arnold Bracy," March 20, 1987.

35. Interview on February 3, 1988, with Del Grosso.

36. Ibid.

37. Bracy's testimony on page 94 of Lonetree's court-martial proceedings.

38. Mecke's cable of August 25, 1986, to the State Department.

39. State Department memo to the file of September 8, 1986, on Bracy's debriefing.

40. The Duchateaus could not recall where the highchair was.

41. Marine Corps transcript of Bracy's press conference on June 12, 1987, at Quantico Marine base, page 14:

> Q. So she [Golotina] invited you to the diplomat's house and you went to tell her—
> A. No, she didn't invite me. She didn't know I was coming. I just showed up there, ma'am.

42. Interview on February 19, 1988, with a State Department security officer.

43. Interview on December 21, 1987, with Lamb.

44. Interviews on February 24, 1988, with NIS officials, and on February 19, 1988, with a State Department security officer.

## 16 Happy Birthday, pp. 175–88

1. Seina's letter of March 17, 1986, was entered as Exhibit 24 in Lonetree's court-martial.

2. Seina's letter of March 26, 1986, was entered as Exhibit 45 at Lonetree's court-martial.

3. Seina's letter to Lonetree of April 12, 1986, was entered as Exhibit 24 in his court-martial.

4. Seina's letter to Lonetree of May 10, 1986, was entered as Exhibit 45 in his court-martial.

5. Lonetree's statement to the NIS of December 26, 1986, which has not been retracted.

6. Ibid.

7. Interview on March 8, 1988, with an intelligence source, and interview on March 9, 1988, with another intelligence source.

8. Lonetree's statement of December 26, 1986, which has not been retracted.

9. Interview on March 7, 1988, with Huddleston.

10. Interview on April 27, 1988, with a staff member of the Senate Select Committee on Intelligence.

11. Interview on February 1, 1988, with Thomas Switzer, a State Department public affairs officer.

12. Interview on April 24, 1988, with a State Department official.

13. Interview on January 6, 1988, with Lamb, and on January 12, 1988, with a State Department official.

14. Lonetree's letter of October 27, 1986.

15. Lonetree's statement of December 26, 1986, which has not been retracted.

16. Lonetree's statement of December 29, 1986, which has not been retracted.

17. Lonetree's statement of December 26, 1986, which has not been retracted.

18. Lonetree's statement of December 29, 1986, which has not been retracted.

19. Interview on April 25, 1988, with an intelligence source.

20. This information on what Lonetree disclosed has not been publicized before and was not specifically included in the charges against him. The charges against Lonetree relating to Vienna were that he gathered names and photographs of covert agents, met with Yefimov and gave him photographs, discussed national defense information with Yefimov and Lysov, and gathered information on floor plans and office assignments. As summarized on page A-8 of the August 23, 1987, *Washington Post*, the charges against him relating to Vienna included giving floor plans and an embassy phone book to the Soviets.

The new information comes from a summary of 200 hours of debriefings of him after his sentencing by the NIS, with the participation of the CIA and other intelligence agencies. The results were verified with polygraph tests.

21. Lonetree's letter of December 5, 1986, to Seina.

22. Interview on April 25, 1988, with Downes.

23. Interview on December 28, 1987, with a State Department security officer.

24. Interview on April 25, 1988, with Downes.

25. Interview on December 7, 1987, with Downes.

26. Statement to the NIS by Corporal Kurt R. Arneson on January 12, 1987, confirmed by Downes in an interview on March 12, 1988.

27. Interview on March 12, 1988, with Downes. The personnel card has a dozen comments in different handwriting about the young woman's sexual activities.

28. Interview on December 7, 1987, with Downes.

29. Pitman's statement of April 23, 1987, to the NIS, confirmed by him on March 11, 1988, in an interview.

30. Interview on January 6, 1988, with Lamb; on December 28, 1987, with Hartman; on December 28, 1987, with a State Department security officer. Additional details came from an interview on December 7, 1987, with Downes, then assistant detachment commander.

31. The Marine Corps, through a spokesman, later denied that the incident was a rape. Major Tony Rothfork, the spokesman, explained on page A-1 of the April 4, 1987, *Washington Post,* that the "lady did not want to file charges."

32. Interview on April 25, 1988, with Downes.

33. Testimony by Enderlin on page 231 of Lonetree's court-martial proceedings.

34. Lonetree's statement to the NIS of December 26, 1986, which has not been retracted.

35. Ibid.

## 17  "Tell Us a Lie," pp. 191–200

1. NIS briefing paper for congressional committees.

2. McCullah's biographical data.

3. Interview on March 8, 1988, with an intelligence source.

4. Ibid.

5. The Justice Department, with the help of the FBI, may elect to preempt the military investigative services.

6. Naval Investigative Service, *This Is the NIS,* page 1.

7. An example is the case of David H. Barnett, a former CIA employee who approached the KGB in Indonesia in 1976 and sold the Soviets classified information. He pleaded guilty to espionage on October 29, 1980.

8. Ronald M. Ferguson, assistant section chief, FBI Laboratory, "Polygraph Policy Model for Law Enforcement," *FBI Law Enforcement Bulletin,* June 1987, page 7. According to the article, "Polygraph effectiveness and accuracy are greatest when relevant issues and the examinee's knowledge of the matter under investigation have been narrowly defined and well defined. . . . Dragnet-type screening of large numbers of suspects should be avoided."

9. The author's conclusions are based on interviews with NIS, FBI, and Justice Department officials. Since the author did not look into all NIS investigations, the comments on the NIS approach necessarily apply only to its investigation of the Marine security breaches.

10. See the author's 1988 book, *Spy vs. Spy: Stalking Soviet Spies in America,* Charles Scribner's Sons, page 4.

11. NIS officials made a similar claim about the Pollard case to the author in an interview on February 24, 1988.

12. Interview with DiGenova on May 3, 1988.

13. NIS cable of December 23, 1986.

14. Lonetree's statement to the NIS of December 24, 1986.

15. Transcript of Lonetree's tape-recorded statement to the NIS of December 24, 1986.

16. NIS evidence custody document dated December 24, 1986, and testimony by Moyer on page 31 of Lonetree's Article 32 investigation.

17. Brannon's testimony on page 356 of Lonetree's Article 32 investigation.

18. Interview on May 2, 1988, with an NIS official.

19. Brannon's testimony on page 365 of Lonetree's Article 32 hearing.

Moyer's version on page 133 of Lonetree's Article 32 hearing is that Brannon said, "Clayton, talk to us, say something, say something, hell, just say something, even tell us a lie."

Lonetree got choked up and said, "What do you want to hear?"

"Clayton, just tell us the damn truth, but say something."

20. Testimony by Brannon on page 365 of Lonetree's Article 32 hearing.

21. Testimony by Moyer on page 135 of Lonetree's Article 32 hearing.

22. Brannon's testimony on page 365 of Lonetree's Article 32 hearing is as follows:

Q. Special Agent Brannon, in the schools that you attended, which of them suggested this technique of suggesting to a subject that he tell a lie?

A. I did not suggest to him that he tell a lie. He asked me if I wanted him to lie.

Q. To which you responded, that that indeed is what you were requesting?

A. In essence, that's correct, yes, sir.

23. Interview on February 24, 1988, with NIS officials.

24. Interview on February 7, 1988, with an NIS agent who helped direct the Marine investigation.

25. Testimony of Moyer on page 33 of Lonetree's Article 32 hearing.

## 18 "Another Spy!" pp. 201–20

1. The first story in the *Washington Post* appeared on January 11, 1987, after the *Los Angeles Times* revealed several details of the case beyond the Marine Corps's press release.

2. Lonetree's charge sheet of January 27, 1987.

3. Interview on November 3, 1987, with Spencer Lonetree.

4. Byrnes's testimony on page 1739 of Lonetree's court-martial proceedings.

5. Byrnes's testimony on page 1741 of Lonetree's court-martial proceedings.

6. Edward Lee Howard's escape to the Soviet Union while under FBI surveillance is the first time in recent history an espionage suspect has escaped while being watched by the bureau.

7. Interviews on February 24, 1988, with NIS officials; NIS briefing statement of January 28, 1988; interview on February 19, 1988, with a State Department counterintelligence official.

8. NIS cables of March 16 and 17, 1987, supplemented by an interview with an intelligence source on March 8, 1988.

9. Interview on April 6, 1988, with an intelligence source.

10. NIS cable of March 16, 1987, from Moyer.

11. Interview on May 3, 1988, with an NIS agent.

12. NIS cable of March 17, 1987, to Twentynine Palms.

13. Interview on May 12, 1988, with an NIS headquarters agent.

14. Interview on April 23, 1988, with an NIS agent.

15. Interview on May 3, 1988, with an NIS agent.

16. Interview on April 23, 1988, with an NIS agent, and on May 3, 1988, with another NIS agent.

17. NIS chronology entitled "Polygraph Examinations of Bracy."

18. Bracy's second statement to the NIS of March 19, 1987, which he has retracted.

19. Bracy's third statement to the NIS of March 20, 1987, which he has retracted.

20. NIS "results of interview" with Bracy on March 20, 1987.

21. The NIS report of investigation in the Bracy case of March 21, 1987, and an NIS analysis entitled "Polygraph Examinations of Bracy."

22. NIS action/lead sheet of March 24, 1987, ordering corrections to Bracy's polygraph exam report.

23. Interview on March 8, 1988, with a senior FBI polygraph examiner.

24. Ibid.

25. Interview on February 24, 1988, with NIS officials, and on April 23, 1988, with an NIS agent.

26. Interview on May 11, 1988, with an NIS agent.

27. Interview on November 29, 1987, with Bracy.

28. Interview on February 24, 1988, with NIS officials.

29. Interviews on March 8, 1988, with an NIS official, and on May 11, 1988, with one of the agents who interviewed Bracy.

30. Bracy's statement to the NIS of March 18, 1987, says Daniloff was on the "access list" and "could have been working for someone in the embassy because he frequented the embassy." An NIS agent said in an interview on May 3, 1988, that Bracy said Daniloff was on the access list to the secure areas of the embassy; an NIS supervisor confirmed that statement in an interview on March 4, 1988. According to other Marines, Daniloff was on the same list any other American journalist was on, a point confirmed by Bracy in an interview with the author. Taking all the facts into account, it seems likely the NIS misinterpreted what Bracy had said.

31. Interview on December 28, 1987, with a State Department security officer.

32. "Lonetree and Bracy Joint Assignment Period All Posts," NIS computer printout showing Bracy's and Lonetree's guard duty.

33. Mandie Stilleke, "Analysis of Bracy Watches at the American Embassy in Moscow," November 23, 1987.

34. Interview on February 24, 1988, with NIS officials.

35. Clarence M. Kelley, then FBI director, confirmed in the July 24, 1975, *Washington Post*, page A-3, that the FBI conducted "surreptitious entries" or burglaries to obtain "information relative to the security of the nation."

36. Hollings asked for the FBI investigation in a letter to President Reagan on May 6, 1987.

37. The information on the FBI's investigation comes from interviews with officials from the FBI and other agencies with knowledge of the investigation, as well as from Marines and civilians interviewed by the FBI.

38. Interview on May 13, 1988, with Bracy.

## 19  Russian Posters, pp. 221–31

1. Marine Corps press release, March 24, 1987.

2. Weinberger made the comment on the Cable News Network, according to the *Washington Post*, March 29, 1987, page A-1.

3. Message from Marine Corps public affairs office, March 30, 1987.

4. *Washington Post*, April 17, 1987, page A-16.

5. *Washington Post*, April 8, 1987, page A-1.

6. *Washington Post*, April 11, 1987, page A-23.

7. *Washington Post*, April 6, 1987, page A-1. Neither lawmaker could spare the time for an interview for this book.

8. NIS cable of March 27, 1987. White was said to carry a copy of her original text to show that the NIS teletype operator had misspelled President Reagan's name. In an interview on March 10, 1988, she said the misspelling was a typographical error by a communicator.

9. Interview on March 10, 1988, with Hartman.

10. Interviews on May 11, 1988, with NIS officials.

11. Stufflebeam's commentary on his statement of March 29, 1987, and an interview on May 11, 1988, with an NIS official.

12. Interview on March 10, 1988, with Stufflebeam.

13. Interview on March 8, 1988, with a senior FBI polygraph examiner.

14. Interview on May 12, 1988, with a senior FBI polygraph examiner.

15. Interview on March 8, 1988, with an NIS official.

16. Interview on May 12, 1988, with an NIS official, and on May 13, 1988, with an NIS official.

17. Interview on November 14, 1987, with Stufflebeam.

18. Ibid.

19. Interview on May 11, 1988, with an NIS official.

20. Interview on April 23, 1988, with an NIS official.

21. Interview on March 8, 1988, with an NIS official.

22. Interview on May 11, 1988, with an NIS official.

23. Ibid.

24. Marine Corps press release, March 31, 1987.

## 20   "A Witch-Hunt," pp. 232–45

1. Downes's statement of May 14, 1987, concerning his NIS interrogation.

2. Interview on December 7, 1987, with Downes.

3. Downes's statement to the NIS of April 16, 1987.

4. Downes's statement to the NIS of April 17, 1987.

5. Interview on December 7, 1987, with Downes.

6. Interview on May 12, 1988, with Downes.

7. Williams's testimony on page 319 of Lonetree's Article 32 hearing.

8. Williams's testimony on page 326 of Lonetree's Article 32 hearing.

9. Williams's testimony on page 322 of Lonetree's Article 32 hearing.

10. Interview on November 20, 1987, with Williams.

11. Laurivuori's statement of July 26, 1986, and May 13, 1987, to the NIS, confirmed in an interview on January 21, 1988.

12. Sink's statement to the NIS of July 31, 1987, confirmed in testimony by him on page 512 of Williams's Article 32 hearing. Sink was given a draft of the book manuscript referring to him and did not suggest any corrections.

13. Interview on December 11, 1987, with Martinson.

14. Interview on December 11, 1987, with Roen.

15. Interview on April 25, 1988, with Downes.

16. Interview on May 12, 1988, with Walton.

17. Ibid.

18. Interview on December 29, 1987, with Weirick.

19. Interview on November 26, 1987, with Weirick.

20. The statute of limitations on espionage in the military has since been extended to five years. The civilian statute for espionage committed on behalf of a foreign country has no limitation on prosecutions.

21. Interview on March 8, 1988, with an intelligence source, corroborated by an interview on February 15, 1988, with a government investigative official; on February 24, 1988, with NIS officials; on May 12, 1988, with a State Department security officer; and on May 13, 1988, with an NIS official. An NIS briefing paper given to congressional staff members lists an East European Marine security guard, identified as "K," as having admitted disclosing top-secret information to a suspected intelligence service. The Marine has been identified by government sources as Diekmann.

22. State Department "Infractions List" showing Marine security guards removed from post.

23. Interview on May 27, 1988, with Diekmann.

24. Interview on December 7, 1987, with Kelley.

25. Memo of April 7, 1987, by Rich.

26. Williams's charge sheet of June 17, 1987.

27. Memo of June 11, 1987, from Ryan to Petersen.

28. Marine Corps transcript of Bracy's June 12, 1987, press conference.

29. NIS memo of June 16, 1987, on the briefing.

30. McKee quoted Aldridge's message in a teletype to NIS agents on September 1, 1987, upon Aldridge's retirement.

31. UPI, June 25, 1987.

32. Del Grosso's memo to Mundy of July 9, 1987, entitled "MSG Program: A Commander's Estimate."

33. Handwritten comment by Mundy on the bottom of a Marine Corps memo of January 26, 1988, entitled "NSIC/USMC MSG Counterintelligence Plan."

34. NIS transcript of Gray's remarks on January 12, 1988.

35. Brahms's memo of February 26, 1988.

36. General Accounting Office preliminary report of February 23, 1988.

## 21   Indian Feathers, pp. 246–53

1. Interview on November 10, 1987, with Kunstler.

2. Interview on October 31, 1987, with Stuhff.

3. Interview on November 13, 1987, with an official of the Marine judge advocate's office.

4. "White paper" of August 11, 1987, signed by Stuhff, Kunstler, and Headley.

5. Page 92 of Lonetree's Article 32 investigation transcript.

6. Interview on November 10, 1987, with Kunstler.

7. *Washington Post*, August 22, 1987, and Kunstler's "white paper."

8. Interview on November 13, 1987, with a member of the Marine judge advocate's office.

9. Interview on November 2, 1987, with Cohen.

10. Interview on May 17, 1988, with Cohen.

11. *The New York Times* on October 18, 1987, reported Kunstler's charges about the abortive "60 Minutes" appearance in an article headlined "Marine Corps Said to Have Urged Spy to Turn Down CBS Interview."

12. Letter of October 16, 1987, from Kunstler.

13. Letter of October 22, 1987, from Lonetree. The letter says it was drafted by Cohen.

14. See page 167 of the author's 1988 book, *Spy vs. Spy: Stalking Soviet Spies in America*, published by Charles Scribner's Sons.

15. Interview on May 17, 1988, with Cohen. Lonetree has not given any interviews to the press. In a call to the author from prison on September 11, 1988, Lonetree said his lawyers have advised him not to give any interviews until his appeals are exhausted. "I'm for what you're doing," he said, "but I have to do what my lawyers say."

## 22   A New Power Line, pp. 254–68

1. *Time*, November 23, 1987; *New York Times*, December 8, 1987; *Washington Post*, January 17, 1988. The most prominently played story was the *Post*'s. "The government has concluded . . . that the entire affair was wildly overblown," the story said. "No evidence has been found that the KGB penetrated the Moscow embassy."

The story originated, according to a State Department official, when he called a *Post* reporter to correct his claim of six months earlier that the embassy had been penetrated. The official did not know of the CIA's and NSA's true findings.

2. Interview on January 19, 1988, with Gerasimov.

3. Interview on January 20, 1988, with Matlock.

4. Interview on January 16, 1988, with Yvonne Dupont, an embassy worker.

5. Interview on January 19, 1988, with Kelly, the administrative counselor of the embassy.

6. Interview on January 22, 1988, with an official of the consulate.

7. Interview on May 25, 1988, with Dzhirkvelov.

8. Memo of June 4, 1987, from Del Grosso to Major General Carl E. Mundy, Jr., on the "Report on Security at the U.S. Missions in Moscow and Other Areas of High Risk."

9. Interview on February 3, 1988, with Del Grosso.

10. Memo of February 4, 1988, from Gordon to the undersecretary of the Navy concerning "Critical Media Coverage Regarding NIS Conduct of Marine Embassy Espionage Investigations."

11. The Executive Protective Service is a branch of the Secret Service. Its guards are paid roughly twice the salaries of Marine security guards.

12. Interview on May 26, 1988, with Lamb. In an attempt to play down the differences, a State Department paper claimed that assistant secretaries report to the secretary and are "coordinated" by undersecretaries.

## Epilogue, pp. 269–72

1. *Washington Post*, May 21, 1988, page A-2.
2. Interview on May 13, 1988, with Bracy.
3. Interview on November 14, 1987, with Stufflebeam.
4. Interview on March 13, 1988, with Parks.
5. Interview on May 12, 1988, with Walton. While an honorable discharge looks better to future employers, there is no other difference between the two types of discharges.
6. Interview on April 25, 1988, with Downes.
7. Interview on May 12, 1988, with Kelley.
8. Interview on May 26, 1988, with Lamb.
9. *New York Times*, May 14, 1987, page B-12.
10. Interview on March 29, 1988, with Hartman.
11. *New York Times*, January 19, 1988.
12. Interview on May 25, 1988, with McCullah.
13. Interview on May 28, 1988, with Mecke.
14. Interview on January 7, 1988, with Faurer.

# Selected Glossary of Intelligence Terms

**Accommodation address**   A sterile address used as a cutout to receive and pick up clandestine messages. See also *Cutout.*

**ACOUSTINT**   Acoustic intelligence.

**Agent**   An individual employed by any agency for carrying out clandestine intelligence or clandestine operations.

**Agent, co-opted**   An agent of one intelligence service co-opted by another.

**Agent, deep cover**   An agent operating under layered legends for long-range operations. See also *Agent, sleeper; Throwaway.*

**Agent, double**   An agent who is recruited to work against his original service, either because he is coerced, becomes disaffected, or has defected.

**Agent, espionage**   An agent who collects foreign intelligence information clandestinely.

**Agent handler**   A case officer or principal agent who directly controls an agent or net of agents.

**Agent, illegal**   An espionage agent using false or deep cover for his activities.

**Agent of influence**   An individual who is in a position to influence public opinion in favor of the Soviet Union, such as a journalist, politician, commentator, labor leader, author, scientist, or academic.

**Agent, legal**   An espionage agent using official cover for his activities.

**Agent, sleeper**   A long-range agent to be activated during wartime or extraordinary emergency. See also *Agent, deep cover.*

**Agent, triple**   A double agent who is redoubled to work again for his original service while ostensibly working for the opposition.

**Agent, unwitting**   An individual who is unaware that he is being used by an intelligence service, or an agent who believes he is working for one service but is actually being used by another.

**Approach**   The method used to entice a likely agent or developed individual for recruitment.

**Archives**   KGB term for central files or central index.

**Artichoke**   In tradecraft jargon, to use drugs, hypnotism, or psychological testing to establish an agent's or defector's bona fides.

**Assessment**   The evaluation of an individual's potential as a clandestine agent.

**Black bag job**   Jargon for breaking and entering.

**Black operator**   KGB and GRU jargon for clandestine agent.

**Bona fides**   Credentials or, in tradecraft jargon, the results of interrogation used to establish the identity, authenticity, and truthfulness of a suspect, defector, or potential agent.

**Bury**   As a verb, jargon for concealing sensitive-source intelligence within a report on a related subject to conceal its source.

**Case officer**   Intelligence or clandestine operations officer responsible for a specific agent, net, or operation in a clandestine agency.

**CIA**   Central Intelligence Agency. The civilian agency of the U.S. government charged with the clandestine collection of intelligence, analysis and dissemination of all types of intelligence, undertaking covert action and executive action directed by higher authority, protecting the security of its own operations worldwide, and countering hostile intelligence threats against American security interests overseas.

**Clandestine mentality**   Paranoid behavior by intelligence officers.

**Clandestine operations**   Intelligence collection, counterintelligence, or covert action operations conducted surreptitiously against hostile or sometimes friendly governments, their military, intelligence, and security agencies.

**Cobbler**   KGB and GRU jargon for a document forger.

**Collection**   The procuring, assembling, and organizing of information for further intelligence processing.

**COMINT**   Communications intelligence.

**Communications security**   A specialized form of information and matériel security that is concerned not only with the safeguarding of classified information transmitted by electrical or electronic means, but also with the safeguarding of the means of transmission and the equipment and devices used in such transmission.

**Compartmentation**   The insulating of personnel, information, operations, and locations on a "need-to-know" basis.

**Concealment devices**   Clandestine devices used to conceal messages, film, poison, secret ink, ciphers, or other material used in tradecraft.

**Contact**   An individual who is not an agent but is used for intelligence information collection.

**Co-option**   The act of recruiting a government employee with diplomatic or official cover by one of the intelligence services of his government to perform specific intelligence tasks.

**Counterespionage**   Operations intended to negate, confuse, deceive, subvert, monitor, or control the clandestine collection operations or agents of foreign governments or agencies.

**Counterintelligence**   All security measures, active and passive, to safeguard information, personnel, equipment, and installations against espionage or sabotage by foreign powers and their agencies.

**Countersurveillance**   The tradecraft technique of detecting hostile surveillance of a person, rendezvous, safe house, or dead drop.

**Country team**   The chiefs of all U.S. government agencies operating in a foreign country, headed by the American ambassador or chief of mission.

**Cover**   The identity and occupation used by an agent, staff officer, or case officer to conceal his espionage or clandestine operational activities.

**Cover, diplomatic**   Staff or case officers holding diplomatic passports and operating out of embassies or consulates.

**Cover name**   An alias, pseudonym, cryptonym, or code name.

**Cover story**   Notional or false biography. See *Legend.*

**Covert action**   Methods used by intelligence agencies to influence countries or political parties overseas, including paramilitary actions, bribery, kidnapping, counterfeiting, and propaganda.

**Cryptography**   Creation of codes and ciphers.

**Cutout**   An intermediary, human or physical.

**Damage report**   The assessment of damage to an agency, station, or base caused by the exposure of an agent net or operation.

**Dead drop**   A concealed physical location used as a communications cutout between an agent and a courier, case officer, or another agent in an agent operation or net.

**Debriefing** The technique of extracting all the information obtained by an individual or group in the accomplishment of an assigned mission.

**Deep cover** Long-range operation involving backstopped documentation, either genuine or legend, usually layered for throwaways. Used for sleeper agents to be activated in time of war or emergency.

**Defector** A disaffected individual who renounces his citizenship and requests political asylum from another government.

**Defector-in-place** An individual who remains in his place of residence and employment as an agent for the opposition. See *Double agent; Defector.*

**Disinformation** Any information fabricated or distorted by a government on a nonattributable basis for the purpose of influencing the actions of one or more governments, international organizations, officials, individuals, or public or private entities in a manner to further the political and military objectives of the former.

**Doubling** Tradecraft jargon for turning an agent to work against his original service on behalf of its opposition.

**Dubok** Soviet term for dead drop.

**ELINT** Electronics intelligence.

**Encryption** Transposition of clear text into a code or cipher.

**Executive action** Murder and assassination conducted by certain intelligence agencies.

**Falling in love** Tradecraft jargon for emotional attachment. The term refers to a case officer who is blind to the faults of his agent and is therefore considered a threat to the operational security of a case.

**FBI** Federal Bureau of Investigation. The U.S. agency responsible for counterintelligence and enforcement of federal laws.

**GRU** Soviet military intelligence agency. Competes with the KGB to obtain military intelligence outside the Soviet Union.

**Honey trap** An attractive female used as bait in an entrapment or recruitment operation. Also known as honey pot.

**HUMINT** Human intelligence, including processed information obtained by overt or clandestine means.

**Illegal**  KGB and GRU jargon for a deep-cover agent in a foreign country.

**Illness**  KGB and GRU jargon for exposure or arrest of an agent.

**Indicator**  A cryptonym used to indicate the sensitive nature of a message's contents.

**Intelligence**  The product resulting from the collecting and processing of information concerning actual and potential situations and conditions relating to domestic and foreign activities.

**Intelligence, acoustic**  Processed information from aural sources that may be electronically enhanced.

**KGB**  Committee for State Security. The Soviet secret police corresponding to a combination of the FBI, CIA, and NSA.

**Legend**  False biography; cover story; backup for false identity.

**Mole**  A penetration agent infiltrated into an opposition intelligence service or other opposing governmental agency.

**Musician**  GRU jargon for a radio operator.

**MVD**  Ministry of Internal Affairs. Soviet agency for internal and state security that performs police and internal security functions not under KGB jurisdiction.

**Open code**  A method of communicating by telephone or written communication using esoteric references known only to the correspondents.

**Operations, illegal**  Espionage operations that are illegal in the country in which they are conducted.

**Pseudonym**  A cover name used by clandestine personnel in official internal communications.

**Raven**  A male prostitute used as a spy, informer, or provocateur.

**Recognition signal**  Tradecraft term for a password or sign used in an agent rendezvous.

**Recruitment-in-place**  Usually a defector who agrees to serve as a double agent by remaining in his position and place of residence.

**Referentura**  Section of a Soviet embassy used exclusively by KGB and GRU personnel.

**Rezidentura**  The Soviet equivalent of a CIA station. Also known as residency.

**Safe house**  A sterile location used to meet or debrief agents.

**Secret writing**  Clandestine communications using secret inks, ciphers, and microphotography.

**SEISMINT**  Seismic intelligence from earth-tremor data.

**Shadow**  Jargon for a tail.

**Shoe**  KGB and GRU jargon for a false document.

**Shopping list**  A list of intelligence requirements, scientific documents, arms, weapons systems, computers, or other items of advanced technology to be purchased on the open market or procured surreptitiously.

**SIGINT**  Signals intelligence.

**Sign-of-life signal**  An indication that an illegal is still alive.

**Soviet realities**  CIA jargon for operational intelligence pertaining to Soviet life, customs, and documentation.

**Spy**  Espionage agent.

**Station**  An intelligence agency post normally located in an embassy.

**Swallow**  A female prostitute used as a spy, informer, or provocateur.

**Swallow's nest**  KGB jargon for a seduction safe house, usually an apartment, equipped with cameras and recorders, used by a swallow in an entrapment operation.

**TELINT**  Telemetry intelligence.

**Throwaway**  A legend or cover story that is layered on top of one or more other legends in the event one story does not withstand hostile interrogation.

**Tripling**  Redoubling a double agent back to his original service.

**Uncle**  Reference by a Soviet-bloc intelligence service to its Soviet adviser.

**Walk-in**  An opposition agent who voluntarily surrenders himself for defection or who offers himself voluntarily for recruitment.

**Wet affairs**  KGB and GRU jargon for murder and assassination.

The above terms are selected from Leo D. Carl's *International Dictionary of Intelligence,* to be published by National Intelligence Book Center, Washington, D.C.

# Index

Made in the USA
Lexington, KY
15 November 2017